INITIAL TEACHER EDUCATION
IN SCHOOLS

Education at SAGE

SAGE is a leading international publisher of journals, books, and electronic media for academic, educational, and professional markets.

Our education publishing includes:

- accessible and comprehensive texts for aspiring education professionals and practitioners looking to further their careers through continuing professional development

- inspirational advice and guidance for the classroom

- authoritative state of the art reference from the leading authors in the field.

Find out more at: **www.sagepub.co.uk/education**

INITIAL TEACHER EDUCATION IN SCHOOLS

A Guide for Practitioners

Edited by
CAREY PHILPOTT,
HELEN SCOTT
and
CARRIE MERCIER

Los Angeles | London | New Delhi
Singapore | Washington DC

Los Angeles | London | New Delhi
Singapore | Washington DC

SAGE Publications Ltd
1 Oliver's Yard
55 City Road
London EC1Y 1SP

SAGE Publications Inc.
2455 Teller Road
Thousand Oaks, California 91320

SAGE Publications India Pvt Ltd
B 1/I 1 Mohan Cooperative Industrial Area
Mathura Road
New Delhi 110 044

SAGE Publications Asia-Pacific Pte Ltd
3 Church Street
#10-04 Samsung Hub
Singapore 049483

Editor: James Clark
Assistant editor: Rachael Plant
Production editor: Nicola Marshall
Production manager: Jeanette Graham
Copyeditor: Carol Lucas
Proofreader: Isabel Kirkwood
Indexer: Anne Solomito
Marketing executive: Dilhara Attygalle
Cover design: Naomi Robinson
Typeset by: C&M Digitals (P) Ltd, Chennai, India
Printed in Great Britain by
CPI Group (UK) Ltd, Croydon, CR0 4YY

Library of Congress Control Number: 2013957189

British Library Cataloguing in Publication data

A catalogue record for this book is available from
the British Library

ISBN 978-1-4462-7584-9
ISBN 978-1-4462-7585-6 (p)

At SAGE we take sustainability seriously. Most of our products are printed in the UK using FSC papers and boards.
When we print overseas we ensure sustainable papers are used as measured by the Egmont grading system.
We undertake an annual audit to monitor our sustainability.

CONTENTS

LIST OF FIGURES AND TABLES

FIGURES

TABLES

ABOUT THE EDITORS

Carey Philpott has taught in both English and Scottish schools. In higher education in England he has been a programme leader for secondary PGCE and secondary undergraduate QTS courses as well as a PGCE for the Lifelong Learning Sector. He currently works in the School of Education in the Faculty of Humanities and Social Sciences at the University of Strathclyde in Glasgow. His main research interests are the nature of professional learning and the role of narrative in learning from experience.

Helen Scott has taught art and design in secondary, further and higher education. Helen currently works at the University of Northampton where she is Deputy Dean for Student Experience in the School of Education. Her previous roles in higher education include Director of CPD & ITE Partnerships at Manchester Metropolitan University and Head of School of Secondary and Post-Compulsory Initial Professional Studies, Programme Leader for MA in Education and course leader of the PGCE in Secondary Art and Design at the University of Cumbria. Helen's research and expertise lie in the professional development of teachers and in the theory and practice of secondary art and design education. She is currently studying for a PhD in the use of critical studies in secondary art and design education.

Carrie Mercier has taught in schools in England, Scotland and in USA and was Head of Department in RE and PSHE in two schools. She has over 20 years' experience in higher education working mainly in initial teacher education. Her publications and research include work in the fields of the Curriculum and Religious Education as well as Initial Teacher Education. Carrie is Senior Lecturer at the University of Cumbria and is engaged in teaching on both the PGCE and MA programmes in the Faculty of Education Arts and Business.

ABOUT THE CONTRIBUTORS

Nigel Appleton taught mathematics in secondary schools in London and Berkshire before moving into higher education. He worked at what is now the University of Cumbria for 18 years, gradually taking on more leadership responsibility for mathematics education and for secondary initial teacher education in general. In 2009 he moved to what is now Bishop Grosseteste University as Dean of Teacher Development. He is committed to teacher education as being to ensure children and young people get the best possible education. He sees teacher development as a continuum in which universities play a vital role. His research interests are in teachers' subject knowledge and their mathematical learning journeys.

Simon Asquith is Head of the Department of Professional Education within the School of Education at the University of Birmingham. He has been the long-standing National Chair of the Association for Partnership in Teacher Education and has held substantive leadership positions at Liverpool Hope University and the University of Cumbria to do with partnership working in teacher education. Simon has taught in schools in Leeds, Bradford and Cumbria and has written a number of publications to do with primary geography and teacher education.

Alison Chapman has extensive experience of working in schools and in higher education. She is currently the Teaching School Coordinator and a Specialist Leader of Education for initial teacher education and newly qualified teachers at The Queen Katherine School in Kendal. She previously worked for six years at the University of Cumbria in a range of leadership roles, the most recent as Director of School Engagement, responsible for the partnerships with schools and the development lead for School Direct. She is a Senior Fellow of the Higher Education Academy and was awarded the Vice Chancellor's Teaching Excellence Award for outstanding contribution to teaching and learning in Physical Education in 2010. Alison has worked in five contrasting secondary schools and is currently leading the development of a cross-phase Teaching School Alliance in South Cumbria. Her research interests are the impact of working with ITE on schools and school leadership.

Kathryn Fox has developed, taught and led a range of initial teacher education (ITE) and continuing professional development (CPD) provision, including teaching mathematics and subject pedagogy with passion. Prior to this she taught secondary mathematics in schools. She is a Fellow of the Higher Education Academy. Her current research interests in education include the development of mathematics teacher identities, professional development in schools and student teachers' contributions to school improvement. Kathryn is currently the Director of School and Business Engagement at the University of Cumbria.

Gail Fuller is a Religious Studies teacher at Ripley St Thomas CE Academy in Lancaster where she is the Professional Mentor for newly qualified teachers. This work involves overseeing the induction programme for new staff and newly qualified teachers, mentoring and coaching recently qualified teachers in early professional development. Gail was ITT Mentor in Religious Education for a number of years before becoming Professional Mentor. Her MA in Education was focused on newly qualified teachers and the journey to becoming a teacher. Her current research interests include relationships in school and the importance of emotional intelligence for teachers.

Robert Heath has taught in both secondary and primary schools and has over 30 years' experience teaching in state schools where he also mentored students during their training. Robert is now a senior lecturer at the University of Wolverhampton where he teaches on the BEd, PGCE and Schools Direct courses in Primary Initial Teaching Education, specializing in science and ICT. Robert is a Fellow of The Higher Education Academy and has an MA in Education. His current research interests are in the use of mobile devices in the classroom and also how students maintain their faith interests when they move to higher education. Robert was ordained as a deacon in the Church of England this year and now also works as a member of the chaplaincy team.

Patrick Smith is currently Associate Dean in the Faculty of Education, Health and Wellbeing at the University of Wolverhampton. He has many years' experience of teaching children in schools and working with trainee teachers in higher education. He is a Fellow of the Higher Education Academy. His specialist subject area is physical education and he has led numerous staff development events for teachers in the UK and overseas. He firmly believes that children who experience high-quality physical education in the early years of education can reap huge benefits so that they may enjoy lifelong physical activity. While at the University of Cumbria he and his subject team were awarded the Vice Chancellor's Teaching Excellence Award for their outstanding contribution to student teachers' learning.

ACKNOWLEDGEMENTS

Kathryn Fox and Patrick Smith would like to thank:

- Ruth Buxton, University of Cumbria, for 'Working Together' to enhance Secondary PGCE Partnership processes and paperwork
- Susan Giacoletto, University of Wolverhampton, for Figure 2.1
- Bill Myers, University of Wolverhampton
- Carole Marshall, University of Wolverhampton.

Alison Chapman would like to thank the following people who have supported research for Chapter 9:

- Kevin Bell, Advanced Skills Teacher and teacher of Design and Technology at The Queen Katherine School, Kendal
- Simon Bramwell, Executive Principal at St Simon and St Jude Primary School, Bolton and Irk Valley C P School, Manchester
- David Chapman, Head of Humanities at Central Lancaster High School, Lancaster
- Rebecca Dunne, Director of Teaching School Prestolee Community School, Bolton
- Paul Smith, Executive Principal at Parbold Douglas Church of England Academy
- Dougie Yarker, Advanced Skills Teacher and Specialist Leader of Education in Mathematics at The Queen Katherine School, Kendal.

SAGE would like to thank the following reviewers whose comments helped shape the proposal for this book:

- Chris Baker, John Cabot Academy, Bristol
- Christopher D'Netto, Seven Kings High School, Ilford
- Lee Gray, Tudor Grange Academy, Solihull
- Rob Higgins, The Kemnal Academies Trust SCITT
- Cristina Taboada-Naya, Brooke Weston Academy, Corby.

CHAPTER 1

INTRODUCTION

Carey Philpott, Helen Scott and Carrie Mercier

By the end of this chapter you should be able to:

- understand the aims of the book, the intentions of the authors and the context for which it is designed
- have a sense of the structure and content of the book and the way in which it is intended to work for teachers and schools
- begin to reflect on the implications of the changes that are taking place in initial teacher education and the ways in which this book might help you to think about these in a systematic way.

Initial teacher education (ITE) is going through a time of rapid change and there are many issues emerging for both schools and universities. The editors of this book all have a long-standing involvement in ITE but their separate institutions have quite different standpoints in relation to recent developments in more school-based ITE such as School Direct. In one university the decision has been to embrace the School Direct initiative with both hands and to work with schools and school alliances to support this shift towards more school-based ITE. As a result the numbers of trainees recruited on the Postgraduate Certificate of Education (PGCE) and other university-based routes into teaching have been much reduced and the university staffing base has been cut. This would suggest that there is no going back to the old system of university-based ITE. In one of the other universities the response to the School Direct initiative has been much more cautious and the traditional PGCE programmes continue to provide the main route into teaching for both secondary and primary ITE. The third university is in Scotland where the recent radical changes under way in England do not apply. However, recent developments in Scotland have also been towards rebalancing the nature of partnerships with schools towards an enhanced role for schools in the ITE process. Given that the editors are starting from different points, it is not surprising that they find much to discuss in these times of change, and this book reflects some of the issues in the debate that is going on around ITE.

This book is aimed at all teachers who work in schools, and tutors who work with schools, who are taking a lead or an increasing role in ITE. With the establishment of School Direct and other employment-based routes, an increasing number of schools are beginning to lead ITE themselves or take a greater role in ITE, with an inevitable decreasing input from universities. Because of the recent history of partnership working in relation to ITE, teachers in many schools are skilled and experienced in the aspects of ITE that have long been located in their classroom and staffroom context. However, within the partnership working model, some aspects of ITE have remained the responsibility of the universities. This publication is intended as a handbook that will give teachers a clear understanding of those aspects of ITE previously led and managed within partnerships by universities.

The book is intended to be accessible to busy teachers who have to balance many demands on their time. The general structure is one where each chapter is divided into three main sections. The first section is to give an accessible and concise overview of research and theories in the area of the topic covered. The second section of each chapter sets out the practical implications that emerge as a result of the research and theories. The third section of each chapter includes specific case studies of how these actions might be implemented. Most of these are from examples of actual practice already used in institutions. In addition to the three main sections there is a further reading section that will assist those who want to explore the issues further.

In Chapter 2 Kathryn Fox and Patrick Smith discuss getting selection processes right. This is an area that schools have mostly been able to leave to universities until now. Many universities have invited teachers and mentors to help in the interview process and others have involved them in the selection process at an earlier stage. However, schools have often found it hard to allow their staff release from the classroom in order to engage in this process of selection. This chapter draws on the breadth of experience that the authors bring with them in devising, using and reviewing selection processes. It also engages with some of the international research related to the issue of teacher recruitment. This chapter will be useful for schools as they discuss the most effective processes for selection of those suitable for teaching.

In the next chapter Carey Philpott reviews models of professional learning and what they mean for those who are concerned with teacher learning in schools. The consequences of each of these models for the practical organization of ITE in the school are set out and practical suggestions emerge on how to implement these actions with specific examples.

In the following chapter Gail Fuller picks up the importance of identity and relationships to teacher learning and emphasizes how they need to be explicitly considered when planning learning experiences for beginning teachers.

Helen Scott follows this with a discussion on the difference between mentoring and coaching. Schools in ITE partnerships are experienced in mentoring trainees during placements. However, the whole ITE process currently includes professionals who have roles other than mentoring. Many of these currently work within universities. This chapter sets out the differences between these different roles (that might all now be taken on by the school) and how they can be implemented effectively.

In his chapter, Nigel Appleton looks at the importance of, and how we might organize, the academic component of ITE. This chapter sets out why it is important to focus on the academic development of trainees rather than just focusing on a narrowly conceived version of professional competence, even for courses that award Qualified Teacher Status (QTS) only. The chapter also sets out how the academic component can be organized and managed in practice.

Carrie Mercier goes on to look at the issue of the assessment of those learning to teach. There has been much debate around the introduction of teacher competences or the 'Teachers' Standards' in the whole process of trainee-teacher assessment. This chapter picks out the main threads of the argument and raises questions for schools to consider in putting together their assessment processes for trainee teachers. In this chapter the author also asks questions about those aspects of teacher development that cannot readily be captured in the Teachers' Standards. Issues emerge in terms of how to integrate the assignments for the university award with the assessment of professional standards and classroom performance. Information technology provides new opportunities for the design of the assessment process and the author draws attention to recent research related to the development of the electronic portfolio as a tool for structuring and enhancing the process of assessment for the trainee teacher.

In his chapter on how to create synergy between different school priorities, Simon Asquith asks us to look at the bigger picture. Most of us would agree that the main priority of the school is to ensure that all its pupils have the opportunity to achieve their potential. However, the role of the school has long been envisaged as bigger than this. According to the law it has a responsibility for the enrichment and education not only of its pupil population, but also of society. So the school cannot keep a focus on the pupils alone. It is therefore quite appropriate that it should take seriously the development not only of its own staff, but also look beyond its own gates to the education of future teachers.

Schools are busy places and teachers are busy people with many competing demands on their time and many targets that they have to reach. The pressures of the Office for Standards in Education, Children's Services and Skills (Ofsted) are never far from the door. In Chapter 9, Alison Chapman focuses on the ways in which ITE is not just another demand that has to be squeezed in alongside all the others. Initial teacher education can play a central role in promoting other priorities in the school including staff development and school improvement.

Carey Philpott goes on to look at the place and importance of action research as an approach for teacher learning, school improvement and enhancing school-led ITE. Action research is a valuable way to meet many of the imperatives of school and teacher education and is one possible solution to the issues explored in Chapter 9.

Pastoral care for trainee teachers is the focus of Chapter 11 by Robert Heath and Carey Philpott. This chapter looks at the importance of anticipating needs as well as solving problems once they occur. The pastoral care dimension of ITE has tradition-ally been a function of the university in the partnership as ITE trainees have been students of the university. The university tutor has often been the person to whom the trainee teacher turns in times of stress or insecurity. In school-led ITE many, if not all, pastoral care issues may be the responsibility of the school.

Taken together, the chapters cover a range of issues and concerns that will emerge for teachers in schools which are taking on greater responsibility for ITE. In the longer term other issues may come to light and schools and universities must continue their dialogue in order to address these. Universities will need to take seriously their responsibilities in terms of managing the research that will be essential if we are to reflect critically on the impact of new developments in ITE. Many university tutors will, of course, regret the fact that their role as course leader for an ITE programme has diminished or even disappeared. There will be a real sense of loss as they will no longer have that close relationship with the trainee teachers at the beginning of the year when they are just starting out with all the enthusiasm and excitement that comes at the commencement of a new endeavour. But it will be important for universities to recognize that the experi-ence and expertise that these tutors bring to the discussion on the future of ITE are much to be valued. There is important work to be done in harnessing the learning from these times of change and there are opportunities for research and development that must not be missed if we are to ensure our readiness to deal with new contexts of teacher education.

CHAPTER 2

GETTING SELECTION PROCESSES RIGHT

Kathryn Fox and Patrick Smith

By the end of this chapter you should have:

- developed a critical understanding of a range of ITE selection related issues
- an appreciation of the context for teacher supply, recruitment and selection
- considered a range of practical examples of selection activity and processes.

This chapter will draw on a wide range of practical experience in devising, using and reviewing ITE selection processes as well as international research evidence to identify the most effective ways of selecting the most suitable candidates for ITE.

WHAT DO WE KNOW ABOUT SELECTING AND RECRUITING TEACHERS?

Selecting the best

Before considering selection and recruitment processes it is helpful to reflect upon the types of knowledge, skills and characteristics that you may envisage as an outcome of that process. You may wish to reflect in the broadest terms on what it means to be an effective teacher as a starting point. This may not be a straightforward question to answer as not only is there little evidence surrounding the characteristics that make an effective teacher, but it may not even be possible to uniquely define 'effective' teachers (SCORE, 2011). SCORE (2011) does go on to note that there is wide acceptance of the notion that good teachers are those with specialist subject knowledge and passion and enthusiasm for the subject, and this may be a useful starting point for this discussion. To develop this further we could add in the characteristics identified in the work of Barber and Mourshed (2007) who examined the characteristics of teachers in the world's high-performing school systems. They suggested that important characteristics are high levels of literacy and numeracy, strong interpersonal and communication skills, willingness to learn and motivation to teach. It is notable to see how this work has influenced current government policy around pre-entry tests in literacy and numeracy, for example.

However, if we consider the relationship between the values and dispositions of potential applicants for teaching and their later success as teachers (Welch et al., 2010) then this suggests that it is valuable to widen the ways in which we identify those with good potential for teaching. Values and dispositions are not straightforward to define and we may, for example, look to Costa's (1991) 'habits of mind' as a useful guide. These are described as intelligent human responses to problem-solving and include persisting, listening to others with empathy and understanding, thinking flexibly, questioning and posing problems as well as learning continuously. Costa argues that these habits of mind are rarely used in isolation and, instead, clusters of habits are used when applied to situations. He goes on to further develop five key characteristics for those who employ habits of mind:

- Inclination: they feel a tendency to employ particular patterns of intellectual behaviours.

- Value: they choose to value and employ the most effective patterns of intellectual behaviours, rather than other, less productive patterns.

- Sensitivity: they perceive opportunities for, and the appropriateness of employing a particular pattern.

- Capability: they possess the basic skills and capacities to carry out the intellectual behaviours

- Commitment: they constantly strive to reflect on and improve their performance of the behaviours.

It is also worth considering not only recruitment and selection for an ITE programme, but also remembering that the time spent in ITE is limited, and so one of the aims of a successful programme is to work with trainee teachers to promote the best possible outcomes for them on their training and for the future, something that Burch (2011) calls 'traction for current and future teaching'. For this reason it is also worth adding the notion of 'resilience' to those under consideration. Day et al. (2007) conceptualize this as a teacher's capacity to 'sustain their sense of positive professional identity and commitment', much like Hymer's 'bouncebackability' (Hymer, 2009). 'The capacity to remain resilient is a key factor in sustaining teachers' effectiveness' (Day et al., 2007: 213) and an essential component is a sense of self-efficacy. A question for us here is how we set about identifying a potential applicant's own judgement of whether they have the ability to promote pupil learning. There is a further question for us about whether we can provide the training environment to nurture and develop self-efficacy.

So, in summary, what we know about the qualities of effective teachers suggests that these qualities are diverse and may not be straightforward to identify during selection processes.

Challenges for recruitment

In addition to the challenge of knowing what qualities effective teachers have and knowing how to identify these, there can also be the challenge of attracting a sufficient number of suitably qualified applicants. There is ongoing debate about the nature of teacher recruitment and the ability of the market supply to meet the demand. Figures published in 2012, for example, suggest that applications to teacher training in England reduced by almost 15 per cent following a reduction in bursaries for those with a 2:2 or less ('Trainee teacher numbers tumble', 2012). Many countries use academic qualifications to screen potential applicants (OECD, 2005), but there is ongoing debate about the extent to which this should be applied and the suitability of the measures used. As mentioned above, in 2010 the Department for Education (DfE) moved to support funding for training only for those with at least a 2:2 degree (DfE, 2010) as part of their stated strategy to raise the quality of entrants to teaching. This is a controversial and contested stance as there appears to be no relationship between the classification of a trainee teacher's first degree and their ability to teach (or outcome as a newly qualified teacher – NQT) (Clarke and Pye, 2012). Indeed, Smith et al. (2005) raise concerns in their research that, while it may be desirable to raise the academic selection criteria, this may lead to the exclusion of those with the potential to be good teachers. Smith notes that this may in particular exclude mature and experienced applicants. The Organisation for Economic Co-operation and Development report, *Attracting, Developing and Retaining Effective Teachers* (OECD, 2005), recommended that the selection criteria for new teachers should be extended to broaden selection processes, typically to include interviews and the demonstration of teaching skills, advocating that greater weight be given to characteristics that may be potentially harder to measure – enthusiasm, commitment and sensitivity to student needs.

The OECD went on to argue that many aspects of teacher quality are not measured through indicators, such as qualifications, experience or tests of academic ability, and listed teachers' characteristics that had the potential to impact upon pupil learning. These are being able to:

- convey ideas in clear and convincing ways
- create effective learning environments for different types of students

- be enthusiastic and creative

- work effectively with colleagues and parents.

You may wish to reflect upon some of the challenges presented by attempting to measure the potential for these in applicants for teaching.

In addition, there are specific challenges for recruitment in some secondary subject areas. For example, the Smith Inquiry (Smith, 2004) recommended that there was a need to look beyond the pool of mathematics graduates in order to fulfil the supply of mathematics teachers, noting, for example, that it would require around 40 per cent of mathematics graduates to opt for ITE per year to fill training places, a challenging outcome to achieve (Smith, 2004: 46). Subsequently several strategies have been employed to address the identified significant difficulties with the recruitment of mathematics teachers. These strategies include pre-initial teacher education courses for graduates with degrees other than mathematics.

So, in summary, in addition to knowing what the qualities of a good teacher are and how we can reliably identify these in candidates during selection, there are challenges relating to the actual profile of the available pool of potential applicants.

WHAT PRACTICAL RECRUITMENT AND SELECTION ACTIONS ARE NECESSARY?

An overview of routes into teaching

In order to qualify as a teacher in England trainee teachers are required to meet the necessary professional standards as set out by the DfE. Qualified teacher status may be achieved through a variety of routes into teaching either via an undergraduate or postgraduate course of study. Having such a wide range of routes into teaching should be welcomed as they enable both ITE providers and applicants to find the most appropriate training programme based on individual needs, experience and qualifications.

The number of undergraduate training places allocated to higher education institutions (HEIs) has been in decline in recent years owing to the growth of employment-based routes such as School Direct. Trainee teachers are charged tuition fees as per those set by the HEI. Numbers are allocated to HEIs from the National College for Teaching and Leadership (NCTL) normally based on Ofsted quality ratings and are reviewed on an annual basis by the NCTL.

Postgraduate ITE programmes include a one-year PGCE which normally confers 60 master's-level credits and the Professional Certificate in Education (PgCE) which may offer some master's-level credits but not the full 60 credits required for the award of PGCE. Both routes enable trainee teachers to reach the necessary standards to achieve QTS. The PGCE is normally offered as a one-year full-time programme that is led and managed by the HEI. The PgCE is more prevalent on employment-based initial teacher training (EBITT) routes. The latter predominantly applies to primary and secondary routes into teaching. Numbers allocated to EBITT providers of primary and secondary teacher training programmes are also regulated by the NCTL based on

Ofsted quality ratings and regional teacher supply needs. Although post-compulsory ITE programmes are inspected by Ofsted, allocations are not regulated by NCTL.

Trainees are subject to fees which are normally in line with traditional postgraduate programmes. Trainees who will complete a PGCE or PgCE course of study may be entitled to receive a bursary in line with current government funding regulations. School-centred initial teacher training (SCITT) providers currently have QTS awarding powers and are subject to the quality assurance requirements as set by Her Majesty's Chief Inspector (HMCI) and Ofsted.

Employment-based initial teacher training routes are those routes that require the trainee teacher to conduct their training in a school. Trainee teachers are employed by the school as unqualified teachers and as such are subject to the employment regulations and conditions of service of the school and/or local authority in which they are based. These posts may be supernumerary but, more recently, trends suggest that this is not necessarily the case. Trainee teachers on EBITT routes normally conduct their training in one school with some additional experience in a second school.

Trainee teachers wishing to undertake employment based routes have a number of options. Until 2012 the Graduate Teacher Programme (GTP) was the main employment-based route into teaching. Since then the DfE, through the NCTL, has introduced and developed School Direct which comprises a salaried route and a training/tuition route. It is the School Direct salaried route that is now the main employment-based route into teaching, alongside Teach First, which seeks to attract 'the very best graduates', based on their degree classification, into the teaching profession. However, can we measure the potential to be an outstanding teacher simply through the degree classification held by applicants? Evidence suggests this is probably not the case.

Other employment routes include the two-year undergraduate Registered Teacher Programme (RTP) and the Overseas Trained Teacher Programme (OTT) both of which supply lesser numbers to the teaching profession but can attract high calibre trainee teachers. The 'assessment only' programme is another qualifying option for future teachers which seeks to attract candidates who have significant classroom experience such as Higher Level Teaching Assistants (HLTA) and do not need further training to be awarded QTS. Assessment for the latter route is normally via portfolios of evidence that include planning, teaching and assessment, classroom observations and interviews.

With such a plethora of routes into teaching all must comply with the Secretary of State for Education's requirements. These essentially focus on:

1. trainee-teacher outcomes

2. the quality of training

3. the quality of leadership and management.

Trainee-teacher outcomes are centred on their ability to meet the current standards for QTS but do not currently include those training in the post-compulsory sector. The quality of training is assessed both in the school and training partnership, as is leadership and management. The latter form the basis for Ofsted in assessing the quality of the training provider.

In summary, whatever the route into teaching, it is the HEI that is responsible for the quality assurance processes and is subject to regulation by Ofsted unless the provider has sought accreditation for QTS-awarding powers through the NCTL. Consequently, HEIs remain cautious when franchising a significant part of the training to partner schools, colleges and early years settings.

Recruitment and selection

Recruitment to undergraduate and postgraduate teacher training programmes has remained mostly buoyant in recent years, although it is difficult to recruit high-quality male teachers to early years and primary training programmes and, in many areas of the country, it is difficult to recruit from ethnic minority groups despite the frequent recruitment drives to do so.

Secondary teacher training programmes, the majority of which are postgraduate, normally recruit well in such areas as physical education and English but struggle to recruit high-calibre applicants to mathematics, physics, physics with mathematics and computer science. Subject knowledge enhancement (SKE) courses have helped enormously in 'bridging the gap' in trainee teachers' subject knowledge through both short and long courses prior to the commencement of PGCE programmes, and the generous bursary awards for first-class and upper second-class degrees in shortage subjects have helped to support recruitment. Applicants for secondary subjects may be asked to complete an SKE course of study, depending on their individual needs, which could necessitate a deferral to the School Direct programme for up to 12 months. The latter is more likely in secondary shortage subjects such as mathematics, physics and physics with mathematics but could include other curriculum areas too. Increasingly there is recognition that subject knowledge development is an ongoing process and so the use of audit tools and regular review is encouraged.

The recruitment and selection process requires rigour in order that the partnership selects the very best candidates for the profession and that due process is followed in line with current legislation. For example, ITE providers are obliged to make appropriate adjustments to the selection process in the case of applicants with particular needs and disabilities. A provider cannot reject people for health reasons without a very robust justification (see *Fitness to Teach; Occupational Health Guidance for the Training and Employment of Teachers* [TDA, 2007a] and *Able to Teach; Guidance for Initial Teacher Trainers on Discrimination Disability and Fitness to Teach* [TDA, 2007b])

It is important to acknowledge applications as early as possible and to notify those candidates that do not necessarily meet the entry criteria so that they may be permitted to apply for alternative programmes. Qualifications of candidates must be checked (original certificates), QTS skills tests passed and appropriate Disclosure and Barring Service (DBS) checks completed. It is also important to check that candidates have not previously failed a QTS programme, as failure may prevent their application proceeding.

If the partnership is between a school and an HEI, university tutors can review the applicant's areas of strength and suitability and advise the receiving school to reject or accept at this stage of the process. The interview process should involve school and university colleagues, and it is advisable to see candidates working with children and young people prior to selection. This may take the form of a mini teaching session but more importantly it is best to observe and assess the candidate's early professional skills through their engagement with adults and young people. Whole-class teaching is not necessarily recommended as this requires higher-level skills than would normally be expected later in their training, during their NQT year and as part of teachers' assessment as they progress in their careers. In short, to ask an applicant to teach a class of children and young people with little knowledge of their specific learning needs is not normally the best solution.

Figure 2.1 illustrates a journey of the application through to the acceptance process from a university and school partnership perspective.

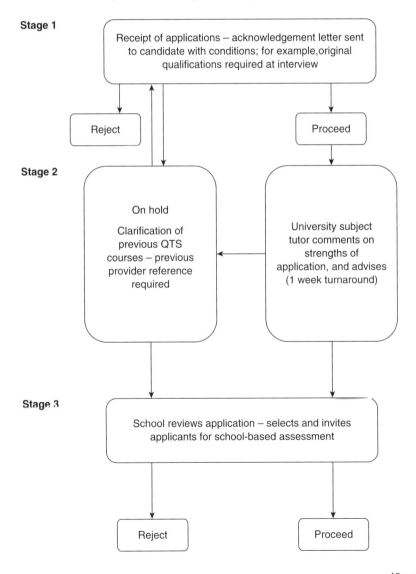

(Continued)

Figure 2.1 *(Continued)*

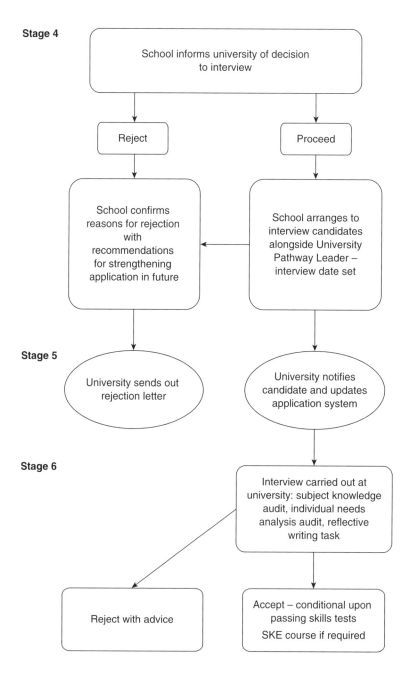

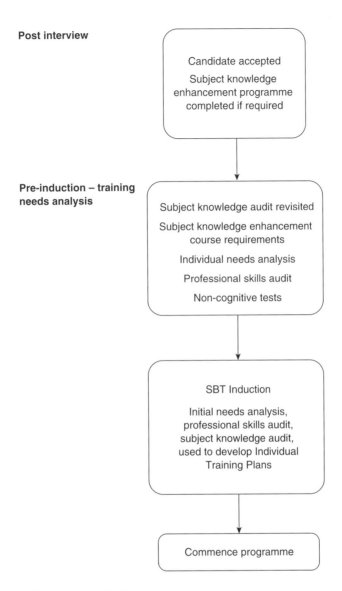

Post interview

Candidate accepted

Subject knowledge
enhancement programme
completed if required

**Pre-induction – training
needs analysis**

Subject knowledge audit revisited

Subject knowledge enhancement
course requirements

Individual needs analysis

Professional skills audit

Non-cognitive tests

SBT Induction

Initial needs analysis,
professional skills audit,
subject knowledge audit,
used to develop Individual
Training Plans

Commence programme

Figure 2.1   Recruitment and selection processes

MAKING THE MOST OF PRE-SELECTION PROCESSES

As outlined above, recruitment to ITE starts even prior to the point of application. There are opportunities to engage with potential applicants early in their decision-making cycle as their wish to enter the profession emerges. One example of this is the use of 'school experience' programmes or placements. A version of this is organized and funded by the NCTL. Alternatively, schools often develop links with local universities who are often keen to link student undergraduate volunteers with school improvement projects. These programmes are an excellent opportunity for a potential applicant to spend focused time in school in order to develop an understanding of the role of the teacher. We would argue that the best of these programmes provide opportunities for structured, targeted school-based activity. For example, a university may link with an ITE provider to set up such a programme. The ITE provider prepares participants to go into school through targeted briefings (for example, professional expectations, developing a focused curriculum intervention). Schools are keen to be involved in the project as they not only see this as an excellent way to focus on school improvement priorities and raise aspirations, but also as a way to engage with potential applicants for school-embedded teacher education courses.

Recruiting to school-embedded ITE involves advertising and promoting the course. This may be through local press engagement, promotion via in-school open evenings, open afternoons in schools and a range of other tools. It is worth considering ways to build relationships with potential applicants for the future. For example, consider your response to a potential applicant for a postgraduate ITE course who explains at your open evening that they are not due to graduate for two years. You may wish to offer school experience and keep in touch as they complete their degree. It is common now for schools to keep in touch with their alumni – could this be a potential source of applicants for the future? However, this is not without its challenges. There is a view that placing trainees in schools they attended as pupils misses opportunities to challenge assumptions arising from their formative experience – arguably an essential part of the development process for an aspirant teacher. Many providers discourage pre-ITE experience within schools applicants previously attended as pupils in order to encourage a breadth of experience. For these reasons this approach needs to be used with caution. Where schools work as federations or partnerships, though, it might be possible to arrange placements in other schools. As well as alumni, many schools have colleagues within the school who they would wish to develop through to an ITE qualification. This is of course subject to existing qualifications.

Overall, whether recruiting locally or more widely, it is necessary to ensure that you undertake strategic planning of the teacher workforce. This is easier said than done in a context with year-on-year ITE allocations, but considering future workforce recruitment issues is vital to ensure an adequate supply of teachers to individual schools and alliances, and to meet system-wide supply needs.

DEVELOPING SELECTION PROCESSES IN PRACTICE

Since November 2013 the NCTL have, through the Universities and Colleges Admissions Service (UCAS), developed a single application system for all routes into teacher training and as such should enable the recruitment and selection process to be streamlined. The House of Commons Education Committee (2012) in the report *Great Teachers: Attracting, Training and Retaining the Best*, sets the parameters for the selection process, which includes the following:

- entry tests for applicants to teaching in numeracy and literacy with a limit on two resits

- a recommendation that all providers of ITE set entry tests that assess applicants' interpersonal skills through, for example, psychometric testing

- applicants must have some experience of working with children before application to an ITE programme and can demonstrate this at interview

- the selection and recruitment process is driven by the schools with support from their nominated HEI where appropriate.

As Figure 2.1 suggests, the recruitment process is complex but, if dealt with logically and systematically through clearly defined and agreed processes, it will enable you to recruit the very best candidates.

In 2010 the government published *The Importance of Teaching* White Paper which outlined the direction of policy for education in England and introduced the intention of using psychometric assessment as part of the selection process for teacher training. In Section 2.11 it stated:

> we know that highly effective models of teacher training (including those of Finland, Singapore, Teach First and Teach for America) systematically use assessments of aptitude, personality and resilience as part of the candidate selection process. We are trialling such assessments and, subject to evaluation, plan to make them part of the selection process for teacher training. (DfE, 2010: 21)

The intention of this was to 'raise the quality of new entrants to the teaching profession' (ibid.: 20). The procedures in place for Teach First applicants include a whole day of interviews and highly structured scenarios to measure the aforementioned characteristics. To enable this they have a team devoted to carrying out these tasks 50 weeks a year, four days a week. Needless to say this use of human resources is far removed from the capabilities of schools or HEI providers.

Recent Ofsted inspections of ITE providers have gathered information about the testing used and it is clear that their use is being monitored by the government.

Implementing the testing of applicants has raised a number of matters for providers of ITE to consider. The tests themselves have to be valid and reliable; they have to be administered in a coherent and consistent manner and have to remain ethical in their content and administration. These criteria make it almost impossible for a training provider to administer these tests without considerable cost of the tests themselves and the human resources required to administer them (a provider would require a licence to use the copyrighted tests and have a psychometrically trained member of staff to administer and score each test). Thus a number of providers have outsourced their testing to private companies at considerable cost. To reduce the overall cost, some providers may test applicants after they have successfully completed the interview stage of the application process and are thus more likely to be taking up an offer of a place on the course. Testing earlier in the process would entail larger numbers of applicants sitting such tests, creating significant financial commitment. The tests themselves are completed online via an emailed login system and the findings are accessible to the provider within hours of completion.

The use of the psychometric testing of applicants is still new and data from trainee progress and outcomes has yet to be correlated with the scores from the tests. Early indications from trainees who have left the course within the first half term show no pattern from the test results but the numbers are so few that no statistical analysis is possible. Realistically no analysis of worth can be started until the system has run its course over a two-year period, when accurate data is more readily available.

Once the initial checks and balances have been completed, such as all academic requirements met, skills tests passed, DBS checks and teaching experience documented, the applicant will normally be taken forward to the formal interview and selection stage. Some applicants may be taken forward to interview without all the necessary requirements in place; this is normal practice, for example, for many postgraduate entrants where the receiving school and/or HEI will be awaiting confirmation of candidates' degree awards if they are in their final year of study at university.

The selection process should involve all partners such as the school or college and the HEI. There is some debate around the merits of observing candidates teach full classes of children as part of this selection process but there is little doubt that it is important to observe candidates working with children and young people at some point in the selection process.

Care should be taken not to overburden candidates during the selection process but a variety of modes of assessment at interview are to be encouraged, such as a presentation to staff of the school on a teaching resource they have found effective in developing children's understanding of a particular mathematical concept, for example. However, informal conversations with colleagues will also reap rewards in terms of assessing candidates' skills and personal attributes as well as observing candidates' interactions with children and young people. In short, do they appear to enjoy working with children?

Additional considerations will be to match candidates' skills to your school and/or department's needs. As such it is also useful to share among the wider school partnership the skills and attributes candidates bring so that they may be suitably matched to the school's needs. In other chapters in this book there are cautions about the limitations of thinking of school-based training as being primarily for a specific school, and you are encouraged to think about your responsibility for training professionals in the broadest sense.

NEEDS ANALYSIS, PRE-ITE AND INDUCTION

We have seen above how the development journey for the teacher of the future starts pre-application. This journey extends as we move from applicant to trainee teacher. During the interview process you will have started to identify areas for the applicant to develop and will hopefully have been able to share and explore these with them. Subject knowledge is one area where we are perhaps more familiar with the notion of 'needs analysis' and a result of the selection process should be a raising of awareness of the areas which they will need to develop, including prior to entry. This may be a condition of entry (for example, the requirement to undertake some form of SKE) or may be a recommendation to continue to develop knowledge in a particular area through self-study, depending on whether the applicant meets the requirements for entry to ITE. Other needs may include additional school experience; you may wish the applicant to attend a particular school for this so that 'fit' with a particular training department and their needs may be ascertained. These needs may be broad, for example, gaining experience of current teaching approaches to the subject of geography, or may be more specific. Needs analysis, whether focused on academic needs or more practical needs, is a good basis for developing the relationship between provider and future trainee teacher prior to the start of the course.

Induction may take place at the very start of the course or, in the case of many providers and schools, during the summer term prior to the start of the course. The aim of induction is both to undertake some of the necessary administrative tasks prior to the course starting and to familiarize the applicant with course expectations and those involved, that is, key staff and peers, thereby developing a community of practice at an early stage and with all-important support and challenge.

Initial teacher education providers will often invite those holding offers to attend for a day during the summer term to work with key staff and to start to fur- ther develop areas to work on prior to the course, for example, by being provided with reading lists or key documents. Peer support networks are encouraged to develop (for example, through the use of a protected online forum). Increasingly, those engaged in school-based ITE, such as School Direct, also run such events in school during the summer term so that applicants can develop an understanding of a particular school. Given current insecurity around allocations and recruit- ment, this is a way to encourage those to whom you have offered places to start to feel part of that cohort or group, both increasing their feelings of security and the provider's confidence that the place will be taken up at the start of the course. We do need to recognize that some secondary shortage subjects are renowned for recruiting late in the recruitment cycle and this poses challenges for the latecomer, and you will need to consider ways to facilitate these trainees being part of this cohort.

CASE STUDIES

The case studies below illustrate the complexity of issues underpinning the suc- cessful delivery of quality ITE that have the potential to impact on recruitment processes. We contend that in deep partnership models all partners work successfully together to engage with the depth of issues and work to find solutions as a partnership.

CASE STUDY 2.1 'WORKING TOGETHER' TO ENHANCE SECONDARY PGCE PARTNERSHIP PROCESSES

A working group was convened to provide an opportunity for university tutors and school-based professional mentors to work together in a 'third space' (Wenger, 1988).

The working group comprising university partnership tutors and school-based mentors (from a range of partnership schools actively working with the university) met to review the observation, assessment and quality assurance processes for the Secondary PGCE programme. The group openly discussed and evaluated the partnership practices and policies to help to secure consistently high-quality outcomes for trainees on the core and the School Direct programmes. All involved were working actively on developing a vision for ITE to underpin collaborative recruitment activity.

The working group discussion led to:

- revised observation paperwork and clearer roles, responsibilities and expectations linked more explicitly to the Teachers' Standards

- improved processes around QTS grading interpretation with a focal point for discussions about trainees' progress towards meeting the standards, through weekly target setting and through lesson observation

- clear roles and responsibilities for colleagues involved in PGCE Core and School Direct courses, including recruitment roles and responsibilities

- quality assurance processes that aim to improve the overall consistency, coherence and quality of all aspects of the training and placements through effective moderation and quality assurance of the judgements that are being made.

This review was felt to not only help to produce improved paperwork and processes for the partnership, but also provide opportunity for tutors, mentors and trainees to engage meaningfully in the underlying pedagogical process of the PGCE programme – thereby leading to the promotion of a 'collaborative' rather than a 'cooperative' model of training. The specific cases below are examples of this partnership at work.

CASE STUDY 2.2

This case study illustrates how an ITE partnership made the necessary adjustments to a trainee with a specific disability in supporting them to achieve QTS.

The trainee secured a place on the programme with a strong academic background and experience of teaching in the further education (FE) sector. She had a severe hearing impairment, and in order to fulfil programme and NCTL requirements would need support from both the school and student enabling centre on campus. All resources were transcribed and signers and interpreters were provided for all subject and professional studies sessions at university.

In order to ensure that the trainee could have access to the same opportunities as other trainees and to develop an appropriate individual training plan (ITP), the programme manager met with the professional tutor. Reference was made to the *Fitness to Teach* and *Able to Teach* (TDA, 2007a, 2007b) guidelines to ensure that the trainee had 'reasonable' support in place, while given the opportunity to demonstrate all of the relevant QTS standards. The supporting school also had a specialist deaf unit, which could provide appropriate resources for the trainee to teach effectively.

The issues relating to the programme included how to ensure the trainee would be able to teach larger classes of mainstream pupils, and demonstrate ability to meet all of the Professional Standards for Teachers. A programme was designed to:

- build up class sizes over time

- teach more mainstream mathematics groups.

Use of the *Fitness to Teach* and *Able to Teach* guidelines supported the programme design, taking into account:

- Are there any barriers?

  o Skills of interpreter impact upon delivery (knowledge of specialist terminology).

- What reasonable adjustments might we make?

  o Speaker/signer within the department to support terminology.

  o Timetable to be built up over time.

- ITP and timetable for next term

  o to increase class sizes by February – teaching full mainstream groups

  o move to teaching in the mathematics department rooms to enable full integration to mathematics team, initially sharing groups (giving subject specialist support).

Challenging targets were set and the above support provided. The trainee completed with a Grade 1 outcome.

Given the nature of the training experience, the school commissioned a training DVD, monitoring the trainee's journey and impact upon classes and attitudes. This was shared with local authorities and university staff at the EBITT Advisory Group and is now available for use within the school and for university training purposes. The trainee subsequently gained permanent employment at the school.

 CASE STUDY 2.3

This case illustrates how an ITE partnership successfully managed the training programme of a support staff member who achieved QTS and who was later employed as a qualified teacher in the same school.

The trainee began the programme with a strong academic background, and had secured the support of a partnership school with relatively high-achieving pupils where he had worked as a science technician and had delivered lessons with Year 9, 10 and 13 pupils. His application included strong references from the supporting school and at interview he demonstrated a good insight into teaching and a dedicated approach.

As the second term progressed, feedback from observations indicated that the trainee was not able to make the expected progress in terms of lesson structure and behaviour management. It was evident that the transition from science technician to teacher was presenting further challenges to the trainee, particularly in relation to behaviour management and the organization of resources.

This led to intervention by the professional tutor and university tutor with initial 'at risk' support and targets put in place. The trainee was guided to an extended second school placement in a long-standing partnership school where pupils provided many more challenges in terms of behaviour and aspirations, though strong subject knowledge was required to deliver the programmes available in the science department.

The programme manager liaised with the professional tutor, headteacher and school-based tutor to provide an extended placement for the trainee. Further intervention and support was provided in the initial weeks of the placement, and a timetable built up for the trainee. This allowed the trainee to develop confidence in a department where his subject knowledge and industrial experience were highly valuable in developing resources suitable for the courses offered by the department, whilst developing skills in behaviour management through observations and co-planning and co-teaching. Further intervention by the programme manager included feedback on the emotional intelligence aspects of his practice and targets were set in relation to non-verbal communication and strategies to develop relationships with more challenging pupils.

Results of observation feedback demonstrated that the trainee gradually improved practice, completing the programme within the designated time frame. Not only did he complete the programme as a Grade 2 trainee, he was subsequently offered a permanent position within the science department at the school where he was originally employed.

CONCLUSION

In summary, we have examined here the context for teacher supply, recruitment and selection, and have provided a range of practical examples of related activities and processes for your consideration. Through critical examination of what we mean by 'recruiting the very best' we have challenged potential assumptions about this concept. We have set out a range of challenges for recruitment with practical considerations for solutions. Finally, we have aimed to convey a sense of the process of recruitment and selection as involving a range of partners and that starts before a potential applicant has decided to apply and continues well into the induction stage of the ITE year.

FURTHER READING

We have argued here that values and dispositions are not straightforward to define. For further reading and a much more thorough treatment readers are encouraged to access Kallick and Costa (2008).

Kallick, B. and Costa, A. (2008) *Learning and Leading with Habits of Mind: 16 Essential Characteristics for Success*. Alexandria, VA: Association for Supervision and Curriculum Development.

REFERENCES

Barber, M. and Mourshed, M. (2007) *How the World's Best-performing Schools Systems Come Out on Top*. Mckinsey+Co.

Burch, J. (2011) 'Secondary programmes quality group: validation briefing document', unpublished, University of Cumbria.

Clarke, J. and Pye, T. (2012) 'Right turn for Gove; wrong turn for Initial Teacher Education', BERA Conference Paper, Manchester University, September.

Costa, A. (1991) 'Habits of mind', in A. Costa (ed.), *Developing Minds: A Resource Book for Teaching Thinking*. Alexandria, VA: ASCD.

Day, C., Sammons, P., Stobart, G., Kington, A. and Gu, Q. (2007) *Teachers Matter. Connecting Lives, Work and Effectiveness*. Maidenhead: Open University Press.

Department for Education (DfE) (2010) *The Importance of Teaching*. White Paper. London: HMSO.

House of Commons Children, Schools and Families Committee (2010) *Training of Teachers. Fourth Report of Session 2009–2010 Volume 1*. London: The Stationery Office.

House of Commons Education Committee (2012) *Great teachers: Attracting, Training and Retaining the Best. Ninth Report of Session 2010–2012 Volume 1*. London: The Stationery Office.

Hymer, B. (2009) *Gifted and Talented Pocketbook*. Alresford: Teachers' Pocketbooks.

Kallick, B. and Costa, A. (2008) *Learning and Leading with Habits of Mind: 16 Essential Characteristics for Success*. Alexandria, VA: Association for Supervision and Curriculum Development.

Organisation for Economic Co-operation and Development (OECD) (2005) *Attracting, Developing and Retaining Effective Teachers*. Paris: OECD.

SCORE (2011) 'Attracting, training and retaining the best teachers: a SCORE response to the Education Select Committee inquiry', available at www.rsc.org/images/training-retaining-teachers_tcm18-209680.pdf.

Smith, A. (2004) *Making Mathematics Count: The Report of Professor Adrian Smith's Inquiry into Post-14 Mathematics Education*. The Smith Inquiry. London: The Stationery Office.

Smith, A., Moran, A., McCully, A. and Clarke, L. (2005) 'A values-based approach to teacher education', an Economic and Social Research Council (ESRC) Programme of Research into Teaching and Learning.

'Trainee teacher numbers tumble' (2012) *Education*, 469: 4.

Training and Development Agency for Schools (TDA) (2007a) *Fitness to Teach; Occupational Health Guidance for the Training and Employment of Teachers*. London: TDA.

Training and Development Agency for Schools (TDA) (2007b) *Able to Teach; Guidance for Initial Teacher Trainers on Discrimination, Disability and Fitness to Teach*. London: TDA.

Welch, F. C., Pitts, R. E., Tenini, K. J., Kuenlen, M. G. and Wood, S. G. (2010) 'Significant issues in defining and assessing teacher dispositions', *Teacher Educator*, 45(3): 179–201.

Wenger, E. (1998) *Communities of Practice: Learning, Meaning and Identity*. Cambridge: Cambridge University Press.

CHAPTER 3

MODELS OF PROFESSIONAL LEARNING AND WHAT THEY MEAN FOR THOSE WORKING WITH TEACHERS

Carey Philpott

By the end of this chapter you should have an overview of:

- different models of professional learning and some of their strengths and weaknesses
- what this means for ways of working with student teachers.

The focus of this chapter is on different ways we can understand how people learn to be teachers. We need to understand this process so that we know how best to support it. When thinking about *how* teachers learn we might also think about *what* teachers learn. This is because there is a connection between what we need to learn and how we most effectively learn it.

Different models of learning to be a teacher are related to wider developments in learning theories. One way of understanding developments in learning theories is as a journey from thinking about learning as something inside the heads of individual learners to increasingly locating learning as something that takes place in, and is influenced by, social contexts. Another way of characterizing these developments is as a movement from scientific or mechanistic models of learning to more emphasis on humanistic aspects of learning such as relationships, identity and aspirations and the ways these influence why, what and how we learn.

LEARNING THEORIES; A THUMBNAIL SKETCH

A potted history of learning theories might include:

- behaviourism (for example Skinner)
- cognitivism (for example Piaget)
- constructivism (for example Bruner)
- social constructivism (for example Vygotsky)
- experiential learning (for example Kolb)
- humanism (for example Maslow)
- andragogy (for example Knowles)
- social practice theories (for example Lave and Wenger, Engestrom).

This is not a strict chronology as some of the ideas overlap historically. However, it does represent a general historical direction of travel. Some of these models also share features with one another rather than being totally distinct. Nevertheless, each does indicate something about the different ways we can understand learning. The purpose of the outlines below is to provide a context for the focus on professional learning that comes after.

Behaviourism

Behaviourism rejected attempts to speculate on what went on inside learners' minds during learning and, as a more scientifically defensible approach, chose to focus on external observable behaviours. Behaviourism studied how behaviours could be modified through the use of externally applied rewards and sanctions. Learning was defined as modified behaviour and research focused on how rewards and sanctions could be used to modify behaviour most effectively.

Behaviourism did not include consideration of the ways in which meaning, identity and intentions might influence the behaviour of individual learners. It was not considered scientific to focus on such elusive, internal phenomena that might not be universal.

Cognitivism, constructivism and social contructivism

Cognitivism and constructivism sought to understand learning by doing the thing that behaviourism would not do, that is, speculate on the processes inside learners' heads that lead to learning. However, cognitivism was still interested in being able to generalize about learning processes that are common to everybody rather than understanding how learners might be different.

Cognitivism was also primarily concerned with solitary learners rather than seeing social interaction and social context as central to models of learning. The models of learning of cognitivism are sometimes likened to information-processing models used in computing. The phrase 'lone scientist' has also been used to characterize learners in some cognitive models because learning is seen as a rational process (rather than an emotional one) that can be understood by focusing on individual learners.

Constructivism can be seen as introducing a greater element of personalization through its argument that what and how we learn is related to what we already know. So a constructivist approach to thinking about learning requires that we think about where individual learners are starting from and how we relate new learning to the learner's existing understanding.

Social constructivism places more emphasis on the centrality of social interaction to the process of learning. Rather than researching learners, as individuals, social constructivism often researches pairs or groups of learners, focusing on how the processes of interaction support learning.

Experiential learning

Approaches to experiential learning focus less on learning that takes place in formal contexts for learning and more on how learners learn from experience when engaged in 'real-world' activities. These models are often conceptualized as a cycle of learning based on reflection on experience that leads to modified action and a new round of reflection on the effect of that modified action.

Humanism and andragogy

Humanistic models of learning and andragogy focus on the importance of individual human aspiration, values and life history in what, why and how people learn. Whereas behaviourism understands learning in terms of rewards and sanctions, and constructivism in terms of learners building theories, humanistic models focus on how feelings, motivations, aspirations, values and life history influence learning for specific learners. Andragogy is related to humanistic models of learning and seeks to understand the ways in which adult learners are different from children. Some of the ways in which they might be different relate to their motivations for learning, their self-directedness, their experience and their life history.

Social practice theories

Social practice theories are a related group of models of learning that recently have been among the most popular. The most prominent of these have been communities of practice, cultural historical activity theory (CHAT) and sociocultural theory. What they share in common is focusing on learning as a social and cultural process that can best be understood if we focus on specific individuals, in specific contexts, engaged in specific activities rather than on abstracted, generalized learners.

Sociocultural theory and CHAT have similarities with social constructivism in that they focus on learning as an irreducibly social process mediated by shared 'tools' such as language. However, they differ from social constructivism in that they also focus on the central role of cultural context as well as social context in learning. A focus on cultural context recognizes that where we are learning (China or the UK) and when we are learning (now or 500 years ago) will alter the tools that we use to make sense of the world and this will affect what and how we learn. Cultural context can also operate at the level of institutions (for example, social services rather than the police service). Learning in each of these will make use of different tools, such as different shared beliefs, practices and conceptual models, and this will influence what is learned and how.

Communities of practice emphasizes the ways in which learning is also about becoming a member of a community by incrementally adopting the practices and identity of that community and becoming an ever more central member of it.

Social practice theories often focus on ideas such as situated rationality and situated cognition (Brown et al., 1989). These ideas explore the ways in which how we think is connected to where we are when thinking and how this might change, even for the same individual, in other contexts. For example, how we think about young people when we are being a parent in the home might differ from how we think about them when we are being a teacher in the classroom.

MODELS OF PROFESSIONAL LEARNING: A CRITICAL DISCUSSION

The broader context of models of learning in the previous section should inform your understanding of what is in this section.

Kolb – experiential learning

Several experiential learning models conceptualize learning as a cycle of reflection on experience. One of the best known of these models is Kolb's experiential learning cycle (Kolb, 1983) (Figure 3.1).

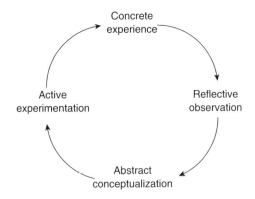

Figure 3.1 Kolb's experiential learning cycle

This model is often used to conceptualize learning as starting from concrete experience. However, learning can start anywhere in this cycle. For the purposes of the discussion at this stage, though, I am going to consider learning starting with concrete experience.

Used in this way, learning starts with an experience. After the experience we reflect on what happened and we use this reflection to build (or adapt) a conceptual understanding of the situation. We use this conceptual understanding to plan our next actions and the cycle starts again. This model has face validity as a model of learning from experience. However, it has some limitations.

One limitation is the possible slippage of this model into a 'lone scientist' model because it apparently emphasizes learning as a purely cognitive process that has no obvious space for values and identity in learning, and also might not consider where the resources for abstract conceptualization come from beyond the individual learner.

Another limitation of this model is that it can lead to restrictive learning (Evans et al., 2006). It is possible to imagine a teacher in this model who reflects on how to increase the test scores of her class. She could travel around this reflective learning cycle several times, each time getting better, on the basis of reflecting on experience, at improving the test scores. However, this learning might be restrictive because she never reflects on whether improving test scores is the most important thing or on whether it should be achieved irrespective of the methods used. A simple version of this model might lead to a view of learning in which we get better at achieving given outcomes without reflecting on their value.

Another risk of restrictive learning for this model relates to situated rationality and situated cognition (Brown et al., 1989). If we accept that the resources for abstract conceptualization are socially and culturally specific, then our learning can be limited by the ways of thinking that are dominant in the context we are in. This could mean that a student teacher learning in one school could come to quite different conclusions about the same experiences to those they would come to in another. This learning is restrictive because it fails to recognize that the understanding of a situation in one institution is not universal but that different understandings of the same experience exist in different places.

A third possible problem with this model is the difficulty in practice of producing paradigm shifts in people's thinking. Kolb's cycle is based on the idea that our experiences will alter the ways we conceptualize the world. However, many researchers (Festinger, 1957; Kuhn, 1996) have concluded that it takes a lot for experience to change our models of the world. In practice we tend to be very good at interpreting our experience to make it consistent with the models we already have.

Argyris and Schön – double-loop learning

Some of the limitations of Kolb's model can be overcome by adopting the double-loop learning model of Argyris and Schön (Argyris, 1976, 1999; Argyris and Schön,

1978). They define single-loop learning as learning that takes place when the goals and frameworks of actions are taken for granted and we are just interested in how to operate more effectively within them. Double-loop learning takes place when we also reflect on those goals and frameworks so that learning might involve changing these as well.

The recognition that we need to go beyond the restrictive cycle of single-loop learning also acknowledges that what we learn might be socially and culturally situated and, therefore, limited by the world view of the particular institutions that we are in. However, the main motivation for going beyond current institutionally specific ways of understanding a situation in the model of Argyris and Schön is the failure of the strategies or techniques currently being used to improve performance. It is this failure that prompts learners to examine the fundamental assumptions they are working within. This means that if the techniques being used appear to be working to achieve the predefined goals of the institution we are in, we may not feel the need to question the value of the goals or of the techniques we are using. Going back to the example of the teacher and the test scores, if the teacher finds that a diet of rote learning motivated by fear of punishment improves test scores, then she might never question the value of the goal or whether the methods are appropriate. We also still potentially have the problem of how difficult it is for our experiences to actually change the models of the world we hold.

In addition, although values and emotions play a part in the double-loop learning model, other models of professional learning give a more central role to the ways in which non-cognitive aspects play an important role in what professional learning is and how it takes place. So this is, arguably, an area that is still under-represented in this model.

Schön – the reflective practitioner

It is largely thanks to Schön's influence that the term 'reflective practitioner' became ubiquitous in teacher education (Schön, 1990, 1994), although Schön rarely, if ever, wrote about teachers. Schön is well known for writing about two types of reflection on practice: reflection-in-action and reflection-on-action. Reflection-in-action is Schön's term for the thinking we do and the ways in which we adjust our actions while in the middle of acting. An example is how teachers modify their approaches during a lesson as a result of what is happening in the room. Reflection-on-action is similar to the reflective observation of Kolb's experiential learning cycle and happens after the event.

Schön also wrote about the importance of framing and reframing problems (Schön, 1990). Framing is how we conceptualize or construct the problem; what sort of problem do we think it is. In some of his work Schön argued that how we frame a problem should receive as much attention as the solutions we suggest (Schön, 1993). It is important to recognize that problems are constructed and that how we construct them will influence the types of solutions we look for.

Another contribution that Schön made to understanding professional learning was to reject what he called 'technical rationality' in favour of the model of the reflective practitioner. Technical rationality is a view of knowledge that believes that there are stable and universal solutions to problems and that these can be unproblematically applied across a range of contexts. A professional practitioner, therefore, just needs to take them 'off the peg' and apply them. As an alternative, the reflective practice model emphasizes the importance of personally generated, contextually specific solutions to ever changing circumstances.

Engestrom – cultural historical activity theory (CHAT)

Cultural historical activity theory is a development of Vygotsky's work on psychology (see Roth and Lee, 2007, for an overview). Vygotsky researched the ways that human thinking is mediated by the use of cultural tools. In a concrete way, these tools can be things like bows and arrows, tractors or computers. However, they can also be tools such as language, mathematical formulae, theories or belief systems, all of which are culturally specific creations to help us do things. In the context of learning, these things influence how and what we learn. For example, if we want to learn how to manage behaviour effectively in a classroom, what we learn from our experiences in the classroom will be shaped by the culturally specific tools (beliefs, theories and values) that we bring to the situation.

Engestrom and others developed this model by making more explicit the ways in which a range of cultural factors influence the nature of the tools (Engestrom et al., 1999). He represents the developed model by the diagram in Figure 3.2. Engestrom calls this an activity system.

An easy way to understand an activity system is to think of it as a group of people (community) engaged in a shared activity (working on an object to achieve an outcome). There are different roles within the community (division of labour), accepted ways of doing things (rules) and different accepted tools (beliefs, theories and standard procedures as much as physical tools) for doing this. The subject in Figure 3.2 is an individual member of that community. The lines connecting each

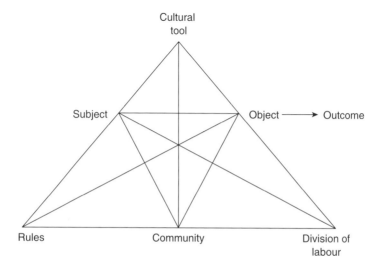

Figure 3.2 Engestrom's activity system

word in the diagram show that each of these things influences the nature of the others. What this means for learning (which is one form of human action) is that what and how we learn is influenced by the culturally and historically specific tools (beliefs, theories and accepted procedures) that we use to help in the learning process. The nature of these tools is influenced by a range of factors about the specific culture and organization where we are learning.

Engestrom's work has been developed by researchers in work-based learning to emphasize his distinction between expansive and restrictive learning (Evans et al., 2006). Restrictive learning is characterized by looking for already existing solutions to known problems. Expansive learning is characterized by the need to generate new solutions to novel problems. Restrictive learning can result from learning within a single activity system and being limited by the rules, tools and so on of the system. It can also mean learning no more than is necessary to carry out our given function within a particular organization.

Lave and Wenger – communities of practice

Communities of practice (Lave and Wenger, 1991; Wenger, 1999) has recently become one of the most influential learning theories. This model emphasizes learning as a holistic process that involves becoming a member of a community. Becoming a member of a community involves not only learning the knowledge and developing the skills used by that community but also means developing the identity and adopting the practices, values and general outlook of that community. Learning in this model is not just a cognitive process but one that can involve all aspects of our identity and behaviour.

A key term for Lave and Wenger is 'legitimate peripheral participation'. This means that to learn to become a member of a community we must be given some legitimate form of participation in it, we must be admitted to it and its practices as a proper member. However, the word 'peripheral' acknowledges that initially the membership and participation will be in a subsidiary or subordinate role, not a central one. Lave and Wenger and other researchers (Hutchins, 1996) have studied a number of working communities and detailed the successive tasks that learners perform and the roles that they take as they move from the periphery as beginners to the centre as experts. Some researchers (Gherardi et al., 1998; Philpott, 2006) have identified what they call a situated curriculum for learning. This is the sequence of tasks and roles that new members of a working community typically engage in as they move from periphery to centre.

Communities of practice is susceptible to a number of criticisms as a model of learning. It might make learners appear too passive as they are apparently moulded into a community identity. This is linked to a more general criticism that many applications of the communities of practice model to specific situations have not analysed in detail below the level of the community (Trowler, 2005). This might make it appear that communities and their members are homogeneous and that there are no differences within communities and no issues such as power and conflict within communities.

Another criticism is that the theory emphasizes learning how to carry out existing practices and roles. It is not clear how it can explain learning to do things in innovative ways that go beyond current community practices.

IMPLICATIONS OF DIFFERENT MODELS OF PROFESSIONAL LEARNING FOR INITIAL TEACHER EDUCATION IN SCHOOL

Experiential learning and reflective practice

The nature of school-based ITE means that learning through experience is a central part of the learning process. What are the best ways to support this process and to enhance its value and impact?

A recurring theme in the previous section is that learning from experience can become restrictive. So the first challenge for school-based ITE is to prevent restrictive learning. The purpose of ITE is not to shape student teachers so that they fit only into the expectations and practices of a single school. It is to assist in the creation of teachers who can work across the education system with its diverse expectations and practices, and who are equipped with the skills, confidence and disposition to reflect critically on any current practice and to generate innovative solutions when necessary.

One of the attractions of school-based ITE might be that schools can 'grow their own' teachers. However, a longer-term view needs to be taken. The teachers that schools train this year could be in other schools next year and might be replaced in their training school by teachers trained elsewhere. For this reason it is important to train teachers with the adaptability to move into different contexts. Also, if 'grow your own' means restrictive learning, new teachers might not have the ability to think beyond existing practices when new challenges arise, even in their training school.

The last section argued that Kolb's cycle of experiential learning provides little detail on how our reflections on experience are formed into abstract conceptualizations. I would argue that they are fitted into ways of understanding the world that are easily available to us as cultural tools or resources. There are a number of ready-made ways of understanding the world in any given culture that can be used for making sense of the experiences we have. When students are new to ITE it is likely that the cultural resources they use for making sense of their experience will be those available in the world outside the context they are learning in. So they might draw on media representations of education and young people. They might draw on the understanding of school they acquired when they were pupils. Or they may draw on 'folk psychology' (Bruner, 1990), that is, general, non-specialist, ways of explaining human behaviour that are prevalent within any culture.

As they gain experience it is likely that they will use the ways of making sense of teaching and learning that are common in their school. Their abstract conceptualization will come from the ways that things are routinely conceptualized by the people they work with. However, there are risks that this will become restrictive learning or single-loop learning. They might become increasingly proficient at fitting in with the expectations of their school. However, what is needed from a process of teacher education is expansive learning; the ability to see beyond the world view and practices of any single school at any single point in history.

One way to minimize this risk is to pay explicit and careful attention to the abstract conceptualization part of the learning cycle. In practice the process of conceptualization can be largely implicit or hidden. Students develop ways of understanding their experience through interacting with more experienced teachers but they rarely expose this conceptualization to explicit examination. One way to minimize the risk of restrictive learning, is to ensure that learners are provided with more than one way of understanding their experiences. This means offering alternative theories or models for experience and subjecting initial conceptualizations of experience to critical scrutiny. Alternative models can come from educational research and theory (Brookfield, 1995). Universities have traditionally been the providers of educational research and theory to student teachers but in a more school-based model this must also be done by the school.

The relocation of this role from the university to the school also raises another consideration. In the first section of this chapter I commented that Kolb's cycle is often used as if the process of learning always starts from experience. However, the learning process can start anywhere in the cycle. One of the possible limitations of traditional ITE courses is that they typically start the learning cycle with abstract conceptualization. This means that students are introduced to educational ideas in a generalized form first and are then expected to apply them to specific situations. Viewed unsympathetically, this can look like a technical-rationalist approach to education in which teacher learning consists of acquiring a body of knowledge and skills that can then be applied to diverse situations of practice. Many students find it difficult to understand how to relate the abstract conceptualizations to the specific experiences they have. This often leads to them considering what they learned in the university as irrelevant and they seek alternative ways of understanding experience through the sense-making resources routinely used in the school (Philpott, 2006). A better model is to use a variety of theories or models after students have had experiences, in order to encourage them to conceptualize their experiences in different ways and to reflect on the relative merits of different conceptualizations. This is more like Argyris and Schön's double-loop learning, in which we are invited to reflect on the value of our current assumptions and goals as well as on how to improve our practice within them. It also links to Schön's argument about not neglecting the importance of how we frame problems before we try to find a solution to them.

Another consideration comes from Brown and Duguid's (1993, 2000) distinction between 'supply-side' and 'demand-side' learning. They argue that much formal education is supply-side learning: what is learned, how and when, is decided by the providers rather than the learners. Therefore, it might not be related to the particular concerns of the learner at that point in their development. However, demand-side learning is led by learners who learn what they want to learn, how and when they want to learn it. If we consider the constructivist model of learning outlined in the first section of this chapter, you might be able to see that learning is likely to take place more effectively where learners are ready to relate new learning to what they currently know and understand. A risk of supply-side learning is that learners cannot assimilate the things they are being told to learn in relation to what they already understand.

Starting the experiential learning cycle with abstract conceptualization could be a form of supply-side learning as student teachers might be asked to make sense of ideas that do not yet relate to any experiences they have had. Using abstract conceptualization retrospectively to make sense of experiences learners have had, and challenges they are wrestling with, is more like demand-side learning. This sequence for learning also relates to Billett's (1996, 1998) idea of 'disembedding' as a useful process for professional learning. Disembedding involves using specific experiences to develop more general understandings of practice rather than starting with the general understanding and trying to apply it.

However, we need to acknowledge that this model is still limited by seeing learning as a fundamentally rational or cognitive process. It has no obvious place for aspects of learning such as the values and identity of the professional community that learners are joining. It is worth making a distinction here between values and identity as things to be learned as part of learning to be a teacher, and as things that might motivate learning. The latter are things that the humanistic and andragogy models of learning take account of. What we can say about demand-side learning is that we can see the motivation for it. It comes from the uncomfortable experience of not feeling properly equipped to deal with the situations we find ourselves in. However, what is still not explained is what motivates us to engage in double-loop learning that questions our goals and assumptions if we are doing a competent job within single-loop learning to produce the kind of performance expected by our cultural context. It might be this situation that accounts for the plateau in student teachers' learning that some researchers have identified (Furlong and Maynard, 1995).

One particular consideration about effective support for school-based learning in ITE arising from reflective and experiential models of learning comes from considering Schön's reflection-in-action and how skilled practitioners reflect on what they are doing and simultaneously modify it. This is a skill of experienced teachers that might not be visible to student teachers. The development of this ability can be supported by making it more visible. Some practical strategies for doing this are included in the third section of this chapter.

Cultural and historical activity theory

The risk of restrictive learning with CHAT comes from how the culturally and historically situated tools or resources that we use for understanding our context, and acting on it, might limit our understanding and actions.

Expansive learning in ITE can be achieved in a number of ways. One of the main ways is to make sure that students have the opportunity to participate in more than one 'activity system'. This can mean different departments within a secondary school, it can mean different schools and it can mean working with different children's services. These need to be more than tokenistic visits but proper opportunities for engagement in the work of these 'activity systems'. An important corollary of this is that differences in understanding and practice in different activity systems should not be downplayed or seen by the students as problematic and signs of confusion. Differences need to be acknowledged and explored because this can lead to the understanding that all ways of understanding a situation and all practices for acting upon it are partial and provisional.

Another way is to build in sufficient space for 'off the job' reflection (Wenger, 1998) and to give official value and status to that reflection. This means not seeing reflection as something that students will mostly do alone in their own time or limiting reflection to single-loop learning on specific classroom incidents or practices. Linked to this need is the need to value the status of students as students; to recognize that they are in the school first and foremost as learners. Although the communities of practice model emphasizes the importance of making learners full members of the community, a risk with this can be that some of the needs of students as expansive learners get overlooked and their process of development primarily becomes one of fitting into the work of the school in the specific role they are given. Another issue is not underplaying the importance of academic learning and qualifications in learning to be a teacher. Also, it is important to emphasize that satisfactorily meeting the expectations of ITE is not the end of the journey. It is the beginning of a longer journey that will involve more inquiry and study, and perhaps further qualifications.

Communities of practice

The communities of practice model has the advantage of giving explicit consideration to the ways that professional learning is not just about developing knowledge and skills, but also about identity, values and relationships as a member of a community. The challenge for using this as our model is to decide how to most effectively facilitate this process of becoming a community member.

One of the first steps is for learners to have legitimate membership of the community and not to be seen as outsiders or temporary visitors. This might seem to conflict with the value of respecting the role of the student as a student. However, this need not be the case. The communities of practice requirement is that students are not kept as outsiders to the community. They should be accorded all the status of a proper member of the community. However, the CHAT requirement is that their participation and opportunities should not be bounded just by carrying out the day-to-day activities of their teacher role but should extend to properly organized and valued opportunities to reflect, read, discuss, gain experience elsewhere, and so on. In practice this means that the distinct role of the *student* teacher needs to be recognized as a full community member.

A second consideration is the opportunities to learn community knowledge, skills and practices that are available through participation in the community. Lave, Wenger and others conducted much of their research in professional communities in which participation in the work of the community was the main form of learning. Although other forms of learning also play an important part in learning to be a teacher, participation in practice is still a key source of learning and one that has become more prominent.

If we see participation in practice as a key source of learning we need to consider how much of the practice of experienced members of the community is visible to learners as they practice. Hutchins (1996) gives an account of two professional communities, one of which had a helpful 'horizon of visibility' in relation to professional practice and one that did not. The community with the helpful practice was US Navy warship navigators. While navigating as they moved in and out of harbour, the teams worked together in such a way that less experienced members could see what it was that more experienced members did and how they did it. This meant that the routine act of practising their profession was in itself a preparation for them to take on more experienced roles and not just an opportunity to improve their performance in their current role. The professional community with the unhelpful horizon was a group of butchers in a large meat preparation facility. The most junior butchers were located where they could not see what the experienced butchers did. This meant that daily practice for them was only likely to result in getting better at their current, limited, role and not in being prepared for more experienced roles. It was a form of restrictive learning.

In ITE the question of horizon of visibility has at least two components. The first is proximity to experienced teachers' practice. How wide a range of experienced teachers' activities are students present at or participating in? The wider the range the better, including things they are not expected to do yet but will be in the future. Learners need to be able to see a professional role beyond the one that they are currently learning. This allows them to understand how their own role fits into the bigger picture and to see a professional trajectory beyond their current learning. The second aspect of horizon of visibility is gaining access to aspects of experienced teachers' practice that are not visible even when students are in proximity. This will mostly be teachers' thought processes. We may be able to observe an experienced teacher's written feedback to pupils but not why they chose to give the feedback they did. We may observe them teaching but not the planning process that produced the lesson, and we may see a teacher responding to a pupil but not see the decision-making that led to that response.

Like other models of learning through practice, the communities-of-practice approach can run the risk of restrictive learning as learners take on the identity and practices of their community without recognizing that it is only one way of thinking and practising. Wenger (1998) emphasizes the importance of 'time off the job' for reducing this problem. This is time for critical reflection away from the immediate pressures of engaging in practice. Some researchers in communities of practice also emphasize the value of 'boundary crossing' which involves working across different communities of practice (Wenger 1998; Wenger et al., 2002).

CASE STUDIES

Note: the names of schools in these case studies have been changed.

CASE STUDY 3.1

This case study shows the planned use of boundary crossing and its benefits for student teacher learning. It focuses on a group of schools who work together as a federation and have good links with other educational institutions in their area, including a special school and a further education college. Nethertarn Federation was not established for the purpose of ITE but its existing infrastructure has been built on to provide this additional benefit. The relationship allows schools in the federation to divide student teacher placements across different institutions. Although each student has a 'home' institution where they spend most of their placement, they spend regular time each week working in a different context. This exchange can be reciprocated between institutions in the federation. Where the alternative context is marked by particularly strong contrasts, the benefits of boundary crossing for student teachers' learning can be clearly seen. Some students spend regular time each week in the special school. They find that the different 'activity system' of the special school means that pupil identities, teacher identities, pupil–teacher relationships, teaching and learning, pastoral issues and home–school links are conceptualized differently. This has given students a broader or alternative view of these issues that has been beneficial to how they think and act in relation to them in the mainstream school that is their 'home' placement. Similarly, student teachers who were regularly placed in a context working with adult learners with learning difficulties have found that it broadened their conception of the purposes and practice of education. This broader conception also benefited their work in the mainstream school.

   The benefits of this planned and sustained boundary crossing are that student teachers:

- have an enriched understanding of educational issues and practices beyond what they could get in a single activity system or community of practice
- understand how their role fits into the larger picture of education and, therefore, get a better understanding of it
- gain a view of possible roles beyond the one for which they are currently training and, therefore, develop an understanding of possible career trajectories.

These are all examples of expansive learning.

CASE STUDY 3.2

This case study focuses on the benefits of making students fully legitimate members of the school community and fully legitimizing their distinctive role as *student* teachers rather than just relatively inexperienced teachers. The first of these relates to the ideas of communities of practice and the second relates to the idea of expansive learning developed from CHAT. Lightmount High School hosts several student teachers. They allocate two fully dedicated high-quality spaces to the student teachers. One of these is a training room and the other is a work room. The training room is equipped with educational displays and notices appropriate to student teachers and has a growing resource library of books useful to student teachers. It is used for regular planned learning activities for the student teachers. The work room has designated space for each student for working and for storing personal property. The provision of these high-quality dedicated spaces for the student teachers signals that they are legitimate and valued members of the community of the school, not visitors, that is, outsiders on sufferance or just passing through. In addition, the provision of a training room, relevant resources and activities recognizes that the primary activity of student teachers is to learn. This also legitimizes the value and role of 'academic' or 'theoretical' learning as well as 'on-the-job' experiential learning for teacher development.

However, this case study also requires a word or two of caution. Some of the student teachers at the school have reported feeling that they are developing a separate community from the community of the rest of the staff. This is because they are often physically separate and are forming a distinct group. The school needs to be careful that the legitimization of the student-teacher role is balanced with full participation in the wider life of the school so that identity formation and the horizon of observation are not limited.

CASE STUDY 3.3

This case study focuses on how to open up hidden processes for the 'horizon of observation'. Egdon Heath Community School has developed the practices of student teachers and experienced teachers sharing planning and marking, and of student teachers continuing focused observations of experienced teachers long into their placement. During shared planning the experienced teacher can articulate their thought processes while planning. The shared planning also allows a rich dialogue about planning. Similarly, during shared marking the experienced teacher can articulate why they make the responses they do during the marking process. The focused observations are followed by a discussion between the student teacher and the experienced teacher so that the student can find out about the thought processes of the teacher, during the lesson, that underlie the actions the teacher took in the lesson.

These are all areas of teacher expertise that could remain invisible to student teachers without the practices that Egdon Heath Community School have developed. Obviously they are time-consuming and, although they are used regularly, they cannot be used on every occasion of planning and marking. The time-consuming nature of these practices also raises another issue of the legitimacy of student teachers and their learning in the school. This is the time that experienced colleagues are given to work with them. If student teachers are a legitimate part of the school community and their learning a central part of what they are there to do, then supporting them properly is a legitimate part of an experienced teacher's role, not just an extra add-on done through goodwill. This means that schools should allocate, as far as possible, proper time to experienced teachers for supporting student teachers.

CONCLUSION

Throughout this chapter a recurring concern has been the impoverished nature of professional learning that can occur if we allow learning to become restrictive. Although the specific term 'restrictive' comes from within one particular model of professional learning, similar concerns are present within other models. Restrictive learning can result from not explicitly considering different ways of making sense of experiences. It can result from accepting the world view of one particular community and not learning about the different world views of others, and it can result from overemphasis of learning from experience and underemphasis on examining underlying theories (perhaps implicit) and assumptions. It can also result from training people with only the skills and knowledge they need to fulfil one role and not giving sufficient opportunities to move beyond this.

If school-based ITE is not to be a restrictive and impoverished model of learning for student teachers it needs to give proper emphasis to educational theories as much as educational practice, it needs to value the academic as much as the practical and it needs to give student teachers the widest experience possible.

FURTHER READING

Evans, K., Hodkinson, P., Rainbird, H. and Unwin, L. (2006) *Improving Workplace Learning.* London: Routledge.
McNally, J. and Blake, A. (2009) *Improving Learning in a Professional Context: A Research Perspective on the New Teacher in School.* London: Routledge.
Philpott, C. (2015) *Theories of Professional Learning: A Critical Guide for Teacher Educators.* St Albans: Critical.

REFERENCES

Argyris, C. (1976) 'Single-loop and double-loop models in research on decision making', *Administrative Science Quarterly,* 21(3): 363–75.
Argyris, C. (1999) *Organisational Learning.* London: Wiley Blackwell.
Argyris, C. and Schön, D.A. (1978) *Organizational Learning: A Theory of Action Perspective.* Reading, MA: Addison-Wesley.
Billett, S. (1996) 'Towards a model of workplace learning: the learning curriculum', *Studies in Continuing Education,* 18(1): 43–58.

Billett, S. (1998) 'Constructing vocational knowledge: situations and other social sources', *Journal of Education and Work*, 11(3): 255–73.

Brookfield, S.D. (1995) *Becoming a Critically Reflective Teacher*. San Francisco, CA: Jossey-Bass.

Brown, J.S. and Duguid, P. (1993) 'Stolen knowledge', *Educational Technology*, 33(3): 10–15.

Brown, J.S. and Duguid, P. (2000) *The Social Life of Information*. Cambridge: Harvard Business School Press.

Brown, J.S., Collins, A. and Duguid, P. (1989) 'Situated cognition and the culture of learning', *Educational Researcher*, 18(1): 32–42.

Bruner, J. (1990) *Acts of Meaning*. Cambridge: Harvard University Press.

Engestrom, Y., Miettinen, R. and Punamaki, R. (1999) *Perspectives on Activity Theory*. Cambridge: Cambridge University Press.

Evans, K., Hodkinson, P., Rainbird, H. and Unwin, L. (2006) *Improving Workplace Learning*. London: Routledge.

Festinger, L. (1957) *A Theory of Cognitive Dissonance*. Stanford, CA: Stanford University Press.

Furlong, J. and Maynard, T. (1995) *Mentoring Student Teachers: The Growth of Professional Knowledge*. London: Routledge.

Gherardi, S., Nicolini, D. and Odella, F. (1998) 'Toward a social understanding of how people learn in organizations: the notion of situated curriculum', *Management Learning*, 29: 273–97.

Hutchins, E. (1996) 'Learning to navigate', in J. Lave and S. Chaiklin (eds), *Understanding Practice; Perspectives on Activity and Context*. Cambridge: Cambridge University Press.

Kolb, D.A. (1983) *Experiential Learning: Experience as the Source of Learning and Development*. London: Prentice Hall.

Kuhn, T.S. (1996) *The Structure of Scientific Revolutions*. Chicago, IL: University of Chicago Press.

Lave, J. and Wenger, E. (1991) *Situated Learning; Legitimate peripheral participation*. Cambridge: Cambridge University Press.

McNally, J. and Blake, A. (2009) *Improving Learning in a Professional Context: A Research Perspective on the New Teacher in School*. London: Routledge.

Philpott, C. (2006) 'Transfer of learning between higher education institution and school based components of PGCE courses', *Journal of Vocational Education and Training*, 58(3): 283–302.

Philpott, C. (2014) *Theories of Professional Learning: A Critical Guide for Teacher Educators*. Oxford: Critical.

Roth, W.-M. and Lee, Y.-J. (2007) '"Vygotsky's Neglected Legacy": cultural-historical activity theory', *Review of Educational Research*, 77(2): 186–232.

Schön, D.A. (1990) *Educating the Reflective Practitioner: Toward a New Design for Teaching and Learning in the Professions*. London: Wiley.

Schön, D.A. (1993) 'Generative metaphor', in A. Ortony (ed.), *Metaphor and Thought*. Cambridge: Cambridge University Press.

Schön, D.A. (1994) *The Reflective Practitioner: How Professionals Think in Action* Farnham: Ashgate.

Trowler, P.R. (2005) 'A sociology of teaching, learning and enhancement: improving practices in higher education', *Revista de Sociologia*, (76): 13–32.

Wenger, E. (1998) *Communities of Practice; Learning, Meaning, and Identity*. Cambridge: Cambridge University Press.

Wenger, E., McDermott, R. and Snyder, W. (2002) *Cultivating Communities of Practice*. Boston, MA: Harvard Business School Press.

CHAPTER 4

EFFECTIVE PROFESSIONAL LEARNING

Gail Fuller

The aim of this chapter is to:

- provide a concise overview of research on the importance of affective and interpersonal factors in fostering effective professional learning
- explore the idea of learning to teach and teaching as a journey linked to the development of a professional identity
- offer practical strategies for ITE within school.

This chapter is concerned with the importance of affective and interpersonal factors in effective professional learning. It will explore the influence of feelings, attitudes, intuitions and relationships on this process. Learning does not take place in a vacuum for pupils or for adults; we bring ourselves and our unique life story to learning experiences, and this inevitably affects the outcome.

THE IMPORTANCE OF AFFECTIVE AND INTERPERSONAL FACTORS

Identity and 'becoming' a teacher

The new teacher's development as a student and subsequently as a newly quali-fied teacher can be viewed as a journey that is influenced by the people they meet and experiences that they have, both good and bad. These experiences, along with their personality and characteristics, will shape the kind of teacher they become. As a student teacher they will be influenced and changed by the experiences they go through, constantly evolving and making decisions and choices based on beliefs, experiences and reflections on those experiences. In fact, their journey to becoming a teacher may already have been shaped in some way by events prior to their training. Childhood and adolescent experiences in school, for example, will have influenced the way they view the role of a teacher (Smith, 2007).

As the new teacher progresses through teacher education and prepares for their first post as a teacher, they will undergo a shift in identity. Further developments in their professional identity as a teacher are bound to occur throughout their teaching career. Therefore, new teachers will continue to grow and change throughout their professional life, and teacher training is a very significant part of this continuous journey.

The academic literature on learning to teach puts much emphasis on the richness and complexity of 'becoming' a teacher and the variety of idiosyncratic and contextual factors involved (Williams, 2003). This process of 'becoming' is often viewed as developing a professional identity. This identity plays a pivotal role in teachers adhering to professional norms and their commitment to their work. 'Teachers' identities are central to the beliefs, values, and practices that guide their engagement, commitment, and actions in and out of the classroom' (Cohen et al., 2007: 80). Research by Beauchamp and Thomas (2009) into the shift in identity as student teachers move into their first year of practice shows the need to more effectively address identity as a component in teacher education.

For many, initial experiences as a student teacher can have a sustained effect on the development of professional identity. The concept of identity is complex, and in this chapter I refer to the combination of the personal and professional aspects of teacher identity. A beginning teacher's journey to becoming a teacher is influenced by people, experiences and their understanding of them. Evidence from research suggests 'beginning teaching is demanding for just about all beginners and is special for each beginner' (McNally et al., 2008: 295).

An idea that recurs within the research literature is the view that identity is dynamic, and that a teacher's identity shifts over time under the influence of a range of factors both internal to the individual, such as emotion (Rodgers and Scott, 2008), and external to the individual, such as the work place and life experiences (Flores and Day, 2006; Rodgers and Scott, 2008). Therefore, teacher identity is not fixed or imposed but is shaped by experiences and also by the sense a teacher makes of those experiences. Sachs (2005) suggests that this sense of identity is a useful starting point for thinking about being a teacher as it not only highlights the importance of identity in the profession, but also points to the different dimensions of identity. These dimensions can be conceived as three overlapping areas for attention: 'how to be', 'how to act' and 'how to understand'. Sachs suggests that teachers' professional identity 'provides a framework for teachers to construct their own ideas of 'how to be', 'how to act' and 'how to understand' their work and their place in society' (Sachs, 2005: 15).

The idea of teacher identity is not new. Research by Nias (1989) suggests there is a huge investment 'of the personal' in teaching for some teachers and teaching 'partakes of and shapes the person'. Researchers such as Clandinin and Connelly (1987) have identified a personal dimension to professional knowledge, suggesting that our professional learning to be a teacher will be influenced by our personalities and character traits.

This brings into focus the significance of the personal in teaching. It seems obvious that the style of teaching new teachers adopt will be influenced by their personality. It is not really surprising that the personal dimension is significant as schools are social settings where people interact all the time. As a result, there is a sense of the personal dimension in school, for example, attitudes, beliefs and relationships. It is not just a professional setting. Teachers are individuals with personalities, experiences and beliefs that have an effect on their professional role as a teacher. It is important to take these affective and interpersonal factors into account during ITE if professional learning is to be effective in the earliest stages.

Creating a list of standards for teaching, such as the Teachers' Standards, has been viewed by some as an attempt to conceptualize the role of the teacher as a list of competences, which all teachers must understand and be able to put into action in order to teach successfully (McNally et al., 2008). These standards reflect areas of professional practice and attributes expected of beginning teachers. This might suggest that by meeting these standards, a teacher's professional identity is stable and their professionalism can be measured against the absolute scale of the standards' criteria.

This model of training is not without its critics. While the 'standards model' of teacher identity has been viewed by some as a powerful tool in the development of teaching as a profession, some have found that it does not fully encompass their lived experience as a student teacher. Teaching is a complex professional role and therefore learning to teach is complex too. It involves the whole of the individual, including beliefs, emotions, identity and personality, and is much more than an abstract set of skills.

Research suggests there are tensions between the formal process of training and the informal learning that takes place outside the parameters of these structures, especially through relationships with pupils and colleagues (McNally et al., 2008; Tickle, 2000). Various studies suggest that the all-encompassing process in learning to teach is about 'becoming' a teacher. It is an organic process through which new teachers have to reinvent themselves, gaining their identity through a range of emotional, relational and cognitive experiences. Beginning teachers, we are told, report an emotional-relational dimension: the nature and quality of relationships in school are important. In other words, how a student feels in school about themself, their role and their relationships with colleagues and pupils are often central concerns in their early teaching experiences – themes that are not always visible in the standards (Flores, 2004; McNally et al., 2008). It is this informal but crucial learning for which there are no standards provided for guidance or measurement. This more three-dimensional model of early professional learning suggests that the experience of beginning teachers is largely dependent on engagement with pupils and colleagues, with a high correlation between job satisfaction and working relationships with colleagues. These social interactions produce the crucial relationships for the new teacher's professional identity and role.

Affective issues and the learning process

During the twentieth century there was significant research and developments in understanding how students learn, and a number of taxonomies or classifications were created. Perhaps the most well known is by Bloom et al. (1956) which identified three domains of learning: cognitive, affective and psychomotor (Anderson and Krathwohl, 2001). Bloom's taxonomy, focusing on the cognitive domain, is still widely used in education today. Affective learning (Krathwohl et al., 1973), developed from Bloom's original idea, refers to the ways in which we deal with things emotionally, such as feelings, values, appreciation, enthusiasms, motivations and attitudes. The third domain, psychomotor learning, refers to the relationship between cognitive functions and physical movement. More recent taxonomies have been devised using different terms including Fink's taxonomy of significant learning (2003) and Marzano and Kendall's (2007) new taxonomy for educational objectives.

Although all three domains have been available since Bloom, the cognitive domain has received the most attention. However, the affective and psychomotor have recently become more recognized as having a powerful influence on learning and are becoming more popular (Anderson and Krathwohl, 2001).

Affective learning is the emotional responses an individual experiences based on instincts, intuitions or feelings. The intensity of the affective response is dependent on a number of factors, both internal and external to the individual. Internal factors such as attitudes, memories of past experiences, likes and dislikes that have developed over time, will strongly influence the affective response a person will have to any given situation. These factors lead to a reaction with little or no cognitive effort or process. External factors such as the time and setting of the interaction, the appearance, language and mannerisms of the individual(s) involved also influence the affective response. In addition, lighting, sound and smell can play a role in determining the intensity of affective response (Kraiger et al., 1993).

Many educators have recognized the links between all three domains. As far back as 1917 a connection between the emotional and cognitive was proposed which suggested that they are inextricably related and perhaps never entirely separate or distinct (Picard et al., 2004). Caine and Caine (1994) support this idea by stating the 'brain does not naturally separate emotions from cognition, either anatomically or perceptually' (cited in Rogers and Renard, 1999: 43). Picard et al. (2004) take this further by concluding that advances in scientific understanding reveal the human brain as a system in which affective functions and cognitive functions are inextricably integrated with one another, rather

Figure 4.1 Borromean rings

than it being a purely cognitive information processing system. This indicates that for professional learning to be effective it must take into account and incorporate the learning teacher as an individual with all their personal characteristics, beliefs and values. Affective and cognitive functions are impossible to disentangle and it is impossible to separate the influence of one from the other.

MacDonald et al. (2012) adapt Bloom's cognitive learning (Bloom et al., 1956), Krathwohl's (1973) affective learning and Simpson's (1972) psychomotor learning to explain the connections between the three learning domains. They use the analogy of Borromean rings (Figure 4.1), where each ring is separate and has its own identity but when all three come together, they lock as one and the best learning takes place. So the most effective learning incorporates each distinct aspect, knowledge, feelings and physical aspects. When all three areas are used in learning experiences this fosters the most productive kind of learning that is likely to last.

Beginning teachers have to practise and refine their teaching skills to meet teaching standards consistently. In addition they also have to develop relationships with colleagues, pupils and parents, become familiar with school routines and practices, as well as perceive and respond to the 'unspoken rules' and expectations within schools. So, emotional, relational and cognitive factors are all key components to successful completion of teacher training (Keates, 2008; Rippon and Martin, 2006). In terms of recent research relating to beginner teachers, there has been growing attention to the place of the personal element in the process of becoming a teacher (Flores, 2004; McNally et al., 2008). All these factors will influence the experience of the beginning teacher and, therefore, to ignore these personal and individual influences on learning may be counterproductive to effective professional learning. Emotional involvement is an essential part of the process of learning to teach. On the one hand, teacher training can be seen as an objective learning process, a process whereby the student teacher learns how to become a participating member of the school workforce and the teaching profession. On the other hand, teacher training can and should involve reflexive engagement, and in some cases a personal struggle, with the experience itself so there is reciprocal interaction between the student and the learning process. Teacher training in this sense is something the beginning teacher is 'involved in', cognitively, emotionally and physically, rather than simply learning the mechanics of how to teach. Every beginning teacher is unique and will experience the process differently. The journey from student to teacher will be subjectively understood according to the individual's background, beliefs and values.

The importance of relationships

Other recent developments in new teacher research have acknowledged the importance of the emotional-relational aspects of becoming a teacher. Developing relationships with colleagues and pupils are seen as vital to the new teacher's sense of efficacy and acceptance in the work place. In some cases, it is argued that for new teachers, relationships 'almost define the job' at these early stages of professional development (Eraut et al., 2004; McNally et al., 2008).

Becoming a teacher and being a teacher are intertwined in developing relationships within school (Capel, 1998; McNally et al., 2008). These developing relationships create a sense of belonging and community which is essential if new teachers are to remain in the teaching profession. The belief that others care about us and will support us in school is, for some, a critical factor in continuing as a teacher. Some research has suggested that a powerful network of personal and professional support is the most critical aspect of teaching. So, alongside providing professional support in teaching skills, the human needs of the beginning teacher must also be addressed. Indeed, Hewitt (2009) argues that the key to successful teachers comes, first, from developing 'powerful, personal relationships', and then a focus on developing professional skills. Cognitive development theory also complements this idea. In order to grow and develop as a teacher, new teachers must socialize and interact personally and professionally, while physical and/or mental isolation can impede teacher development (Lundeen, 2004). Some new teachers view themselves as changing from 'outsiders' to 'insiders', in other words, they see themselves as accepted members of the group rather than someone who does not belong. This sense of belonging will, of course, be more important to some people than others.

Teaching is a human experience, involving daily interaction with others in a social and psychological setting, where relationships, personal characteristics and emotions have a significant impact on the learning that takes place. It is impossible to separate entirely the personal from the professional; each will influence the other, and it is important to take both into account in training new teachers.

PRACTICAL IMPLICATIONS OF THE RESEARCH FOR SCHOOL-BASED ITE

If professional learning is to be effective we need to do more to encourage discussion on how to 'be a teacher' and not just focus on the 'doing and knowing' aspects.

The vital role of reflection in teacher development and success has been acknowledged for some time by a number of writers (Beauchamp and Thomas, 2009) and therefore this must have an impact in ITE alongside the 'how to teach' learning. From research we can identify some practical implications for organising ITE in school that will allow these discussions to take place. During training student teachers need to:

1. explore and be involved in the learning process

2. investigate past experiences and identify how these may have informed their initial beliefs about how to be a teacher and what teaching is about

3. recognize both the personal and professional aspects of a beginning teacher's professional identity

4. become familiar with relationship skills and understand how these relate to the role of the teacher.

Student teachers need to explore and be involved in the learning process

Learning to teach is complex and, for some, conceptualizing the role of the teacher as a list of skills and competences is too narrow a focus and obscures reality. It is helpful for beginning teachers to realize that they need to be involved in the learning process, rather than view it as something that happens to them, and they need an awareness of the importance of engaging with learning in all three ways – cognitive, emotional and physical.

Reflection and discussion throughout the training year are useful in helping the student to combine their new and previous experiences and to refine their beliefs and, consequently, their actions in their role as a teacher. An experienced mentor who can guide and engage in directing the discussion using listening skills is valuable in allowing the student to grow and develop through these reflections. Some students will be more comfortable with the process than others and some may need more guidance and help.

For the student, learning to be a teacher and the first year in teaching can be very powerful in terms of learning who they are as a teacher and how they want to teach. Findlay (2006) suggests that the first year of teaching has a very significant effect on the personal and professional life of a teacher, even going as far as saying it 'imprints and embeds perceptions and behaviours' concerning the role of the teacher. This is not to say that every beginning teacher will have a crisis or find the experience traumatic but it is for most a transformative experience owing to the emotional labour involved. Learning to teach is an emotional experience, as can be seen by the language often used by new teachers to describe their early experiences; for example, 'butterflies', 'overwhelming panic' and 'a rollercoaster ride'. McNally et al. (2008) view beginning teaching as a deep process of personal change in which there is an emergence of a teacher identity.

The social and psychological aspects of school life are often 'hidden' and implicit rather than explicitly discussed in teacher training. Lundeen (2004: 552) suggests that 'Powerful social processes operate within school contexts that can be foreboding and often intimidate novice teachers'. Allowing students to explore these aspects of school life and their interpretation of them in a safe environment with an experienced teacher is an ideal opportunity to open up a dialogue of how the student might cope with any issues or difficulties in these areas.

Student teachers need to investigate their past experiences and identify how these may have informed their initial beliefs about how to be a teacher and what teaching is all about

The journey of 'becoming a teacher' will be different for everyone; each person brings their own ideas and views about teaching with them. These views are informed by teaching placements, previous individual experiences of being a student, as well as beliefs and expectations about the profession. It would be advantageous to discuss the student's views and ideas about teaching and the role of the teacher early on in their training to identify the beliefs they have. It is likely the training experience will cause students to rethink some of their ideas about teaching. In this way their new experiences and knowledge will allow them to develop their beliefs and views about teaching.

This concept of re-analysis, suggested by Freeman (2002), is where the new teacher changes their thinking and practice based on new learning in the work place. This is true in any work place as people are influenced by past experiences and beliefs that are then later reformed and adapted due to new experiences.

Previous skills, and perhaps learning in other work places, will affect the needs that the student has as a beginning teacher and therefore, the journey and experiences along the way will be unique to them. Other personal factors may also determine the needs of the beginning teacher, for example, age, gender, financial status and family support. In order to foster effective professional learning for student teachers they will need support and guidance tailored to them as individuals, as the highs and lows of teacher training will be unique to each one.

Student teachers need to recognize the personal and the professional aspects of their professional identity as a teacher

Teaching is a complex job and often involves skills learnt through informal learning for which there are no standards. There is a potential for the complexity of 'becoming a teacher' to be obscured if the focus is solely on meeting teaching standards as a list of competences, without engaging the affective aspect of teaching. Having completed teacher training, many new teachers enter their first post believing the hardest work is over and this can cause anxiety in the first year when expectations are not met and things do not always go smoothly. Teaching involves emotional, relational and cognitive aspects and all these factors need to be addressed during training if it is to be as successful as possible.

The language that new teachers use to describe their early experiences is often emotional. Statements such as 'I found it a little overwhelming at times' and 'I had to fight my ground in September, but now I've made it' tell the story that sometimes the early years can be, as suggested by Hodkinson and Hodkinson (2003), a personal struggle. Teaching does involve an emotional investment, the student has to process daily the formal and informal learning that takes place and adjust their view of themselves as a teacher as reflected to them by colleagues and pupils. For some teachers, teaching is a lifestyle choice and a personal choice, supporting the idea of the personal and the professional being involved in teaching.

All teachers are assessed against standards, for example, those set out in the Teachers' Standards. However, the motives that lie behind the actions taken by the student should not be related to ticking off standards on a list during their training. Perhaps this is the 'X' factor in teaching; a good teacher meets all the standards but does so because they believe it is the right thing to do, therefore involving personal integrity, intrinsic motives and commitment. Children are very adept at recognizing those teachers who are genuine in their interactions with them, and this helps build the relationship between teacher and pupil and has a knock-on effect on pupil welfare and their learning experience.

It seems clear that teaching does involve the personal as well as the professional, with some teachers engaging in this process more than others. I would argue that it is impossible to separate entirely the personal from the professional. Whatever job an individual has, something of their personality will come through, you bring yourself to every role you take on in life. Many new teachers also mention integrity and morality as being part of their personal investment in teaching, supporting research carried out by Clandinin and Connelly (1987) and Nias (1989) highlighting the personal dimension to professional knowledge.

Much research maintains the view that a teacher's identity is dynamic, and shifts over time. There is a range of factors both internal to the individual, such as emotion, and external to the individual, such as the pupils and life experiences, which shape and continue to affect the student's identity as a teacher; teaching is a two-way process where pupil and teacher continually affect each other (Fuller, 2010). Smith (2007) recommends that teacher training should include some reflective learning relating to identity and knowledge growth. Despite the difficulties inherent in trying to match the personal with the professional it would seem advantageous for beginning teachers to engage in this process. There needs to be recognition that personal skills, and not just teaching skills, are important for a teacher, as social interactions are necessary to build relationships with colleagues. Schools are social and psychological settings, as well as physical settings and formal institutions.

Student teachers need to become familiar with relationship skills and understand how these relate to the role of the teacher

New teachers often report on the importance of relationships in school during their first year, with some identifying that relationships in school were the most important part of their teaching. This adds weight to conclusions by McNally et al.

(2008) and Eraut et al. (2004) who argue that, for most new teachers, relationships define the job. Relationship-building takes energy and emotional intelligence, and making connections with pupils and colleagues is critical in teaching and learning. Successful teaching seems to result from building personal relationships first, followed by the development of professional skills. The building of relationships creates a sense of belonging, which is a human need, and when we feel we belong and others care about us we thrive and grow, not only personally but also professionally, as we gain confidence and become more at ease in our surroundings.

This leaves us with the question 'What kind of teachers are those who cannot build relationships?' An initial response might be to say the teacher who finds it difficult to develop relationships with colleagues and pupils may be viewed as cold and clinical, even distant. Perhaps it is important to bear in mind that this definition of relationship is not referring to just being liked by the pupil, it is impossible for every pupil to like every teacher, as with some pupils there is a better rapport than with others. More accurately, in this instance, it refers to the pupil feeling that there is a level of care, interest in and knowledge of them as a person. This is a basic human need; we all want to be noticed and valued. Beginning teachers need to be aware that it is possible to have relationships with pupils who constantly misbehave in the classroom; the pupils may not like you but will hopefully understand at some point that you noticed because you cared and wanted them to do well.

Some new teachers may struggle between the processes of looking after themself as a developing adult and teacher while caring for the needs of pupils in the classroom. Research by Watzke (2003) found that over time, for most new teachers the focus shifted from self as a teacher towards student needs and creating a productive classroom environment, although initially teaching and nurturing of pupils was overshadowed by classroom management issues (Lundeen, 2004). Here again we can see the importance of self-awareness for the teacher, how they are feeling and how this affects their teaching in the classroom. It is an important area for new teachers to be aware of, this balance between taking care of themself and their pupils.

If relationships are so essential in teaching then there is a need for new teachers to undertake some reflective tasks based around emotional intelligence, and how to build and sustain quality relationships. Research (Smith, 2007) indicates that development of the self and self-understanding would be advantageous for the classroom teacher personally and professionally. It is also significant in terms of helping to improve relationships in school.

CASE STUDIES

How can these recommendations be implemented in schools?

For each of the four areas identified in the previous section this section has some recommendations on how these ideas might be implemented in school, alongside some findings from case studies involving new teachers in school. The suggestions can be used for individual students as well as in a group setting.

CASE STUDY 4.1 STUDENT TEACHERS NEED TO EXPLORE AND BE INVOLVED IN THE LEARNING PROCESS

This idea underpins and intertwines the other three recommendations for school-based ITE. It is a starting point and can be referred back to throughout the year as an ongoing theme. New teachers need to know that they are going to be actively involved in the learning process and that it is not something that just happens to them. If it is to be effective it will require them to be actively engaged in the process, recognizing and reflecting on both cognitive and emotional aspects. Each student will bring with them their individual personalities, characteristics and life story and, therefore, the learning process also needs to be individualized if it is to be beneficial.

Practical guidance for mentors

During your meetings with a student, discuss their assessment of their level of self-awareness and create a dialogue where the student is allowed to be open about their findings as well as challenged to change and grow. Encourage the student to share their reflections on the learning process; how and why it has changed them as a person, their beliefs and behaviour. Engaging the student in the learning process will allow them to develop good habits of reflective practice which will have long-term benefits in their teaching career. This open discussion will be further complemented if the mentor can engage listening skills and reflect back accurately to the student their thoughts and feelings. Further information on the '10 Principles of Listening' can be found at www.skillsyouneed. com/ips/listening-skills.html.

Suggested tasks and critical reflection questions for the student teacher

- Complete a self-assessment of emotional intelligence (see at http://helpguide. org/mental/eq5_raising_emotional_intelligence.htm).

- Explore the topic of self-awareness.

- Keep a reflective journal ongoing throughout the year on your learning journey to becoming a teacher.

- What kind of emotional experiences do you think you may have in school?

- What kind of 'informal' learning do you think will take place in school?

- Be prepared to think critically and discuss your insights and learning on the above tasks.

Group learning task

'Schools are social and psychological settings as well as physical settings and formal institutions'.

- Working in small groups, record responses to the above statement and then follow this with a group discussion about the issues raised and the students' thoughts and feelings.

- This could be followed up with an individual writing task that focuses on personal learning drawn from the task and how it will impact their teaching practice.

Responses to this task from a group of new teachers

'I never thought about schools being a social setting as such, although I know pupils make friends and so on, but, when I thought about school I just pictured lessons most of the time.'

'This phrase made me rethink about the physical aspect of school, especially my classroom, how does it make me feel as well as my students – I had thought about the classroom before but somehow this task gave it more clarity and meaning.'

'Thinking about the formality of school made me think about why some pupils might find it difficult to 'fit in' at school and follow rules, and how I need to respond to them.'

'I'm wondering how I will fit in with colleagues and a bit panicky about whether or not the pupils will like me.'

'The unpredictability of students, the responsibility and the social/emotional environment make it very different to other work places.'

'It's interesting to think of school as a psychological setting, it made me think in a different way about me at school as well as the pupils, about our interactions and responses to each other.'

(Fuller, 2010)

CASE STUDY 4.2 INVESTIGATE PAST EXPERIENCES AND IDENTIFY HOW THEY MAY HAVE INFORMED INITIAL BELIEFS ABOUT HOW TO BE A TEACHER AND WHAT TEACHING IS ALL ABOUT

Practical guidance for the subject mentor

During your meetings with your student, discuss their views about the role and expectations of a teacher and where these may have originated. Ask questions about different kinds of teachers and styles of teaching, and where they see themself fitting into these views, assisting them to identify which beliefs are helpful and can be kept and which beliefs are unhelpful.

Suggested tasks and critical reflection questions for the student teacher

- What does the phrase 'become a teacher' mean to you?

- Can you identify any experiences from your past that have influenced the way you view teachers and teaching?

- Has your view of the role of a teacher changed?

- In what ways has your view of yourself as a teacher altered?

- What does a 'good' teacher look like?

- What does a 'bad' teacher look like?

Responses to some of these questions from a group of beginning teachers

'I'll feel like I've become a teacher when I have an identity with colleagues – are you dependable, can you take on roles in the department – and an identity in the classroom – having excellent lessons to stretch the pupils, so I think professional identity is a mixture of lots of things you do in school.'

'What makes a person a person is experience, so I'll be a different teacher tomorrow, always developing and character evolving, you change and grow as you change as an individual.'

'Some days I feel like I'm a bad teacher, the pupils don't do what I ask, but then when I make a connection with one student, it's like now I feel like I can teach, I'm very up and down at the moment.'

'I'm still struggling to decide what kind of a teacher I want to be, it's hard as you want to be liked by pupils and sometimes my personal feelings get in the way of being tough.'

'The unpredictability of students, the responsibility and the social/emotional environment make it very different to other work places.'

'I suppose I have a mental picture of my favourite teacher and want to be like them.'

(Fuller, 2010)

 ## CASE STUDY 4.3 RECOGNIZE PERSONAL AND PROFESSIONAL ASPECTS OF THE BEGINNING TEACHER'S PROFESSIONAL IDENTITY

Practical guidance for the subject mentor

Provide opportunity for students to consider the personal characteristics they bring to the classroom and recognize those which are beneficial and those which they need to develop further. It may be that the new teacher might need additional insight into the three ways of learning and the emotional investment in teaching. Encourage them to read around the issues and begin to analyse for themselves the emotional, relational and cognitive aspects of teaching and how these areas relate to their learning journey.

Suggested tasks and critical reflection questions for the student teacher

- Can you identify the personal as well as professional skills you are bringing to your role as a teacher?

- What is the difference between personal characteristics and professional skills?

- Can you identify personal characteristics that may influence how a teacher performs in the classroom?

- What is your view of the Teachers' Standards?

- How do the teaching standards fit in to your experience of teaching?

- Can you identify areas of learning not included in the standards?

Responses to some of these questions from a group of new teachers

'Standards cover the formality of being a teacher, you need to know them and be aware of them, measured against them, and they have a reality in the classroom but are also somewhat removed from what happens in the classroom.'

'Standards are in place to ensure standards in school but they're not the be all and end all of teaching – you can tick off a list but it's not why you do things, it's more than that.'

'You can't teach some things about teaching; it's experience that brings the knowledge of how to be a good teacher.'

'Some elements of the job can't be taught only experienced, I think I've changed personally, I'm much more aware of how I come across to others, it's been a struggle at times and challenging on a personal level.'

'I never thought of the personal side of teaching, I just thought I would learn how to teach and that would be it, but it's been a lot more than that and a lot harder than I thought it would be.'

'There's no standard for the constant pressure and how to keep all the balls in the air.'

'A lot of learning this year was not covered by the standards, they're just the basics, and any good teacher sees them as that – far more to teaching than that.'

(Fuller, 2010)

CASE STUDY 4.4 IDENTIFYING RELATIONSHIP SKILLS AND RELATING THOSE TO THE ROLE OF THE TEACHER

Practical guidance for mentors

In your meetings with your students you may find it useful to discuss relationships within school, with pupils and colleagues, and the importance of self-awareness, as knowing how you present yourself to others is essential. Use these meetings as an opportunity to discuss the reflection questions. Encourage students to talk to other colleagues, family and friends, who are 'good' at relationships, and ask them for guidance and advice. Use the reading at the end of this chapter to help your students increase their self-awareness and encourage them to work on areas of personal growth that will enhance their classroom skills. Effectiveness as an individual is not based on any particular personality style; it is really about how well we know ourselves and others. We are the central person in all our relationships so knowing ourselves leads to better relationships. Prompt the student to ask someone they trust to give them feedback on personal character traits.

Suggested tasks and critical reflection questions for the student teacher

- How are you going to build relationships in school?

- What do 'good' relationships look like?

- How well can you 'read' others?

- Examine your views about the importance of relationships within school.

- Are you good at building and sustaining relationships? Can you identify why you are or are not?

- Do you need to develop more self-awareness? Use the websites below to explore your level of self-awareness and how to improve self-awareness

- www.whatsnext.com/content/self-assessment-tests

- www.3smartcubes.com/pages/tests/selfawareness/selfawareness_instructions.asp.

Responses to some of these questions from a group of new teachers

'Relationships with pupils are vital, you can't teach without it, planning and organisation can be overcome but the ability to develop relationships is essential.'

'Teaching takes an emotional hurdle, you have to feel something, interact with pupils, build up relationships and that's not always easy – you may have someone who doesn't want to speak to you and hates your subject and you've got to make it work and take the time.'

'I suppose it was realising that my relationships with the kids is the most important thing and their enjoyment of my subject.'

'I've found it interesting and illuminating finding out about self-awareness – I have to admit I was reluctant at first, I just wanted to teach, but it has been beneficial, in the long run it's made my classroom practice more successful as I've begun to notice what my 'triggers' are.'

'It's an investment of time and energy to build relationships in school – pupils and staff – you have to make an effort to learn and take part, that gives you a sense of belonging when you do.'

(Fuller, 2010)

CONCLUSION

The key learning from this chapter is that teaching is a human experience, involving daily interaction with others in a social and psychological setting, where relationships have a significant impact on the learning that takes place. It is impossible to separate entirely the personal from the professional, each will influence the other, and it is important to take both into account in ITE.

For the beginning teacher it is a steep learning curve. Not only is the school arena new, but the pupils, colleagues and parents are all new, and relationships must be forged and developed, which takes time and emotional energy. Skills of compromise, cooperation, debate, communication, flexibility and negotiation, among others, will be needed daily. The unwritten rules of the school and its own particular culture will need to be taken on board and acknowledged, as well as a heavy teaching workload with numerous practical and administrative tasks that mostly have to be done at once. Schools can often overwhelm new teachers by expecting them to juggle all the responsibilities and duties that experienced teachers do. Instead, it is important to give new teachers time to grow.

Secure and self-confident teachers are essential if they are to care for pupils as well as provide quality learning experiences. The crucial variables in order to provide educational quality are teachers, their education and training, so it is essential that these are based on their needs, personal and professional. There needs to be more recognition that becoming a teacher is a lifelong learning process, new teachers are not the 'finished products' but are at the beginning of their teaching journey during which they will change and grow. In addition to pedagogical support from more experienced colleagues, new teachers need emotional support and encouragement to foster continued growth.

The most effective professional learning takes place when we acknowledge and discuss the emotional-relational aspect of teaching and include some reflective work on relationship skills and highlight the importance of relationships in school. Incorporating the idea of informal learning as part of the ITE process raises awareness of this important aspect of learning.

Many established as well as new teachers feel relationships are the key to being a good teacher. This has been my own educational philosophy since becoming a teacher as well as my philosophy in life. Relationships are the key to a happy, ful-filling life. It is vital to remember that schools are social and psychological settings as well as institutions of teaching and learning. If we can provide our new teach-ers with training that recognizes the personal as well as the professional aspects of their professional identity, we will have accomplished the goal of giving them the best possible start on their journey to becoming good teachers.

FURTHER READING

Beauchamp, C. and Thomas, L. (2009) 'Understanding teacher identity: an overview of issues in the literature and implications for teacher education', *Cambridge Journal of Education*, 39(2): 175–89.

Hodkinson, P. and Hodkinson, H. (2003) 'Individuals, communities of practice and the policy con-text: schoolteachers learning in their workplace', *Studies in Continuing Education*, 25(1): 3–21.

McNally, J., Blake, A., Corbin, B. and Gray, P. (2008) 'Finding an identity and meeting a standard: connecting the conflicting in teacher induction', *Journal of Educational Policy*, 23(3): 287–98.

USEFUL WEBSITES

http://helpguide.org/mental/eq5_raising_emotional_intelligence.htm

This website is an introduction to emotional intelligence.

www.wwnorton.com/college/psych/psychsci2/content/activities/ch10a.asp

This website can be used to develop awareness of non-verbal communication. Increasing skills in this area will help build and sustain relationships.

www.learnmyself.com

This site has ideas to help the beginning teacher become more self-aware. Being aware of emotions and knowing how to channel them is to be proactive rather than reactive and, therefore, more in control in the classroom.

REFERENCES

Anderson, L. and Krathwohl, D.A. (2001) *Taxonomy for Learning, Teaching and Assessing: A Revision of Bloom's Taxonomy of Educational Objectives*. New York: Longman.

Beauchamp, C. and Thomas, L. (2009) 'Understanding teacher identity: an overview of issues in the literature and implications for teacher education', *Cambridge Journal of Education*, 39(2): 175–89.

Bloom, B.S., Engelhart, M.D., Furst, E.J., Hill, W.H. and Krathwohl, D.R. (1956) *Taxonomy of Educational Objectives: The Classification Of Educational Goals; Handbook I: Cognitive Domain*. New York: Longmans, Green.

Caine, G. and Caine, R. (1994) *Making Connections: Teaching and the Human Brain*. New York: Addison-Wesley.

Capel, S. (1998) 'The transition from student teacher to newly qualified teacher: some findings', *Professional Development in Education*, 24(3): 1.

Clandinin, D.J. and Connelly, F. (1987) 'Teachers' personal knowledge: what counts as personal in studies of the personal', *Journal of Curriculum Studies*, 19(6): 487–500.

Cohen, L., Manion, L. and Morrison, K. (2007) *Research Methods in Education*. 6th edn. London: Routledge.

Eraut, M., Maillardet, F., Miller, C., Steadman, S., Ali, A., Blackman, C. and Furner J. (2004) 'Learning in the professional workplace: relationships between learning factors and contex-tual factors', paper presented at the AERA Conference, San Diego.

Findlay, K. (2006) 'Context and learning factors in the development of teacher identity: a case study of newly qualified teachers during their induction year', *Journal of In-service Education*, 32(4): 511–32.

Fink, L.D. (2003) *Creating Significant Learning Experiences*. San Francisco, CA: Jossey-Bass.

Flores, M.A. (2004) 'The impact of school culture and leadership on new teachers' learning in the workplace', *International Journal of Leadership in Education*, 7(4): 297–318.

Flores, M.A. and Day, C. (2006) 'Contexts which shape and reshape new teachers' identities: a multi-perspective study', *Teaching and Teacher Education*, 22(2): 219–32.

Freeman, D. (2002) 'The hidden side of the work: teacher knowledge and learning to teach. A perspective from North American educational research on teacher education in English language teaching', *Language Teaching*, 35(1): 1–13.

Fuller, G. (2010) in Mercier, C., Philpott, C. and Scott, H. (eds) (2013) *Professional Issues in Secondary Teaching*. London: SAGE.

Hewitt, P.W. (2009) 'Hold on to your new teachers', *Leadership*, 38(5): 12–14.

Hodkinson, P. and Hodkinson, H. (2003) 'Individuals, communities of practice and the policy context: schoolteachers learning in their workplace', *Studies in Continuing Education*, 25(1): 3–21.

Keates, C. (2008) 'NQTs get a helping hand', *Teaching Today*, 64.

Kraiger, K., Ford, K. and Salas, E. (1993) 'Application of cognitive, skill-based and affective theories of learning outcomes to new methods of training evaluation,' *Journal of Applied Psychology*, 78(2): 311–28.

Krathwohl, D. R., Bloom, B. S. and Masia, B. B. (1973) *Taxonomy of Educational Objectives, the Classification of Educational Goals. Handbook 11: Affective Domain*. New York: David McKay Co Inc.

Lundeen, C. A. (2004) 'Teacher development: the struggle of beginning teachers in creating moral (caring) classroom environments', *Early Child Development and Care* 174(6): 549–64.

MacDonald, L.L., Schönwetter, D.J. and Nowakowski, A. (2012) 'Actively engaging students in affective, cognitive, and psychomotor learning domains: knowing, being, and doing—trinity or trilogy?', University of Manitoba, Faculty Development Workshop, American Dental Educators Association.

Marzano, R. and Kendall, J.S. (2008) *Designing and Assessing Educational Objectives: Applying the New Taxonomy*. Newbury Park, CA: Corwin Press.

McNally, J., Blake, A., Corbin, B. and Gray, P. (2008) 'Finding an identity and meeting a standard: connecting the conflicting in teacher induction', *Journal of Educational Policy*, 23(3): 287–98.

Nias, J. (1989) *Primary Teachers Talking*. London: Routledge.

Picard, R.W., Papert, S., Bender, W., Blumberg, C., Cavallo, D., Machover, T., Resnick, M., Roy, D. and Strohecker, C. (2004) 'Affective learning: a manifesto', *Technology Journal*, 22(4): 253–69.

Rippon, M. and Martin, M. (2006) 'Call me teacher: the quest of new teachers', *Teachers and Teaching: Theory and Practice*, 12(3): 305–24.

Rodgers, C. and Scott, K. (2008) 'The development of the personal self and professional identity in learning to teach', in M. Cochran-Smith, S. Feiman-Nemser, D.J. McIntyre and K.E. Demers (eds), *The Handbook of Research in Teacher Education*. London: Routledge. pp 732–55.

Rogers, S. and Renard, L. (1999) 'Relationship-driven teaching', *Educational Leadership*, 57(September): 1.

Sachs, J. (2005) 'Teacher education and the development of professional identity: learning to be a teacher', in P. Denicolo and M. Kopf (eds), *Connecting Policy and Practice: Challenges for Teaching and Learning in Schools and Universities*. London: Routledge. pp. 5–21.

Simpson, E. J. (1972) *The Classification of Educational Objectives in the Psychomotor Domain*. Washington, DC: Gryphon House.

Smith, R.G. (2007) 'Developing professional identities and knowledge: becoming primary teachers', *Teachers and Teaching: Theory and Practice*, 13(4): 377–97.

Tickle, L. (2000) *Teacher Induction: The Way Ahead*. Buckingham: Open University Press.

Watzke, J.L. (2003) 'Longitudinal study of stages of beginning teacher development in a field-based teacher education program', *The Teacher Educator*, 38(3): 209–29.

Williams, A. (2003) 'Informal learning in the workplace: a case study of new teachers', *Educational Studies*, 29(2–3): 207–19.

CHAPTER 5

WHAT IS THE DIFFERENCE BETWEEN MENTORING AND COACHING?

Helen Scott

This chapter aims to:

- explore the differences and similarities between mentoring and coaching
- examine particular issues and challenges in relation to each
- suggest and explore useful strategies associated with both roles.

Over the past 20 years, as beginning teachers have spent more time in school as part of their training, there has been much interest in and focus on the role of the school mentor and what mentoring means in theory and practice. In current models of teacher training, school mentors collaborate with university tutors in supporting students, for example, undertaking joint observations of lessons and end of placement reviews. Some mentors also become members of university committees, interview applicants for teacher training courses and teach university-based sessions on a number of issues. A university-based tutor also mentors and coaches student teachers in common with school mentors, and some universities and schools make joint appointments of individuals who work across both settings. While university-based sessions aim to help student teachers put their teaching in context (among other things), school experience affects their development much more significantly (Adams, 2007; Collanus et al., 2012; Furlong and Maynard, 1995). Immediately, therefore, we can see that there is a good deal of fluidity and overlap in who acts as mentor, coach or tutor in the complex work of supporting student teachers as they navigate the different cultures of schools and university.

Whilst the role of the mentor of the student teacher has become established and valued within ITE over the past 20 years, there has also been growing interest in both mentoring and coaching as means of developing teachers at all stages of their careers. The terms mentoring and coaching are sometimes used interchangeably. This chapter aims to explore the differences and similarities between them, as well as examining particular issues and challenges.

This exploration is worthwhile in order to develop greater understanding of the important work of supporting beginning teachers. As experienced teacher educators or teachers we may think we know all there is on the subject; but as the mentor–student teacher relationship is recognized as being so central in ITE, it deserves continual re-evaluation. In the context of a changing landscape of ITE where it is proposed the training of teachers should be more 'school led', we need to re-examine these key roles and revisit familiar themes; to consider if we might need to question or change our practices, and whether we are working with student teachers in school or university or both. As many teachers other than the person named as the mentor may give advice and guidance to student teachers, perhaps we also need to consider *all* teachers as mentors, coaches or tutors on some level (Hobson, 2002).

RECENT LITERATURE AND RESEARCH ON MENTORING AND COACHING

There is an enormous amount of literature and research on coaching and mentoring not just within education but also related to other professional settings, so it is difficult to know where to begin. Inevitably the sources referenced here will only represent a fraction of the available material. There is a plethora of 'how to' mentor and coach guides offering tips and pointers but many do not address the associated complexities. Interestingly, some authors note that being a mentor is often written about in a wholly positive way, what Colley (2002: 270) describes as a 'rose-tinted aura of celebration'.

However, supporting student teachers is widely recognized as involving multiple challenges, as every school mentor–student relationship is different with 'a complex interplay of cognitive, affective and interpersonal factors' (Hawkey, 1997: 332). As noted, it would be easy to assume that because school teachers have supported student teachers for a long time there is nothing new to know; however, some believe there is a lack of research on what mentors or coaches actually *do* that is effective for those they work with. This is incredibly important because preparing teachers for their careers not only impacts on them but also influences what kind of teacher they become, which in turn impacts upon their pupils. LoCasale-Crouch et al. (2012) believe that when new teachers feel supported by their mentor they are much more likely to have a highly developed sense of self-efficacy and reflect on their practice; this results in greater job satis-faction and longer-term commitment to the teaching profession. On the matter of self-efficacy, it is important that mentors also feel this to be able to undertake their role well (Hall et al., 2008).

This part of the chapter is divided into two subsections to help the reader gain a sense of current thinking about issues in mentoring and coaching as reflected in recent literature. The first considers different definitions and descriptions of the terms; the second aims to identify some key challenges in supporting student teachers effectively.

Defining the terms

It is useful to consider what we might mean by mentoring and coaching before we go much further. It has been noted that mentoring and coaching are used interchangeably and in practice, they can look and feel similar (Connor and Pokora, 2012). You will have noticed that I have already used the term 'mentor' or 'school mentor', rather than 'coach', as this reflects its common usage in ITE. At first sight, terms such as 'helping', 'learning', 'teaching but *not* 'telling', 'advising' or 'instructing' are used equally to describe mentoring and coaching and feature frequently in the literature (for example, Connor and Pokora, 2012; Furlong and Maynard, 1995). I have observed a good deal of all those processes in action by school mentors and university tutors with their student teachers. I have also undertaken them myself.

Connor and Pokora (2012) believe learning is at the heart of any professional relationship where there is a necessity and desire to develop a person whatever the particular context; mentoring and coaching both involve learning with others. Cain (2009: 56–7) explores two different theories of mentoring related to learn-ing: 'learning by reflecting' and 'learning through apprenticeship'. Learning by reflecting on experience encourages student teachers to examine a problem by considering their 'ideal situation' and what might be preventing them from achiev-ing this; that is, mentoring is inquiry based and discussions are likely to involve linking issues to wider contexts and theories of teaching and learning. In the learning through apprenticeship model students observe mentors and imitate their teaching practices; mentoring in this situation is very directive and conversations focus on technical or functional aspects of teaching.

Cain notes that the apprenticeship model has been heavily criticized over the years and, although much *can* be learned by watching others teach (for exam-ple, see Scott in Mercier et al., 2013), simply copying another teacher does not allow for any deep understanding of the reasoning behind more experienced col-leagues' actions. Student teachers do not always question *why* their mentors do things in a certain way unless specifically asked to do so, instead focusing more on *what* they do (Zanting et al., 2003).

Furlong and Maynard (1995: 180) examine mentoring and coaching as essen-tially no different from any other kind of teaching, needing 'to start from where the learners are'. Bullough and Draper (2004: 286) also suggest mentoring is a kind of teaching as both require 'deep emotional investment … intimate human interaction, [and] commitment to others' development'. Like Cain, Furlong and Maynard consider the apprenticeship model of learning to be a teacher to be inadequate and partial; the mentor needs no special skills beyond acting as a model to be copied. Furlong and Maynard believe if we think teaching is a complex and developmental process, learning to teach and working with those learning to teach also demands a developmental approach.

Connor and Pokora (2012) propose mentoring and coaching both require skills and abilities such as building trust, showing empathy and offering support, working on the basis that all people are capable of change and learning in their work. According to Connor and Pokora, some key differences are that a mentor is usually a more experienced colleague supporting a less experienced one and the mentoring relationship is usually longer term than a coaching one. Similarly, Atjonen (2012: 40) suggests that, while mentoring in ITE usually means a more experienced teacher advising a less experienced one, there is now 'a shift towards the constructivist understanding of mentoring …so that it is reconceptualised as a more dialogic relationship where the mentors can learn from the conversations as well'. So perhaps we can say mentoring enables the mentee to learn *with* mentors, as well as *from* them.

In terms of further differences between coaching and mentoring, a National College for School Leadership (NCSL) document proposes that mentoring might involve coaching but mentors are usually embedded (and recognized as knowledgeable) in the culture and organization in which the mentoring takes place, while a coach does not need to be working within the same organization or to be more experienced than the person they are coaching (Creasy and Paterson, 2005: 8). Bizarrely in my view, Creasy and Patterson (2005: 8) suggest in their statement 'coaching is usually informed by evidence' that mentoring is not! In my experience, successful mentoring also uses 'evidence', such as students' resources and planning and observation of their teaching.

Furlong and Maynard (1995: 186) see coaching student teachers as having a particular flavour; they adopt Schon's (1990) view of coaching through 'reflection-on-action'; for example, careful debriefing following lesson observations 'can help students find a language with which to establish their own conceptualisation of the teaching processes they have been engaged in'. This kind of coaching involves recognition of the '"sedimented" knowledge of classroom practice that is often taken for granted by experienced teachers' (Furlong and Maynard, 1995: 185).

LoCasale et al. (2012) believe that the most effective mentors have shared experiences with the person they are mentoring (for example, teaching the same age groups and subject); so perhaps a key difference between mentoring and coaching is that the former requires a common experience between the two parties and the latter does not. It would seem a coach can be an external facilitator who builds a relationship with a person in an organization to offer assistance in a specific area of their work (Wainwright, 2006: 68); a mentor needs to have complex contextual knowledge and experience of the situation in which the person they will be mentoring is working and learning. In much of the literature on coaching, it is suggested that a coach asks questions of the person being coached, rather than offering answers (for example, see Broughton, 2013; Flaherty, 2005) but I would suggest effective support for student teachers also includes asking questions. Perhaps we can propose that mentoring *encompasses* coaching to a degree rather than being fundamentally different to it, in practice.

It is interesting to consider how mentors and coaches describe or define their roles; 'mother figure', friend, protector, a resource for ideas, a therapist, someone who can step in or step away; the sheer variety of activities and stances adopted is so varied as to be both potentially stressful and rewarding (Bullough and Draper, 2004: 285). Mentors also cast themselves as a trouble-shooter, scaffolder, instructor or guide (Hawkey, 1997). Bullough and Draper (2004: 278) reference Fairbanks et al.'s (2000) view that 'mentoring is like dancing: the music changes frequently and with each change a new step is required and one never knows if a stumble and an unintended injury or a graceful lift and two joyous smiles will result'.

Challenges of effective mentoring

Mentoring or coaching student teachers is complex and challenging work. Hall et al. (2008: 342–3) summarize it well: 'ultimately the mentor teacher must work to create a context that will facilitate the beginning teacher's learning, engage in discussion, reflection and criticism of teaching'.

Perhaps at the root of the challenges is one fundamental conundrum; how can a mentor work with a student teacher as both their supporter and their assessor? This central tension makes getting the relationship right between mentor and student particularly important. Bullough and Draper (2004) found that mentors invest a lot of emotional energy in their mentees through their actions, but this is not always reflected in the ways they speak to their mentees; at times, mentors feel the need to hide their emotional investment from students, which is very draining. It is also important that mentors demonstrate emotional intelligence in their work with student teachers: 'to process emotional information accurately and efficiently, including the capacity to perceive, assimilate, understand, and manage emotion' (Mayer and Cobb, 2000: 165).

Mentors often feel the pressure to be the one who 'has all the answers' but sometimes they encounter problems they have not come across before and cannot always offer easy solutions. In being a role model to a student teacher, mentors become increasingly aware of their own inadequacies. Bullough and Draper (2004: 280) note that in taking on the role of mentor, it may be assumed individuals are excellent teachers, which some mentors find daunting and uncomfortable. This chimes with mentors I have worked with, who speak of feeling a spotlight on their practice in the presence of student teachers that can cause anxiety. As noted above, most mentors can articulate and identify the kinds of personal qualities, skills and abilities that are needed to be a good mentor, but they cannot always live up to their own ideals (Jones et al., 1997: 256).

A further particular challenge of the mentoring situation in ITE is what Hale (2000) calls 'forced pairings'; you never know who you are going to be mentoring or mentored by. Experienced mentors feel a further pressure that comes from knowing how important the mentor–mentee relationship is to whether the student teacher succeeds or fails (Maynard, 2000). Understanding how to build an effective mentoring relationship with a variety of individuals who all come with their own personalities, abilities and expectations of the relationship as well as different prior experiences can be difficult. Rajuan et al. (2010) suggest that it is not always necessary for mentors and mentees to hold the same beliefs and values; differences in opinions may become opportunities for discussing the bases of such views. If mentor and mentee get on too well, the relationship may become too 'comfortable' and unchallenging for the mentee (Tang, 2003). However, Rajuan et al. (2010) conclude that in situations where there are either *extremes* of divergence or convergence in views between mentors and their mentees, the possibilities for development are limited.

An additional layer to the challenge of being both a supporter and an assessor, noted above, is how a mentor balances being prescriptive with the student teacher, while allowing them to develop some independence. At the heart of this issue lie deeply held beliefs and values, for example, about how people learn to be teachers and the degree to which the mentor demands that their mentee becomes a carbon copy of themselves, either unconsciously or consciously; what Rajuan et al. (2010) refer to as a 'pastiche'. This is a very easy trap to fall into as student teachers put enormous efforts into 'fitting in' to the school culture to ensure others (their mentors, tutors and peers) perceive them as successful (see Maynard, 2000). However, a student who simply attempts to copy what their mentors do will be severely limited in their development as already noted (Zeichner and Gore, 1990). Atjonen (2012: 40) asks that we consider mentoring from 'an ethical perspective … (which) raises significant questions regarding one's rights to influence another person … and the boundaries of trust and autonomy'. Atjonen (2012: 44) further suggests 'mentors should encounter their protégés as individuals with different needs, emotions and expectations of support'; every mentoring situation is different, meaning there is not a perfect 'recipe' which will work in every case.

Furlong and Maynard (1995: 181) helpfully suggest that at different stages, four stances or approaches to mentoring student teachers can be usefully employed. The first is the role model, demonstrating (through the student observing them, for example) the 'rules, rituals and routines' of teaching to help the student ease into the role as teacher. Secondly, the mentor acts as a coach, focusing on the student's teaching competencies and giving them feedback. The third role is a 'critical friend', helping the student to understand not only their own learning, but that of their pupils'. Finally, in the last stages of school experience, the mentor adopts the role of 'co-inquirer'; as a student's confidence grows, the mentor works as more of an equal professional. However, Furlong and Maynard acknowledge that the four roles or stages do not function in a neat, delineated way; it is likely that approaches will be revisited at different times with some overlap.

Another challenge is to be found in how mentors *believe* they should act, compared to how they *actually* work. Cain (2009: 58) notes that while many mentors state they aim to be reflective with their approach to their mentee, in reality, for all sorts of reasons, they enact a much more directive approach. However, Cain also suggests that it is not necessary to always be reflective *or* directive – both can be used effectively depending on the stage and needs of the student teacher; the important thing is for the mentor to 'tune in' to what is needed by an individual and adjust their approach accordingly. It is also important for mentors to be critically reflective themselves about the approaches they take; for example, they may believe they are asking their student lots of questions but in reality they are actually doing a good deal of 'telling' (Clarke, 1995).

It is interesting to consider what student teachers believe makes a good mentor. This does not mean they are always right (or always agree) in their thinking, or that knowing their views, we should entirely build our approach to our work with them around what they say they want or need from being mentored; all the same, it is as important to consider others' perspectives as it is to acknowledge our own. Maynard (2000) asked student teachers what they believed created a good mentoring relationship and they included: feeling welcomed, accepted and supported (before, during and after their teaching – not just afterwards); they needed constructive but not continual criticism (which resulted in reduced self-confidence and a tendency to do things like their mentor). However, a lack of constructive criticism, or providing emotional support alone was also considered unhelpful, as was expecting the student to be a carbon copy (Maynard, 2000). The students' views presented here chime with Atjonen's (2012) idea of the 'ethical mentor' who asks good questions, gives feedback, listens, is flexible and respectful of students, and explains the bases of their views and advice.

Langdon (2011: 243) believes new teachers need a mentor 'who has the capacity to make transparent … what expertise looks like'. This is a similar notion to the 'horizon of visibility' discussed in Carey Philpott's 'Models of professional learning and what they mean for those working with teachers' (Chapter 3 in this volume); it is important that beginning teachers are able to see different kinds of practice and responsibilities experienced teachers undertake and how they deal with them. Langdon goes further to suggest that simply being a good teacher will not automatically mean you will be a good mentor; it is also important to have knowledge and understanding of how new teachers learn and develop, which goes beyond your own experience, so training is important. Langdon references Norman and Feiman-Nemser's (2005) work on mentoring, which suggests an effective mentor is a person who regards the classroom as 'site of inquiry', contrasting this with a narrow mindset of mentoring as chiefly concerned with helping the new teacher 'fit in' to the culture and ways of the school, echoing the points above. LoCasale-Crouch et al. (2012) also emphasize the importance of time spent between the mentor and mentee, as this develops a sense of collaboration between both parties.

Hall et al. (2008: 329) identify six areas in which mentors of student teachers need to feel confident: the mentoring relationship, classroom teaching practices, quality feedback, mediation, impact and school organization. Mentors must feel a sense of self-efficacy in these areas to operate effectively. However, mentors cannot act with self-efficacy if they do not fully understand what their role as a mentor is, so, as noted above, training is very important. Hobson (2002) notes an effective mentor needs to get feedback on their work from those they are mentoring; they need to know what students understand and know because mentors can challenge and support them more if they understand their beliefs and attitudes.

CASE STUDIES

The case studies below are adapted from real situations encountered supporting student teachers and working with school mentors over the past few years, and are intended to illustrate and illuminate some of the issues noted above in the literature.

CASE STUDY 5.1 MAKING MENTORS' KNOWLEDGE VISIBLE AND 'LEARNING, RE-LEARNING AND OVERLEARNING' (HATTIE AND CLINTON, 2008: 319)

All three teachers in a subject department agreed to teach Ally's scheme of work for six different classes in the same year group for the duration of her placement. They hoped this would be a good learning experience for them and the pupils. The head of faculty was doubtful – what if things went wrong with the pupils' work, or even worse, the examination results suffered and/or the parents complained? Jack (the head of department) explained that the scheme of work, although planned by Ally initially, would be jointly reviewed after each class, and decisions made about how to develop and change things in the light of each teacher's lesson. The pupils knew they were learning the 'new teacher's' project and were encouraged to give feedback to each teacher on content, how well they understood things and what they thought might help them understand better as necessary. Ally, Jack and the other two teachers (Jayne and Raj) also had the opportunity to observe each other's lessons and feed their views into subsequent lesson planning.

Things did not always go to plan. At one stage, Ally felt quite strongly that she wanted to do lesson four in the scheme in a certain way and two of the other teachers disagreed, believing she was over-complicating a stage of the pupils' work. In the end, they agreed to disagree – and all tried the lesson differently; no one's lesson worked particularly well but the subsequent discussions developed the scheme from then on.

Ally was very positive: 'The risks I was encouraged to take were a bit scary sometimes but very valuable to me – I was treated as an equal, everyone listened to me, but also explained why they thought things might work or not. Observing each other's lessons and giving (and getting) feedback was amazing – just getting a sense of such a wide range of perspectives on different aspects of teaching and learning in the same scheme of work was so helpful – I could understand so much of *why* each teacher did things. I wasn't expected to conform to any particular way of doing things – I was encouraged to have my own views and be comfortable with my way of being a new teacher.'

CASE STUDY 5.2 FORGETTING AND REMEMBERING

A subject mentor became ill a few days before a student teacher (Robert) was to begin his placement and had to take time off. The Head of Department (Gill) suggested a much less experienced colleague (Mal) take on the role of subject mentor at the last minute. Gill was not worried about Mal; he was a very good teacher, highly organized and very conscientious. Mal had also done the same course as Robert only a few years before so was likely, in Gill's view, to show good levels of empathy with him. The paperwork about Robert received from his first placement school, seemingly confirmed by excellent first impressions, indicated he was a strong student and likely to do very well.

However, things quickly went wrong; Robert and Mal did not get on well and Gill overheard heated exchanges following a lesson observation. When Gill spoke to Mal he said, 'Robert is very defensive, and he actually isn't as good as he thinks he is – he has a lot to learn and needs taking down a peg or two. I went through my list of all the things he needs to work on after his lesson and he didn't like it – I was being incredibly helpful – no one ever gave me so much of their time and advice'.

Ironically, Gill realized that she needed to coach and support Mal before things could improve; she believed without her intervention the relationship between Mal and Robert would be damaged beyond repair. She used a coaching technique encouraging a person to tell their 'story' (see, for example, Connor and Pokora, 2012). The aim of this approach is to try to uncover (as much as is ever possible) where certain views might have originated, and to try to explore or challenge them. While at first dismissive of the offer of coaching, Mal eventually opened up to Gill, to describe his own very negative mentoring experience as a student teacher, which was influencing his approach as a mentor. Mal's subject mentor had been very 'laid back' in their approach and viewed Mal as a highly competent person who did not need much support, time, encouragement or challenge. While Mal as a student was highly organized, he was also struggling with many aspects of teaching but did not want to appear too 'needy'. After initial attempts to seek constructive feedback on different issues failed, he admitted to Gill that at the time he had decided 'just to get through it', unfortunately a fairly common experience for student teachers. Long et al. (2012: 621) examined why some new teachers prefer to remain 'invisible' in their teaching placement schools when they feel excluded from the school's culture due to mentors' lack of interest in them; they adopt various stances which Long et al. characterize as 'fragile', 'robust' or 'competitive' as a means of shutting out or disguising their vulnerability.

Mal's university tutor had picked up that something was wrong and tried to raise her concerns with him, but Mal was clear he would get through things on his own and did not want to make a fuss. Now a mentor himself, he was both determined to 'do a much more thorough job' and frustrated that his technique was backfiring spectacularly.

Over time, with the help of some careful coaching with Gill, Mal realized that he had forgotten some important things his own mentor lacked: empathy, genuine interest in the person being mentored and a willingness to listen. Although his own mentor had acted very differently from Mal, the outcome was in danger of being the same – the person being mentored felt lost, frustrated and overwhelmed with what they felt they needed to learn. Mal's memory of his own negative experience made him over-compensate with his own mentee – for example, in telling him everything (instead of nothing) he possibly *could* work on. Mal remembered it is easy to feel overwhelmed as a student teacher, whatever kind of mentor you have; it was important to work with Robert to prioritize what he needed to improve rather than present him with an avalanche of criticism and then walk away. Mal also remembered that telling too much is as unhelpful as saying nothing; in fact telling as a strategy does not really help at all – some space has to be left for the individual to work things out for themselves.

Practical strategies for effective mentoring

In this final section, I would like to suggest some practical strategies for use with student teachers, or in supporting colleagues as mentors/coaches, taking account of and drawing together some key points from the literature and the case studies above.

Case study 5.1 suggests that it can be incredibly empowering to collaborate with a student teacher in their learning to teach and that we should be prepared to take some risks to develop alongside them; taking that role of 'co-inquirer' proposed by Furlong and Maynard above. Ally experienced and accepted that all teachers fail in their aims sometimes, yet when things go wrong something can always be learned. This resonates with Langdon's (2011) view that support for beginning teachers focuses too much on the kinds of 'coping strategies' of the classroom, which might be a short term 'humane' approach to helping them, but it seriously neglects pupil learning and also constrains new teachers' development (Furlong and Maynard, 1995).

Langdon (2011: 242) believes student and newly qualified teachers *are* able to 'focus on student learning and grapple with complex content knowledge to support learning' and mentors can 'help beginning teachers to reframe problems and to use multiple ways of understanding classroom challenges'. In other words, mentoring needs to be much more than helping student teachers simply survive their placements. In tune with the approach taken by the teachers and student in case study 5.1, Hattie and Clinton's view is that beginning and new teachers need to experience and see 'the expert teacher' at work; this might involve the student seeing a range of teaching behaviours and styles, trial and error and 'often a process of learning, re-learning and over-learning' (Hattie and Clinton, 2008: 319). In mentoring student teachers there is understandably a focus on them and what they need to do to develop or improve. However, sometimes this focus neglects the possibilities that there are in the mentor being explicit about how and what *they* have learned in similar situations, in other words, making their own knowledge 'visible' to their mentee. Case study 5.1 gives an example of teachers who made a conscious effort to work with their student in this way.

So, what can we take from case study 5.1 in terms of practical suggestions for mentoring or coaching? You may be able to do the same as Jack and his colleagues – teach a scheme of work or even one or two lessons designed by the student teacher. You may consider other ways you can enable students to move beyond 'survival', and 'tips' for classroom management (useful as these are at times) to make your expertise 'visible', for example, by reflecting *with* them on why you do certain things that you have probably done successfully, yet intuitively or unquestioningly, for years.

Langdon (2011: 252–4) proposes three key areas essential to successful mentoring of new teachers from which we can draw some ideas for practice: the school's learning culture (where expectations of teachers and pupils are high and teachers formally and informally discuss their work), the mentor themselves (being open to different ways of doing things, giving time, being honest about their own mistakes) and the strategies that mentors use (goal-setting, opportunities to observe and be observed, role-modelling of reflective practice such as evaluating their own teaching).

You could work with other mentors to try to articulate what the 'learning culture' of your school is; is it conducive to working with student teachers? If you have overall responsibility for the mentors in your school, are you providing opportunities for them to have training, regular updating and to share their practices and concerns? As a mentor, are you able to meet with other mentors in your school to develop a shared sense of what works well with beginning teachers in your particular context? You probably already use the strategies suggested by Langton, but could your use of these benefit from a review or 'brush-up'? Are you willing to approach the mentoring role in ways which could transform your own practice as well as that of your student teachers?

Case study 5.2 reminds us that it is incredibly important to remember our own experiences of being mentored, or coached, as these will inevitably affect the kind of mentor we will be. As mentors and coaches we need to be continually aware of the enormous potential and power we have to influence and shape new teachers' beliefs, practices and performance.

A simple exercise I asked new secondary subject mentors to do in mentor training was as follows: 'Consider lesson observation and feedback arising from that process; discuss the most negative and most positive experiences you have had of this in your teaching career so far'.

This activity led to a long, and sometimes quite emotional, discussion about the extremes of both negative experiences of this very common activity used with teachers at different stages of their careers, to inspirational 'light bulb' positive instances. Negative experiences of lesson observation included:

- feeling there was a 'hidden agenda' to the observation (usually down to lack of communication prior to the observation)

- receiving no feedback, or very little; being 'talked at' during feedback with no chance for discussion

- feedback being overly critical; feedback focusing too heavily on relatively minor issues

- no sense of possible development or 'next steps'; the person was left wondering how to act in the light of the feedback.

Positive experiences included:

- an agreement beforehand about what would be useful for the observer to focus on (that is, linked to perceived areas for development)

- an opportunity to discuss things in depth and ask questions of the observer after the lesson, revisiting issues in the future as needed

- a focus not just on the teacher but *on the effects of their behaviour and actions on the pupils.*

Those teachers who had experienced the last point felt that this would be especially important when working with student teachers. We discussed that, as mentors and tutors, we tend to focus most closely on students' behaviour, rather than its *effects*, especially early on in training. This is not to say that conversations about pupils' learning do not take place, but perhaps they are not as foregrounded as they could be in lesson observation feedback. Mentors were determined to avoid a replay of their own negative experiences but, as we have seen in case study 5.2 above, simply having had a bad experience of being mentored does not mean we will automatically be a better mentor. The exercise above could be applied to discussing many other areas of mentoring student teachers, for example, lesson planning, developing subject knowledge, and so on.

Case study 5.2, like Hobson's (2002) and Bullough and Draper's (2004) ideas noted above, points towards beginning the relationship between mentor and student teacher by exploring what each party expects and trying to anticipate some of the difficulties. This is not an easy thing to undertake as some students may feel uncomfortable having a frank conversation with a person they have only just met who has power and influence over them. However, these kinds of discussions may save many tricky misunderstandings later on and reassure students that they have a reflective mentor who takes their role (and them) seriously.

CONCLUSION

In this chapter, different definitions of mentoring and coaching have been explored with a view to revisiting certain challenges of helping students to learn to become effective teachers in their own right. However the student and mentor/ coach relationship is theorized or put into practice, it is complex work. For example, if mentoring can be seen as a kind of teaching, what does the associated learning look and feel like and how can it be assisted? Mentors and coaches bring their own views and experiences to the relationship, having been mentored or coached themselves in ways which may have been a mixture of good, bad and indifferent. Furlong and Maynard (1995) note that the resources and activities for students learning about teaching from working with mentors in schools are in themselves quite limited. Students can observe others teach, talk about teaching, plan, teach and evaluate their work on their own or with others; it is *how* this small range of activities is put to work by the mentor or coach that makes the difference.

I would like to leave the last word to McIntyre and Hagger (1996) who wrote at a time when the implications for school mentors in the light of significant increases to the time spent in schools by student teachers were being considered. They (and the other authors in their book, *Mentors in Schools: Developing the Profession of Teaching*) considered varied issues, such as how mentoring students in primary and secondary schools might be different and what kinds of mentor training and development might be needed if schools were to embed supporting new teachers rather than seeing it as a 'bolt-on' to the school's main business. It is their particular thoughts on the conditions needed to enable mentors to work effectively that I leave with you: 'mentoring, like teaching, can only be a successful activity if those who are engaged in it are deeply committed to it and confident in its value and feasibility' (McIntyre and Hagger, 1996: 163).

 ## FURTHER READING

Burley, S. and Pomphrey, C. (2011) *Mentoring and Coaching in Schools: Collaborative Professional Learning and Inquiry for Teachers*. London: Routledge.
Porter, H. (2008) *Mentoring New Teachers*. Thousand Oaks, CA: Corwin Press.

REFERENCES

Adams, J. (2007) 'Artists becoming teachers: expressions of identity transformation in a virtual forum', *International Journal of Art & Design Education*, 26(3): 264–73.
Atjonen, P. (2012) 'Student Teachers' Outlooks upon the Ethics of Their Mentors during Teaching Practice', *Scandinavian Journal of Educational Research*, 56(1). 39–53
Broughton, T. (2013) *The Perfect Teacher Coach*. Bancyfelin: Independent Thinking.

Bullough, R. V. and Draper, R.J. (2004) 'Mentoring and the emotions', *Journal of Education for Teaching: International Research and Pedagogy*, 30(3): 271–88.

Burley, S. and Pomphrey, C. (2011) *Mentoring and Coaching in Schools: Collaborative Professional Learning and Inquiry for Teachers*. London: Routledge.

Cain, T. (2009) 'Mentoring trainee teachers: how can mentors use research?', *Mentoring & Tutoring: Partnership in Learning*, 17(1): 53–66.

Clarke, A. (1995) 'Professional development in practicum settings: reflective practice under scrutiny', *Teaching and Teacher Education*, 11(3): 243–61.

Collanus, M., Kairavouri, S. and Rusanen, S. (2012) 'The identities of an arts educator: comparing discourses in three teacher education programmes in Finland', *International Journal of Education Through Art*, 8(3): 7–21.

Colley, H. (2002) 'A "rough guide" to the history of mentoring from a Marxist feminist perspective', *Journal of Education for Teaching*, 28(3): 257–73.

Connor, M. and Pokora, J. (2012) *Coaching & Mentoring at Work Developing Effective Practice*. Maidenhead: Open University Press.

Creasy, J. and Paterson, F. (2005) *Leading Coaching in Schools*. Nottingham: National College for School Leadership.

Fairbanks, C.M., Freedman, D. and Kahn, C. (2000) 'The role of effective mentors in learning to teach', *Journal of Teacher Education*, 51(2): 102–12.

Flaherty, J. (2005) *Coaching: Evoking Excellence in Others*. 2nd edn. London: Elsevier Butterworth-Heinemann.

Furlong, J. and Maynard, T. (1995) *The Growth of Professional Knowledge Mentoring Student Teachers*. London: Routledge.

Hale, R. (2000) 'To match or mis-match? The dynamics of mentoring as a route to personal and organizational learning', *Career Development International*, 5(4): 223–34.

Hattie, J. and Clinton, J. (2008) 'Identifying accomplished teachers: a validation study', in L.C. Ingvarson and J. Hattie (eds), *Assessing Teachers for Professional Certification: The First Decade of the National Board for Professional Teaching Standards*. Vol. 11. Oxford: Elsevier. pp. 313–44.

Hall, K.M., Draper, R.J, Smith, L.K. and Bullough Jr, R.V. (2008) 'More than a place to teach: exploring the perceptions of the roles and responsibilities of mentor teachers', *Mentoring & Tutoring: Partnership in Learning*, 16(3): 328–45.

Hawkey, K. (1997) 'Roles, responsibilities and relationships in mentoring: a literature review and agenda for research', *Journal of Teacher Education*, 48(5): 325–35.

Hawkey, K. (2006) 'Emotional intelligence and mentoring in pre-service teacher education: a literature review', *Mentoring & Tutoring: Partnership in Learning*, 14(2): 137–47.

Hobson, A.J. (2002) 'Student teachers' perceptions of school based mentoring in initial teacher training (ITT)', *Mentoring & Tutoring: Partnership in Learning*, 10(1): 5–20.

Jones, L., Reid, D. and Bevins, S. (1997) 'Teachers' perceptions of mentoring in a collaborative model of initial teacher training'. *Journal of Education for Teaching: International Research and Pedagogy*, 23(3): 253–62.

Langdon, F. (2011) 'Shifting perception and practice: New Zealand beginning teacher induction and mentoring as a pathway to expertise', *Professional Development in Education*, 37(2): 241–58.

LoCasale-Crouch, J., Davis, E., Wiens, P. and Pianta, R. (2012) 'The role of the mentor in supporting new teachers: associations with self-efficacy, reflection, and quality', *Mentoring & Tutoring: Partnership in Learning*, 20(3): 303–23.

Long, F., Hall, K., Conway, P. and Murphy, R. (2012) 'Novice teachers as "invisible" learners', *Teachers and Teaching: Theory and Practice*, 18(6): 619–36.

Mayer, J.D. and Cobb, C.D. (2000) 'Educational policy on emotional intelligence: does it make sense?', *Educational Psychology Review*, 12(2): 163–83.

Maynard, T. (2000) 'Learning to teach or learning to manage mentors? Experiences of school-based teacher training', *Mentoring & Tutoring: Partnership in Learning*, 8(1): 17–30.

Maynard, T. and Furlong, J. (1995) 'Learning to teach and models of mentoring', in T. Kerry and A.S. Mayes (eds), *Issues in Mentoring*. Buckingham: Open University Press.

McIntyre, D. and Hagger, H. (eds) (1996) *Mentors in Schools: Developing the Profession of Teaching*. London: David Fulton.

Norman, P.J. and Feiman-Nemser, S. (2005) 'Mind activity in teaching and mentoring', *Teaching and Teacher Education*, 21(6): 679–97.

Porter, H. (2008) *Mentoring New Teachers*. Thousand Oaks, CA: Corwin Press.

Rajuan, M., Beijaard, D. and Verloop, N. (2010) 'The match and mismatch between expectations of student teachers and cooperating teachers: exploring different opportunities for learning to teach in the mentor relationship', *Research Papers in Education*, 25(2): 201–23.

Salovey, P. and Mayer, J.D. (1990) 'Emotional intelligence', *Imagination, Cognition and Personality*, 9: 185–211.

Schon, D.A. (1990) *Educating the Reflective Practitioner: Toward a New Design for Teaching and Learning in the Professions*. London: Wiley.

Tang, S.Y.F. (2003) 'Challenge and support: the dynamics of student teachers' professional learning in the field experience', *Teaching and Teacher Education*, 19(5): 483–98.

Zanting, A., Verloop, N. and Vermunt, J.D. (2003) 'How do student teachers elicit their mentor teachers' practical knowledge?', *Teachers and Teaching: Theory and Practice*, 9(3): 197–211.

Zeichner, K.M. and Gore, J.M. (1990) 'Teacher socialization' in W.R. Houston (ed.), *Handbook of Research on Teacher Education*. New York: Macmillan.

CHAPTER 6

WHY IS THE ACADEMIC COMPONENT OF ITE IMPORTANT AND HOW DO WE ORGANIZE IT?

Nigel Appleton

By the end of this chapter you should have an overview of:

- research and thinking about the types of knowledge teachers need and how they might develop it
- what this means for school-based initial teacher education (ITE).

There are two common uses of the word academic:

1. relating to education, learning and scholarship (such as an academic understanding)

2. of no practical use at all (such as a largely academic debate).

In this chapter we explore the role of the academic component of ITE and conclude that it is important in the sense of the first usage above rather than the second. In fact, we see that, far from being of no practical use, the academic component underpins the practice of teaching and provides the teacher with the wherewithal to make informed judgements and decisions in their day-to-day work.

Teaching, as we see below, is an intellectual and practical activity that requires, among other things, a combination of knowledge, understanding and skills. For a beginning teacher to acquire that combination and learn how to deploy it in the complexities of their professional lives they must engage in academic study as well as in practice. It is important to realize that this applies regardless of whether or not the training programme leads to an academic award. So, even if you are involved in a QTS-only programme, you still need to consider the students' needs for the academic element. Most ITE programmes do also include an academic award – such as Postgraduate Certificate of Education (PGCE), Professional Graduate Diploma in Education (PGDE), BA(Hons) – and this award will be made by the university or other higher education institution with whom you may be working in partnership. In this chapter we consider what this academic element might contain and how it can be managed by school and university working together.

WHAT ACADEMIC LEARNING IS NEEDED?

There have been a number of attempts to establish what professional knowledge teachers require in order to be effective. This is a complex and contested area and it is important for student teacher and teacher trainer alike to understand the notions of teachers' professional knowledge upon which the training course has been constructed. These notions of requisite teacher knowledge are themselves dependent on beliefs about the curriculum, about how learning takes place, about the purpose of education and about the role of the teacher. Thus a deeper engagement is needed with the philosophy of education that underpins the ITE course. Student teachers will come to their ITE course with their own set of beliefs which may or may not match those underpinning the course. Perhaps the first academic challenge, therefore, is to identify and examine some of these beliefs in the light of research and current thinking and subject them to challenge by peers and by experts. Then a process of reconstruction of these beliefs is needed, based on a combination of theoretical perspectives and research findings drawn from academic study and mediated experiences in the school and classroom.

Many programmes of initial teacher education have a stated aim to produce teachers who are reflective practitioners in the sense of Schön (1983) – teachers who reflect on their practice in the light of experience and theory in order to improve their practice. Some also aim to help these new teachers on the road to becoming teacher researchers. The latter are neatly described by Loughran (2002): 'Teacher-researchers can be characterised as those practitioners who attempt to better understand their practice, and its impact on their students, by researching the relationship between teaching and learning in their world of work.' Such goals imply a need for academic study in relation to both the theory of learning and teaching and research methods appropriate to the teacher researching their practice and that of others in the workplace. These goals may not be shared by the student teacher, who may have more immediate concerns about managing in the classroom. Indeed, they may not be understood by the student teacher as legitimate and desirable goals, and part of any academic element needs to be to understand the purpose of the academic element!

A typical starting point for a student teacher is to focus on what to teach and how to teach; on their own subject knowledge and some notion of how to get it across. For a teacher with a subject specialism there is, of course, an expectation that they know their subject well, which if not the case can make the student teacher anxious. This subject knowledge will usually be covered, at least in part, by their degree and other prior learning and experience, and would have been explored as part of the selection process. However, there are likely to be gaps and vulnerabilities in that subject knowledge which will need attention if they are to be secure in what they are teaching. A needs assessment process is commonly used to identify areas that need attention and a plan put in place to support the required learning. Similarly, for a teacher who teaches across the curriculum there is an expectation that their subject knowledge is sufficiently broad and complete for them to teach the whole curriculum but, again, a process of audits and supportive interventions is commonly used to secure this. The nature of subject knowledge is not straightforward, however. The school curriculum in a subject may be quite different from the subject as studied in university. Ellis writes:

> Subject knowledge is communal, a form of collective knowledge. The 'subject', specifically, is the school subject, which has an important relationship with, but is not identical to, the university subject, or governed by it. Those who teach the subject in schools (just as those who teach the university subject), collectively, are the principal sources of authority over the production of the subject in schools. (Ellis, 2007: 458–9)

Bruner (1966) writes about the structure of knowledge as consisting of the subject's ideas, concepts, principles and their relationships, and that these are important for learning. These big ideas may vary according to the context; thus big ideas in school physics may involve Newton's model of gravity rather than Einstein's. Student teachers need to be aware of this distinction between school subject and university subject when considering their subject knowledge learning needs (Deng, 2007). There is evidence that some student teachers find it challenging to attend to their own subject knowledge development while in training. They may find their confidence affected by their perceived shortfall (Kind, 2009) but at the same time be reluctant to admit their needs to those within the school and the university who may be able to help them (Youens and McCarthy, 2007). This may occur across any subject specialism as well as in general primary training. It is clearly important for all trainers to be aware of student teachers' behaviours in relation to subject knowledge and to help them to take a proportionate view of it in relation to their overall learning needs. Various possible approaches to supporting subject knowledge development are offered. Stotko et al. (2005) recommend a collaborative approach between university subject departments and education departments and using a portfolio approach to assessment. Ellis (2007: 459) similarly suggests a collaborative approach but also asserts that she has 'been arguing for much more serious attention to subject knowledge and for a stronger focus on the collective processes by which this form of knowledge might be warranted, accessed and developed where it matters most – in classrooms'. Youens and McCarthy

> propose that the role of school mentors in the subject knowledge development of student teachers needs to be accorded a higher profile, and part of the process for achieving this higher profile needs to be an exploration of the tensions that exist in the dual support and assessment roles of school mentors. Student teachers need structured opportunities before starting their practical teaching placements to articulate and explore their perceptions of the roles of school mentors and university tutors in relation to supporting and assessing their subject knowledge development. By the adoption of such strategies, we can better prepare student teachers to work more openly with staff in schools and so develop more collegial relationships with university tutors and school mentors. (2007: 305)

Unlike with subject knowledge, Burn et al. (2007) found that too close a collaboration between school-based and university-based trainers prevented student teachers from appreciating differing conceptions of the subject held within the school department.

Knowing whatever subject knowledge it is that you want your learners to come to know, is not enough. It is also necessary to know how to help those learners to come to know. Though broadly termed as pedagogy, further analysis reveals that some aspects of pedagogy are specifically related to the subject content being taught and other aspects are more general and transferable. Seeing that pedagogy and subject knowledge were intertwined, Shulman (1986) introduced the idea of 'pedagogical content knowledge' (PCK) as part of an attempt to classify and differentiate between elements of teachers' professional knowledge. (Thus inadvertently picking up on a thread central to education in German-speaking and Nordic countries since the seventeenth century, *die Didaktik* – Kansanen, 2009) Pedagogical content knowledge refers to the content-specific pedagogy that a teacher needs to have in order to teach that content effectively. Thus, for example, it is not enough to understand how place value in mathematics works, either from an advanced mathematical perspective or from a practical usage perspective, but it is also necessary to understand the associated learning issues and the role of place value in underpinning the learning of much of arithmetic. Over the years, Shulman developed his ideas (Shulman, 1991) and they are now widely accepted as a useful framework for thinking about teachers' knowledge. As Ornstein and Scarpaci put it, quite apart from having pure subject knowledge, 'If beginning teachers are to be successful, they must wrestle simultaneously with issues of specialized pedagogical content (or knowledge) as well as issues of general pedagogy (or generic teaching principles)' (2011: 504). Banks et al. (2005) offered a development of these ideas, adding in the central view of the teacher of themselves and their relationship to the subject content and its pedagogy (see Figure 6.1). It is the centrality of the teacher's personal subject construct that determines their interpretation and application of the different

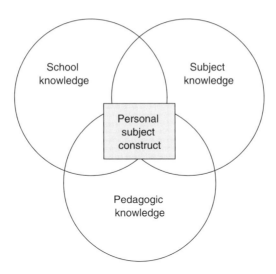

Figure 6.1 Personal subject construct

types of professional knowledge. The importance and challenges of working with subject knowledge, pedagogic knowledge and school knowledge in initial training have been explored across many subjects in secondary (for example, English by Green, 2006, mathematics by Steele, 2005, science by Sperandeo-Mineo et al., 2006, geography by Brooks, 2006, 2010, drama by Kempe, 2009, and physical education [PE] by Sloan, 2007) and primary (for example, science by Anderson and Clark, 2012, information and communications technology [ICT] by Chai et al., 2011, and general by Alexander, 2010).

Craft knowledge is another aspect of teachers' knowledge. Grimmett and MacKinnon describe it thus: 'Craft knowledge represents intelligent and sensible know-how in the action setting' (1992: 395) and 'Craft knowledge is essentially the accumulated wisdom derived from teachers' and practice-oriented research-ers' understanding of the meanings ascribed to the many dilemmas inherent in teaching' (1992: 428). Craft knowledge develops as one makes sense of experi-ence, but experience is limited in the case of a beginning teacher, so much of this knowledge has to be acquired from those who already hold it. For that rea-son, school-based work makes a major contribution to the development of craft knowledge, complementing the academic study, much of which needs to take place out of the school classroom. However, there is not simply a divide between the location of learning, in the classroom or outside the classroom. Much of the accumulated wisdom is captured in the literature on teaching and learning, and much of the student teacher's academic learning will involve reflecting on and conducting research in the classroom. The beginning teacher needs to access a knowledge base that is broad, international, complex and contemporary; that covers knowledge, understanding and skills; that includes subject pedagogy and subject knowledge; and that includes general pedagogic understanding and craft skills. The academic element of the training programme has an important role in providing access to that knowledge base beyond the local expressions of it available within the small number of schools in which they train.

A further helpful distinction is between procedural and declarative knowledge. Put simply, having declarative knowledge is 'knowing what and why' and having procedural knowledge is 'knowing how to'. The relationship between the two has been much discussed (Berge and Hezewijk, 1999; Bruning and Bruning, 2008; Yilmaz and Yalçin, 2012) but there is some consensus that to be an effective teacher the procedural knowledge should be derived from and connected to secure declarative knowledge. This applies, not just to the way a teacher deals with subject knowledge, but also to their pedagogy. The link between theory and practice, if retained, even when practice has resulted in unconscious application of procedural knowledge, can allow the teacher to respond to new situations with confidence. Once again, there is a key role here for the academic element of the training course to provide declarative knowledge that will support and enable the development of the procedural knowledge needed for effective classroom practice.

Consideration needs also to be given to the situated and social nature of knowledge. Putnam and Borko (2000) refer to cognition as being 'situated', 'social' and 'distributed'. Learning is situated in the sense that 'how a person learns a particular set of knowledge and skills, and the situation in which a person learns, become a fundamental part of what is learned' (2000: 4), social in the sense that 'interactions with the people in one's environment are major determinants of both what is learned and how learning takes place' and distributed in the sense that 'the distribution of cognition across people and tools [makes] it possible for the [group] to accomplish cognitive tasks beyond the capabilities of any individual member' (2000: 5). Lave and Wenger (1991; Wenger, 1998) refer to these social learning contexts as 'communities of practice' and this is a helpful model for the school or the ITE provider or the teacher education partnership as a learning community focused around common practice. These ideas of learning as a social activity apply as much to the learning of beginning teachers as they do to that of their pupils, and thus the nature of their training programme needs to be designed with careful consideration given to the situations in which planned learning experiences occur, the involvement of other learners (teachers and other student teachers) and group learning activities.

To summarize this section, the student teacher has much to learn, the complexity of which requires academic study as well as practical activities in and around the classroom. They need to acquire knowledge that has length (extending beyond their own experience), breadth (extending beyond the immediate context) and depth (extending below the surface). Alongside this they need to develop advanced learning skills that will enable them to continue learning as they develop through the stage of reflective practitioner and on to become a teacher researcher.

Teaching in the UK is a graduate profession, going on Master's profession

In common with most countries, teaching in the UK is a graduate profession, meaning that only graduates may join that profession. Non-graduates are able to train to join the profession by undertaking a degree integrated with preparation for the award of QTS so that they become graduates at the same time as they qualify as teachers. For graduates, entry to the profession has traditionally been through a PGCE, an integrated academic and professional preparation for teaching. In 2007 the idea of moving teaching to a master's-level profession was mooted in the Children's Plan: Building Brighter Futures (DCSF, 2007: 4.24) which states that, 'to help fulfil our high ambitions for all children, and to boost the status of teaching still further, we now want it to become a masters-level profession'. Although a master's degree is an entry requirement for joining the teaching profession in some countries (for example, Finland), it was envisaged that in England, Wales and Northern Ireland teachers would still be able to enter as graduates with a first degree but would undertake study for a master's degree in their early career. This aspiration has not to date become statutory but it has informed thinking in relation to teachers' initial and continuing professional development. It has also led to the PGCE being made available at master's level.

What do the levels 6 and 7 mean?

Following the 1999 Bologna Agreement, the frameworks for awards in higher education in the UK were revised by the Quality Assurance Agency for Higher Education (QAA, 2001, 2008) to provide a greater degree of commonality across institutions and nations and to clarify the differences between expectations in undergraduate study (first-cycle qualifications) and postgraduate study (second-cycle qualifications). At the same time, credit accumulation and transfer agreements were developed, assigning a volume of credit to different qualifications based on the amount of study involved (120 credits = one year's full-time study). Among other things, this clarified, and restricted, the terminology so that, for example, the term 'postgraduate' could only be used to imply after degree in level rather than after degree in time. It also brought into question the volume of credit that was appropriate for a one-year full-time course in which a substantial element of professional learning was undertaken in a work place. This led to a review of the PGCE which had traditionally been assumed to be at the same level as an honours degree. In order to comply with the new frameworks, PGCEs in England and Wales became separated into Postgraduate Certificate in Education (at master's level, level 7) and Professional Graduate Certificate in Education (at honours degree level, level 6). In Scotland, consideration of the volume of credit led to the replacement of the PGCE with either a Postgraduate Diploma in Education or a Professional Graduate Diploma in Education (PGDE).

The levels and volume of credit for a PGCE vary between universities, and most universities offer the PGCE at both postgraduate and professional graduate levels. It is important for you to understand the nature and demands of the academic awards your students are working towards, especially if you are working in partnership with more than one university, and understand also the way the academic award integrates with the professional preparation. Student teachers who are on an undergraduate route will typically be studying at levels 4–6 during their course, although some four-year courses include some master's-level work.

Table 6.1 National qualification frameworks – general level descriptions (derived from QAA, 2008)

Descriptor for a higher education qualification at level 6: bachelor's degree with honours	Descriptor for a higher education qualification at level 7: master's degree
The descriptor provided for this level of the FHEQ is for any bachelor's degree with honours which should meet the descriptor in full. This qualification descriptor can also be used as a reference point for other level 6 qualifications, including bachelor's degrees, graduate diplomas etc. For example, Professional Graduate Certificate in Education	The descriptor provided for this level of the framework is for any master's degree which should meet the descriptor in full. This qualification descriptor can also be used as a reference point for other level 7 qualifications, including postgraduate certificates and postgraduate diplomas. For example, Postgraduate Certificate in Education
Bachelor's degrees with honours are awarded to students who have demonstrated:	**Master's degrees are awarded to students who have demonstrated:**
• a systematic understanding of key aspects of their field of study, including acquisition of coherent and detailed knowledge, at least some of which is at, or informed by, the forefront of defined aspects of a discipline	• a systematic understanding of knowledge, and a critical awareness of current problems and/or new insights, much of which is at, or informed by, the forefront of their academic discipline, field of study or area of professional practice
• an ability to deploy accurately established techniques of analysis and inquiry within a discipline	• a comprehensive understanding of techniques applicable to their own research or advanced scholarship
	• originality in the application of knowledge, together with a practical understanding of how established techniques of research and inquiry are used to create and interpret knowledge in the discipline
• conceptual understanding that enables the student: ○ to devise and sustain arguments, and/or to solve problems, using ideas and techniques, some of which are at the forefront of a discipline ○ to describe and comment upon particular aspects of current research, or equivalent advanced scholarship, in the discipline	• conceptual understanding that enables the student: ○ to evaluate critically current research and advanced scholarship in the discipline ○ to evaluate methodologies and develop critiques of them and, where appropriate, to propose new hypotheses
• an appreciation of the uncertainty, ambiguity and limits of knowledge	
• the ability to manage their own learning, and to make use of scholarly reviews and primary sources (for example, refereed research articles and/or original materials appropriate to the discipline)	
Typically, holders of the qualification will be able to:	**Typically, holders of the qualification will be able to:**
• apply the methods and techniques that they have learned to review, consolidate, extend and apply their knowledge and understanding, and to initiate and carry out projects	• deal with complex issues both systematically and creatively, make sound judgements in the absence of complete data, and communicate their conclusions clearly to specialist and non-specialist audiences

- critically evaluate arguments, assumptions, abstract concepts and data (that may be incomplete), to make judgements, and to frame appropriate questions to achieve a solution – or identify a range of solutions – to a problem

- communicate information, ideas, problems and solutions to both specialist and non-specialist audiences

- demonstrate self-direction and originality in tackling and solving problems, and act autonomously in planning and implementing tasks at a professional or equivalent level

- continue to advance their knowledge and understanding, and to develop new skills to a high level.

And holders will have:

- the qualities and transferable skills necessary for employment requiring:

  o the exercise of initiative and personal responsibility
  o decision-making in complex and unpredictable contexts
  o the learning ability needed to undertake appropriate further training of a professional or equivalent nature

And holders will have:

- the qualities and transferable skills necessary for employment requiring:

  o the exercise of initiative and personal responsibility
  o decision-making in complex and unpredictable situations
  o the independent learning ability required for continuing professional development

The national qualification frameworks give general level descriptions (see Table 6.1 for those applicable to England, Wales and Northern Ireland). From the table it is possible to compare the differing expectations of the two levels. The difference in levels is less about what they know and more about how they know, how they show what they know and how they grow what they know. Despite the movement towards the master's level PGCE, teacher educators and student teachers are not all convinced of the value or appropriateness of study at that level within initial teacher education. Jackson (2009) tracked perceptions of master's-level study in the PGCE during the academic year 2007–08. She surveyed student teachers, school-based mentors, headteachers and university-based teacher educators across 10 higher education institutions offering ITE. In her report she makes 12 recommendations, including the following recommendations that may usefully guide the school-based teacher educator:

1. Prospective students of Masters level PGCE courses or other teacher education courses should be made more fully aware of what Masters study is and why it is presented to those intending to become teachers. This could be done through the prospectus and at base interview.

2. Attention should be paid at all levels to ensuring a link between Masters and classroom practice in order to dispel the perception that Masters is an unrelated adjunct.

3. In order for Masters to be meaningful in the job market, headteachers, school mentors and all teachers need to value it; this to be developed through closer

working between trainers in schools and HEIs or other teacher education providers.

4. The initial enthusiasm of student teachers for Masters and their trust in its benefit should be encouraged by greater collaboration between training providers and policy makers.

5. Through the strength of the English partnership between schools and teacher training providers, develop greater 'joined-up thinking' about Masters.

(Jackson, 2009: 5–6)

Jackson's and others' subsequent consideration of the wider implications of master's-level study continues and can be followed via the Teacher Education Advancement Network (TEAN) at www.cumbria.ac.uk/Courses/SubjectAreas/ Education/Research/TEAN/TeacherEducatorsStorehouse/Home.aspx.

Jackson found that some student teachers were less certain of the value of the academic element of their training once they had completed the training than they had been before they started. Other research shows that student teachers are open (before they start) to engaging with theoretical aspects of their training. Knight (2013) offers an optimistic view based on a study of pre-service primary teachers. The challenge is how not to lose that openness during the training course. Many student teachers find the transition to studying a PGCE at level 6 difficult and one at master's level doubly difficult. This is often related to their prior experience and particularly their degree discipline. The PGCE is firmly located in the discipline of education which shares its discourse and its research methods with other social sciences. McLain (2013) raises questions about the equity of expecting all student teachers to be able to engage in the study of education at master's level when their prior education could have been in a number of other disciplines with a substantially different type of discourse and approaches to research. In particular, students coming from practical or vocational degrees may not be used to more theoretical approaches, and those from mathematics and scientific disciplines may be unused to the uncertainties and contested nature of ideas in education and, at a more practical level, be unused to writing essays.

How does the academic learning take place?

The traditional PGCE in England and Wales provided an integrated academic and professional preparation for teaching. With the introduction of competences and then standards for the award of QTS in the 1990s, and the repositioning of the PGCE in the Framework for Higher Education Qualifications in the subsequent decade, there began a drift towards the separation of the academic and professional elements. The PGCE was seen as the academic part and QTS the professional part. Although many PGCE providers resisted this, the sector began to provide QTS-only courses as well as PGCE with QTS courses, and the PGCE was in some instances reduced to a couple of master's-level modules studied alongside the QTS course, often with the QTS part taught in schools and the master's modules taught in a university with little or no overlap. There is much that can be learned through practice, separately from academic study. Kolb's (1984) model for experiential learning offers a cycle of 'experiencing – reflecting – generalizing – applying – experiencing …' as a representation of the ways adult learners in particular can learn from their experience. Such a learning process is often referred to as praxis, which Freire defines as 'reflection and action upon the world in order to transform it' (1970: 33) and uses it to represent access to learning that is not dependent on education provided by those with power. Clearly, such approaches to learning and developing reflective practice are essential tools for the developing teacher throughout their career, but the nature of teachers' requisite knowledge is such that without engagement with theory the process of learning is likely to be slower and more reactive to potentially incomplete sets of experiences. In the light of the above discussion of the nature of teachers' professional knowledge, it is suggested that the two elements, academic and practical, need to be integrated, perhaps like the two strands in the double helix structure of DNA – intertwined, identifiable but multiply connected.

PRACTICAL GUIDANCE ON MANAGING THE ACADEMIC ELEMENT

Designing and planning the academic element

It is important to ensure that the academic elements are built in from the very beginning of the process of designing and planning the training programme. Where the programme as a whole, or the academic award within it, is validated by a university it will be important to adhere closely to the approved documents. Universities have to have tight controls over their academic awards as part of their need to protect the integrity of these awards and their power to make them. However, these documents are often written in such a way as to allow some freedom in terms of content and delivery. Universities tend to follow a process of 'constructive alignment' (Biggs, 1999) in the design of courses. They start with the learning outcomes and work back through the construction of the assessment tasks to then design the learning activities. (A useful guide is available from the Higher Education Academy at www.heacademy.ac.uk/hlst/resources/a-zdirectory/constructive_alignment) This is different from the course design typically used in school learning where there are externally set assessments and/or a prescribed curriculum. Constructive alignment is designed to support the development of students as independent learners taking a share of responsibility for navigating their route to achieving the learning outcomes. The degree of prescription in terms of content can vary between levels and between universities but it will be designed to support the professional outcomes for the beginning teacher as well as the academic outcomes. If a training programme does not lead to an academic award, the academic element can still be designed on the same principles. The learning outcomes and assessment criteria need to reflect the level (6 or 7) shown in Table 6.1 through the use of appropriate language. The programme content will need to support the student teachers in acquiring the desired understanding, knowledge and skills to be effective teachers for the age range and/or subject specialism for which they are training in any relevant school or setting. In particular, it will need to ensure all aspects of teachers' professional knowledge are developed as discussed earlier in this chapter. The content and planned experiences incorporated in the programme design will need to ensure the students have the opportunity to develop and demonstrate that they meet the relevant professional standards as well as meeting the learning outcomes of the academic element.

Keeping the integration of theory and practice in mind, learning activities can be planned so that reading and discussion of relevant theory and research evidence is used by the student teachers to plan an activity with pupils, implement the plan, review and reflect. Much professional learning is serendipitous, however, so students also need to be encouraged to reflect on the unexpected, the critical incidents, and use them as a basis for further reading and learning. Assessment of the academic element is considered in Chapter 7 but at the planning stage it is important to design assessment tasks that match the learning outcomes whilst also providing evidence towards the professional standards. There is not much time within a busy PGCE so two to four assessment items is typical. In order to still achieve breadth of coverage, portfolios of smaller tasks are sometimes used.

Teaching the academic element

As discussed earlier, there is not a clear division between the academic and the practical, between the theory and the practice. Therefore it is important to see all the student teachers' learning as contributing to both academic and professional elements of their professional formation. The teaching programme needs to be seen as an integrated whole. However, for practical reasons much the academic element may be contained within learning that takes place outside the school classroom. Where this happens in the university, students will also have access to other learning resources and, importantly, to academics. It is also important that the students have the opportunity to meet and learn with their peers when they can share and compare learning experiences and contexts, and can challenge and support one another. This can be most effective when it happens reasonably frequently during the course, typically once a week apart from periods of continuous classroom teaching.

The importance of reading and writing

Student teachers need access to literature to support their learning. This includes, but is not limited to, the printed page. In the ideal scenario the student has access to a well-stocked education library and associated access to electronic library resources, such as electronic journals and e-books. There is literature available freely online but much of the commercially expensive materials remain accessible only through a licensed gateway such as a library. These include many books and peer-reviewed journals. Even where a student teacher is training in a school close to the university, access may be difficult if they have a very busy timetable in school. It is important to create space in the students' programme for them to access the library and to have time to read and think. Where a student is training in a school some distance from the library, they should be able to access the online resources, but arrangements will need to be made for them to travel to the library for other materials. This could be at weekends and in the school holidays but the programme would need to take account of this when setting tasks and assessments. It may be possible to arrange for students to access a suitable library nearer to the school but this may only provide limited borrowing and access rights. Of course, students should be encouraged to purchase their own copies of texts that will be valuable for reference in the future.

In order to learn effectively and meet the expectations of level 6 or 7 study, students will also need to record their thinking, usually in writing. Many graduates find this challenging, especially those whose degree did not involve much essay writing. It is possible to use alternative assessment types, such as presentations, but a written essay remains an effective vehicle for students to marshal evidence and thought and produce a cogent extended argument. Universities usually provide support in academic writing and either the student teachers can access this, possibly via email, or it can be provided locally by teachers who are experienced in writing at this level.

Students with additional needs

Provision will also need to be considered for students with additional needs. A university would expect to provide this for its students, and the logistics of access to the university service would need to be resolved or local provision put in place.

Who will do the teaching and assess the academic element?

Although most university-based teacher educators are qualified and experienced school teachers, they also have additional qualifications, skills and experience, together with an academic community which can support them in their work in higher education. School-based trainers are less likely to have this additionality, although their school teaching experience is likely to be more current. A useful approach is to consider the school and university staff as a single community of practice, with frequent movement of staff between the university and school to contribute to differing aspects of the training as fits best. In some cases, such partnerships appoint staff who are jointly employed by the university and school. This can lead to difficulties over conditions of employment but these can be overcome if both employers and the individual are flexible. Perhaps a more sustainable solution, however, is for there to be a programme of professional development within the community of practice that develops within the school-based and university-based trainers the knowledge, understanding and skills needed for the effective preparation of the new teachers.

CASE STUDIES

 ## CASE STUDY 6.1

The value of the academic elements of ITE can go far beyond the impact on the individual student. Take Rik, for example.

Rik (not his real name) had been a professional sportsman, but a serious injury brought an early end to his career and this had led him to consider PE teaching. He studied for a degree and then signed up for an employment-based graduate training route operated by the local authority in the area where he wished to work. Although the training programme contained a strong academic element which was fully integrated into the professional training, there was no academic award attached; it led to QTS only. However, there was an arrangement with a local university for students to undertake some additional supported study at the end of the training year, based on the academic strand of the training programme, leading to assessment for a postgraduate certificate. This required additional commitment from the student in terms of time and finance, and had to be managed during the period when they were preparing for and beginning to work as a newly qualified teacher. Through undertaking this master's-level study, Rik developed a deeper interest in the use of mobile technologies in teaching PE and used social media to disseminate his findings. He achieved high marks in his academic modules but, more importantly, gained greater knowledge and skills. Not only did this enhance his employability, but it also led to him running professional development sessions for other teachers from early in his teaching career. In this case, the academic study had brought benefits to the wider teaching profession as well as to the individual. Unusually for a new teacher, he was in demand to develop other teachers.

> I'm still in the infancy of my teaching career, but I'm already seeing the students progress as a result of my teaching and feel really proud of that. I've now got whole school responsibility as lead coach for creating innovative and invigorating ideas to be using in teaching and learning to enhance lessons across any subject.

In Rik's case the QTS-only course had a strong academic thread which meant that the academic award was well within reach. He opted into this award and reaped the benefits of the additional study that he undertook. Others on the course did not take that option. Even though the academic element was evident for all, the additional study and discipline required to complete the assessment for the award was what made the difference for Rik.

Case study questions:

1. What does this offer as a model for including master's-level study alongside a QTS-only course?

2. What did Rik gain that other students missed out on by not taking the additional study option?

3. How would the school and university need to collaborate to ensure no dislocation between elements?

CASE STUDY 6.2

A group of primary schools in a rural area were pleased to be able to work in partnership with a university to provide ITE in their area. They believed they had a lot to offer to students, but principally they hoped that involvement in ITE would help with their recruitment of new, high-quality teachers and enhance the professional development of all the staff in their schools. The partnership was offering a PGCE with 60 credits at master's level. Training sessions were planned to be delivered locally, using space at one of the schools, with contributions from school staff and from university tutors. The schools would manage all the school experience and had some innovative ways to ensure all the students would see outstanding practice across all areas of the curriculum. The challenge, however, was how to support the academic element of the training programme with the schools being so far from the university. Having identified the detailed needs of the students, the schools and university, in partnership, put in place the following:

*   Blocks of time for the students to be based at the university campus so they could access library and other learning resources, student advice and support, academic services and, of course, their university tutors. These were placed at times (for example, the ends of terms) when university accommodation was likely to be available for the students to stay overnight.

*   Arrangements for students to access the library of a nearby further education college where there was a reasonable collection of education texts for the primary phase owing to the courses for teaching assistants and early years professionals that were offered there.

*   A local base for the students which was equipped with Internet access so that students could access the university's virtual learning environment, online resources, e-books and journals through the university portal as well as access university support services for both personal and academic support.

*   A private room where the students could have Skype tutorials with their university tutors and also those with specific learning difficulties, such as dyslexia, could access their support services.

*   School staff with master's degrees were invited to mentor students in relation to their academic work and those without master's degrees were encouraged to sign up with the university to study for their master's degree alongside the students for their own professional development and also to raise awareness

of the needs of those undertaking academic study. A master's-level study group was set up within the group of schools, facilitated by the university.

Although this attention was paid to the academic elements, it was agreed by all partners that the training sessions would not be assigned to either the academic or professional elements. Instead, learning would be seen to be integrated, with separation only occurring at the points of assessment. Even then, the design of the academic assessment tasks (a portfolio of curriculum tasks with critical commentary and a small piece of classroom-based research) was such that they provided evidence towards the teaching standards and drew from students' professional learning journeys.

Case study questions:

1. How might this model be adapted for a group of schools in an urban setting closer to the university?

2. What are the benefits to the students of studying and training in this model? What might they miss out on?

3. Much of the academic provision depends on good access to information technology (IT). What challenges might this present and how might they be overcome?

CONCLUSION

It is difficult to see how a graduate can become an effective teacher without an academic element to their training. Whether or not this element leads to an academic award, it needs to be designed to complement and extend the learning which occurs through practice. It needs to lift the learning from the specific, local and contextual to the general, global and transferable. It needs to encompass the different types of knowledge, understanding and skills required of a beginning teacher. It also needs to provide the tools to allow the new teacher to continue to read, think and reflect on their practice in the light of research and theoretical contributions from others as they develop as reflective practitioners and teacher researchers. The benefit of the academic element being part of an academic award is that the student teacher is required to respond to questions and construct arguments at a high academic level, leading to deeper learning for themselves and their pupils.

At its most effective, an initial teacher education programme blends theory and practice in such a way that they are barely separable, other than at the points of assessment for the two elements – academic and professional. All trainers on such a programme are committed to making their own contribution to the student teachers' development of professional knowledge, understanding and skills. There is one community of practice without division between school and university and one common goal – to provide children and young people with the best possible teachers.

FURTHER READING

Banks, F., Leach, J. and Moon, B. (2005) 'Extract from new understandings of teachers' pedagogic knowledge', *The Curriculum Journal*, 16(3): 331–40.

Knight, R. (2013) '"It's just a wait and see thing at the moment". Students' preconceptions about the contribution of theory to classroom practice in learning to teach', *TEAN Journal*, 5(1), available at http://bit.ly/AtMwtr (accessed 6 December 2013).

REFERENCES

Alexander, R. (ed.) (2010). *Children, Their World, Their Education: Final Report and Recommendations of the Cambridge Primary Review*. Abingdon: Routledge.

Anderson, D. and Clark, M. (2012) 'Development of syntactic subject matter knowledge and pedagogical content knowledge for science by a generalist elementary teacher', *Teachers and Teaching: Theory and Practice*, 18(3): 315–30.

Banks, F., Leach, J. and Moon, B. (2005) 'Extract from new understandings of teachers' pedagogic knowledge', *The Curriculum Journal*, 16(3): 331–40.

Berge, T. ten and van Hezewijk, R. (1999) 'Procedural and declarative knowledge: an evolutionary perspective', *Theory & Psychology*, 9(5): 605–24.

Biggs, J. (1999) *Teaching for Quality Learning at University*. London: Open University Press.

Brooks, C. (2006) 'Geographical knowledge and teaching geography', *International Research in Geographical and Environmental Education*, 15(4): 353–69.

Brooks, C. (2010) 'Why geography teachers' subject expertise matters', *Geography*, 95(3): 143–8.

Bruner, J. S. (1966) *Toward a Theory of Instruction*. Cambridge, Mass: Belknap Press of Harvard University.

Bruning, R.H. and Bruning, R.H. (2008) *Cognitive Psychology and Instruction*. 5th edn. Upper Saddle River, NJ: Pearson/Merrill/Prentice.

Burn, K., Childs, A. and McNicholl, J. (2007) 'The potential and challenges for student teachers' learning of subject-specific pedagogical knowledge within secondary school subject departments', *The Curriculum Journal*, 18(4): 429–45.

Chai, C., Koh, J., Tsai, C. and Tan, L. (2011) 'Modeling primary school pre-service teachers' Technological Pedagogical Content Knowledge (TPACK) for meaningful learning with information and communication technology (ICT)', *Computers & Education*, 57(1): 1184–93.

Department for Children, Schools and Families (2007) *The Children's Plan Building Brighter Futures*. Norwich: Stationery Office.

Deng, Z. (2007) 'Knowing the subject matter of a secondary-school science subject', *Journal of Curriculum Studies*, 39(5): 503–35.

Ellis, V. (2007) 'Taking subject knowledge seriously: from professional knowledge recipes to complex conceptualizations of teacher development', *The Curriculum Journal*, 18(4): 447–62.

Freire, P. (1970) *Pedagogy of the Oppressed*. Freiberg: Herder and Herder.

Green, A. (2006) 'University to school: challenging assumptions in subject knowledge development', *Changing English*, 13(1): 111–23.

Grimmett, P. and Mackinnon, A.M. (1992) 'Craft knowledge and the education of teachers', in G. Grant (ed.), *Review of Research in Education*, vol. 18, Washington, DC: American Educational Research Association. pp. 385–456.

Jackson, A. (2009) 'Perceptions of Masters level PGCE: a pilot investigation. The University of Cumbria and the ESCalate Initial Teacher Education Subject Centre of the Higher Education Academy', available at: www.cumbria.ac.uk/Courses/SubjectAreas/Education/Research/TEAN/TeacherEducatorsStorehouse/TeachingAMastersProfession.aspx (accessed 7 December 2013).

Kansanen, P. (2009) 'Subject-matter didactics as a central knowledge base for teachers, or should it be called pedagogical content knowledge?', *Pedagogy, Culture & Society*, 17(1): 29–39.

Kempe, A. (2009) 'Resilience or resistance? The value of subject knowledge for drama teachers', *Research in Drama Education: The Journal of Applied Theatre and Performance*, 14(3): 411–28.

Kind, V. (2009) 'A conflict in your head: an exploration of trainee science teachers' subject matter knowledge development and its impact on teacher self-confidence', *International Journal of Science Education*, 31(11): 1529–62.

Knight, R. (2013) '"It's just a wait and see thing at the moment". Students' preconceptions about the contribution of theory to classroom practice in learning to teach', *TEAN Journal*, 5(1), available at http://bit.ly/AtMwtr (accessed 6 December 2013).

Kolb, D.A. (1984) *Experiential Learning*. Englewood Cliffs, NJ: Prentice Hall.

Lave, J. and Wenger, E. (1991) *Situated Learning: Legitimate Peripheral Participation*. Cambridge: Cambridge University Press.

Loughran, J. (2002) 'Teacher as researcher: the PAVOT project', in J. Loughran, I. Mitchell and J. Mitchell (eds), *Learning from Teacher Research*. Crows Nest, NSW: Allen & Unwin.

McLain, M. (2013) 'The challenges facing postgraduate trainees in initial teacher education coming from practical or vocational degrees', *TEAN Journal*, 5(2), available at: http://bit.ly/AtMwtr (accessed 6 December 2013).

Ornstein, A. and Scarpaci, R. (2012) *The Practice of Teaching: A Narrative and Case-Study Approach*. Long Grove, IL: Waveland Press.

Putnam, R. and Borko, H. (2000) 'What do new views of knowledge and thinking have to say about research on teacher learning?', *Educational Researcher*, 29(1): 4–15.

Quality Assurance Agency for Higher Education (QAA) (2001) *The Framework for Qualifications of Higher Education Institutions in Scotland*. Gloucester: QAA.

Quality Assurance Agency for Higher Education (QAA) (2008) *The Framework for Higher Education Qualifications in England, Wales and Northern Ireland*. Gloucester: QAA.

Schön, D. (1983). *The Reflective Practitioner: How Professionals Think in Action*. London: Temple Smith.

Shulman, L. (1986) 'Those who understand: knowledge growth in teaching', *Educational Researcher*, 15(2): 4–14.

Shulman, L. (1992) 'Ways of seeing, ways of knowing, ways of teaching, ways of learning about teaching', *Journal of Curriculum Studies*, 23(5): 393–6.

Sloan, S. (2007) 'An investigation into the perceived level of personal subject knowledge and competence of a group of pre-service physical education teachers towards the teaching of secondary school gymnastics', *European Physical Education Review*, 13(1): 57–80.

Sperandeo-Mineo, R., Fazio, C. and Tarantino, G. (2006) 'Pedagogical content knowledge development and pre-service physics teacher education: a case study', *Research in Science Education*, 36(3): 235–68.

Steele, M. (2005) 'Comparing knowledge bases and reasoning structures in discussions of mathematics and pedagogy', *Journal of Mathematics Teacher Education*, 8(4): 291–328.

Stotko, E., Beaty-O'Ferrall, M. and Yerkes, A. (2005) 'Subject matter knowledge in a master of arts in teaching program: ensuring candidates' content knowledge through an arts and sciences/education collaboration', *Teaching Education*, 16(3): 245–55.

Wenger, E. (1998) *Communities of Practice: Learning, Meaning and Identity*. Cambridge: Cambridge University Press.

Yilmaz, I. and Yalçin, N. (2012) 'The relationship of procedural and declarative knowledge of science teacher candidates in Newton's laws of motion to understanding', *American International Journal of Contemporary Research*, 2(3): 50.

Youens, B. and McCarthy, S. (2007) 'Subject knowledge development by science student teachers: the role of university tutors and school-based subject mentors', *Research in Science & Technological Education*, 25(3): 293–306.

CHAPTER 7

THE ASSESSMENT OF STUDENT TEACHERS

Carrie Mercier

During this chapter we will:

- reflect critically on the role of teacher competences or 'standards' in the process of assessing student teachers
- review the research related to the assessment of the student teacher
- reflect on practical implications and how the findings of research might inform a school-based approach to the assessment of student teachers.

The question of how to assess the progress of the student teacher has been a matter of considerable debate. One of the reasons for the debate is the fact that there are different views about what it is that we are assessing. This chapter begins with an overview of the research related to the assessment of the student teacher. The second section of the chapter looks at some of the practical implications of the research findings and how these might inform the development of the assessment process in the context of school-based initial teacher education (ITE). In the final section of this chapter we will look at two case studies and reflect on the model that might best fit the context of a school-based approach.

THE MAIN AREAS OF RESEARCH

There are several key areas of research to look at in relation to the assessment of those learning to teach. First is the debate on the identification of teacher competences and the question of whether these provide an appropriate assessment tool in ITE. Related to this is the question of how we assess professional values and attributes that are not easily captured in the Teachers' Standards or competence-based approach. We should also look at the research related to lesson observations and their role in the assessment of the student teacher. We need to ask about the research on academic assignments for student teachers and the place of these in the overall assessment process. Lastly we should look at a recent area of research in initial teacher education on the development of electronic-portfolios to help with the assessment process.

Assessing teacher competences

Perhaps we should involve school pupils in the assessment of their teachers as 'in a dream school we could tell the teachers what we think of them. So we could write them reports and give them good or bad marks' (Burke and Grosvenor, 2003: 88). However, instead of pupils setting the standards, we have to contend with the Department for Education and their teacher competences (DfE, 1992). When these were introduced it was intended that they would enhance accountability and make the process of assessing the student teacher transparent. The list of competences were identified as essential for Qualified Teacher Status (QTS) in 1992 and were later restructured and redefined as 'standards' (TDA 2007; DfEE, 1997; TTA, 2002) the most recent version being the DfE 2011 'Teachers' Standards'. Critics have expressed concern that a competence-based approach risks undermining the professional status of the teacher, reducing their role to that of a kind of technician (Arthur et al., 1997: 14). Some argued that the assessment of teachers on the basis of a set of competences is essentially behaviourist in approach (Elliott, 1991: 118) and that reducing teaching to a set of observable actions puts too much 'emphasis on the assessment of performance rather than knowledge' (Norris, 1991: 331). It has been suggested that that the competence-based approach was set up to facilitate greater control from the centre (Jones and Moore, 1993) so that the 'political and bureaucratic masters' could keep teachers on their toes (Tickle, 1992). Others have expressed interest in a definition of teacher competences and have been more open to the idea that they might have a constructive part to play in the overall assessment of the performance of the student teacher (Brookes and Sikes, 1997: 125; Tomlinson, 1995a; Whitty, 1991). The competence-based approach is now embedded in the most recent set of Teachers' Standards (DfE, 2011) and these are now a key part of the assessment of the student teacher whatever route they take into teaching.

   A number of issues are raised in relation to the use of teacher competences. The intention of the competence-based approach was to establish transparency and secure a set of objective criteria against which performance might be judged with a view to assessing student teachers on an equal basis. However, these competences do not take any account of context (Arthur et al., 1997: 32) which is problematic. A strategy or action performed in one lesson might be quite inappropriate in another classroom context. As Tomlinson (1995a: 185) points out 'teaching intent, process and achievement are highly contextual and teaching can therefore only be judged adequately in context'. There is also an issue in terms of how teachers' standards or competences are interpreted by those using them to assess student teachers. There is no guarantee that there will be a single interpretation in any one school let alone across different schools (Arthur et al., 1997: 37; Brooks and Sikes, 1997: 128). Questions arise as to whether teacher competences or standards can be interpreted in terms of actions performed or whether they are about outcomes achieved. Some suggest that the Teachers' Standards should be viewed as a set of 'skills and techniques' (Blatchford, 2013: xiii). However, if we think of the competences as skills, then we need to ask whether these skills can be learned just through practice and repetition, and so be assessed by simple observation of performance, or do we need to have some insight on the thinking behind the skills and the student teacher's ability to know when to use this skill or that strategy in a changing classroom context? Are we looking to assess what Tomlinson (1995b: 167) calls 'intelligent skilfulness'? And so researchers ask, how do we assess the student teacher's 'intellectual readiness' (Song, 2006) in becoming a teacher?

Another area of research related to the use of competences in the assessment of the student teacher focuses on the issue of development (Arthur et al., 1997: 32). We all recognize that student teachers do not learn to do everything in one go. Indeed, there is often a cyclical pattern in learning to teach (Tomlinson, 1995b: 40). For many it can be an uneven journey. Nevertheless, researchers have identified phases in the development of the teacher. For example, Berliner (1994) identifies the stages from novice to expert practitioner. Furlong and Maynard (1995) outline five stages in teacher development but argue that these stages are not completely discrete; they may overlap or the pattern of progression may vary. The stages in teacher development present a challenge for those involved in assessing the progress of the student teacher. To try to employ the identical list of teacher competences to assess the student teacher at each stage of development is inappropriate. Is the answer, therefore, to break down the Teachers' Standards to make each one relevant and attainable for each stage? Is there a danger in doing so that the whole process becomes too unwieldy (Brooks and Sykes, 1997: 129) with an endless number of tick boxes (Tomlinson, 1995a)? Yet we do need assessment tools that take account of the complexity of the process of becoming a teacher. If we try to assess the beginner against the competences expected of the qualified teacher we risk reinforcing a culture of failure which would be discouraging for the student teacher (Stern, 1995: 110). Also, individual development will vary greatly and research suggests that student teachers learn to teach in different ways and that 'different types of learning may characterise different phases in a teacher's career' (Calderhead, 1989: 49). The rate of progress and development of any student teacher will depend on their existing skills, on previous experience, on personality and on the context in which they are learning to teach. Pupils are changing, and schools are changing, so perhaps we need to revisit what 'accomplished teaching' looks like in practice (Norman, 2010).

While it is clear that there are issues regarding the assessment of the student teacher owing to the developmental nature of learning to teach, we do need to come to some agreement on what counts as evidence that any given standard has been attained. Indeed, we will need a whole range of evidence (Kerry and Mayes, 1995: 216) and we need to recognize that some of the evidence is 'much less tangible and more difficult to handle' than some would have us believe (Tickle, 1992: 9).

One might want to argue that the knowledge component of learning to teach should be straightforward to assess. For example, we should be able to assess whether a student teacher has sufficient knowledge and understanding of their curriculum areas. Yet, there has been considerable debate about what might constitute a 'national curriculum' for initial teacher education (Furlong et al., 2000: 154). Attempts have been made to set down exactly what it is that primary teachers need to know about 'early reading' and 'systematic and synthetic phonics' (DfE, 2011) but this area of educational theory is highly contested. The 'Teachers' Standards' talk not only about secure curriculum knowledge, they also require teachers to *know* how pupils learn and *understand* how to assess and 'know when and how to differentiate' (DfE, 2011). All this might be regarded as general or professional knowledge and understanding. Researchers have looked at how to assess this pedagogical knowledge and have begun to develop instruments to measure the progress of the student teacher in terms of this knowledge and understanding (Voss et al., 2011). However, there is surprisingly little in the way of research in this field to help us with this area of assessment of teacher development.

Perhaps the most difficult and controversial aspect of assessment using the Teachers' Standards relates to the question of assessing the 'professional values', 'attributes' or 'dispositions' that are essential to becoming a good teacher (Johnston et al., 2011). Student teachers are not training as technicians, they are learning to become members of a professional and a moral community. Many would argue that a list of competences will not capture everything we are looking for in a teacher and that we need a more holistic approach to assessment because we are looking for 'the embodiment of certain qualities' (Brooks and Sykes, 1997: 124). In the preamble to the Teachers' Standards there is some recognition of the moral or values dimension of becoming a teacher: 'Teachers make the education of their pupils their first concern … teachers act with honesty and integrity; … forge positive, professional relationships' (DfE, 2011). In part two of the same document we find there are expectations in terms of moral conduct, for example: 'Teachers uphold public trust in the profession and maintain high standards of ethics and behaviour, within and outside school'. Research has shown that the professional development of the student teacher 'does not only depend on the acquisition of a body of knowledge; it is also dependent on students undergoing certain forms of personal learning as well as confronting fundamental issues associated with values' (Furlong and Maynard, 1995: 169). The questions are, how do we assess this personal development and 'how do we know about their attitudes and beliefs' (Shively and Misco, 2010: 9)? Others have asked how we acknowledge in the assessment process 'that teaching includes the demonstration of professional qualities and values that go beyond the demonstration of classroom competence' (Moon and Mayes, in Kerry and Mayes, 1995: 236). If we are assessing these dispositions, then the student teacher certainly needs to know the kinds of attributes and qualities that are expected of them, but these are certainly not all listed in the Teachers' Standards. For example, how do we assess 'that quiet sort of enthusiasm for commitment and integrity' (Sotto, 2007: 148) that is essential in a good teacher?

Lesson observations and the assessment process

For many years the assessment of student teachers was carried out by tutors from higher education institutions. Tutors went into schools, observed students on teaching practice and wrote up their comments and judgements. The tutor would be able to compare the performance of one student teacher with that of others, take account of the context and the report from the school and draw conclusions about the progress of the student teacher. This system changed during the 1980s as the teachers took on the role of mentoring and began to carry out lesson observations and provide feedback. The routine of lesson observation and the opportunity for formative assessment that this provides is valued by student teachers and those in schools where this is not happening can feel that they are missing out on professional development. Research indicates that there are different approaches to lesson observation (Montgomery, 1999: 31) and raises questions about what we are looking for when we observe and assess a lesson. One of the questions raised in the research on lesson observation is to what extent we are able to judge the performance of the student teacher by attending to the pupils' learning (Norman, 2010). Findings from research suggest that a direct correlation between the quality of the teaching and the quality of the learning is hard to prove and assessing the effectiveness of the teaching observed on the basis of what pupils have learnt in the lesson is far from straightforward (Arthur et al., 1997: 31; Tomlinson, 1995b: 167). Most would argue that the quality of what the pupils have learnt is going to provide at least some of the evidence in the process of assessing the student teacher and the pupils would certainly agree with this.

As the responsibility for assessing student teachers has shifted from the higher education institutions (HEIs) to the school, mentors have developed different ways of approaching the observation and assessment of student teacher performance in the classroom (Arthur et al., 1997: 95). Some have seen the task as one of making judgements and then making suggestions on how to improve behaviour management or teaching strategies. This kind of feedback is a one-way activity (Brooks and Sykes 1997: 104) and it is regarded as not conducive to learning as the student teacher is a passive receiver (Bubb, 2005: 54). Others have seen the observation and assessment of a lesson as an opportunity to engage the student teacher in dialogue and to enable them to reflect on their teaching. This has been described as a 'discursive' approach (Arthur et al., 1997: 98) that can develop an ongoing critical discourse that is essential to professional development and good practice in teaching. Some research indicates that student teachers make best progress when they reflect through developing a narrative that helps them unpack their experience in the classroom (Beck and Bear, in Adamy and Milman, 2009: 11). Other research highlights the fact that 'student teachers tend towards higher self-evaluation than their supervisors' (Briggs et al., 1985; Montgomery, 1999: 54). This would appear to reinforce the message that observation should not only serve as a tool to assess student teacher progress but also as an opportunity to encourage a readiness to be 'self-critical' (DfE, 2011) and to take responsibility for their own professional development. Research on mentoring in schools (Furlong et al., 2000: 84) suggests that in many partnerships the higher education tutor retained the authority in terms of the final assessment of student teacher and often, in the eyes of the student teacher, the school-based mentor was regarded as the informal assessor and the tutor from the HEI was seen as the person making the final assessment (Kerry and Mayes, 1995: 105). With a school-based model, the task of both formative and summative assessment will now be carried out by staff in school and so we need to be aware of the implications involved in this.

The academic assignment and the student teacher

Higher education providers in ITE traditionally have required written academic assignments as a part of the assessment process. The nature of the assignment has varied from one institution to another. Research suggests that in the past, assignments were often intended to bring together the school-based experience and the academic work at the university (Furlong et al., 2000: 36). In some cases there was an expectation that there should be some positive 'spin-off' from the assignment for the school, perhaps in terms of some curriculum development project. In recent years, the tasks have been about looking for evidence of critical reflection on practice (Furlong et al., 2000: 137). As a response to the call for 'a new professionalism' in teaching under the Labour government in 2005, many Postgraduate Certificate of Education (PGCE) programmes required that the academic work for the student teacher be assessed at master's level (Bailey and Sorenson, 2013). One area of inquiry has been the question of what higher education providers are looking for in these master's level assignments (Bryan et al., 2010: 154). There has been considerable discussion around the importance of developing skills in critical reflection and reflexivity (Bryan et al., 2010: 78) and some higher education providers look for these skills to demonstrate 'master's levelness'. Other PGCE programmes have required an 'action research' or 'practitioner research' project for the assignment. It was believed that this would both secure the master's-level status of the coursework and at the same time carry master's-level credits that could be taken forward to a further postgraduate qualification, such as an MA in Education or a Masters in Teaching and Learning (MTL). Recent inquiry in this field (Cain et al., 2007) highlights the need to ensure that the practitioner research project set as an assignment is achievable within the context and time frame. Other research encourages those involved in initial teacher education to model practitioner research so that student teachers can learn from the example and begin to see this kind of research as essential to good practice in teaching (Lockney and Proudfoot, 2012). There are other issues to consider with regard to academic assignments. For example, there is the fact that the student teacher is having to write for 'two audiences' (Stern, 1995: 8) and the challenges that this presents. There is also the question of the overall experience in terms of the pressures of the assessment process (Furlong and Maynard, 1995: 85). It is important to ask whether the student teacher has a sense of the overall coherence of the assessment process and understands how the different components link together and can be seen to be relevant (Furlong and Maynard, 1995: 175). Assessment should of course model good practice in terms of the balance between formative and summative assessment.

The use of electronic portfolios in assessment

If we look back over this brief summary on the findings of research some key questions emerge. For example, how can we judge the quality of the thinking and the level of critical reflection of student teacher? We have also asked how we are to assess the professional values and attributes of the beginner teacher. We have suggested that checking performance against a list of teacher competences is not going to give us the holistic approach that we need to assess their progress. We have also raised the issue of how to ensure our process of assessment will take account of the different stages in the teacher's development. Another issue is the need to develop a formative approach to assessment so that the feedback we provide serves as a platform for further progress and development. In the previous section we have asked how the academic strand of student teacher assessment joins up with the school experience. All these questions and challenges emerge in the research and discussion on the use of electronic portfolios in the assessment of student teacher progress.

Professional portfolios have been developed as a part of the overall assessment of the student teacher in a number of ITE partnerships (Brooks and Sikes, 1997: 135). Exactly what the student teacher had to gather together for the portfolio has depended on the individual higher educational institute or school partnership. The student teacher has usually been required to select a range of material to demonstrate that the Teacher's Standards have been met. The following items have been accepted as evidence: a reflective journal of initial school experience, notes and reflections on lessons observed, lesson plans and self-evaluations of lessons taught, examples of teaching resources, feedback and observations from the mentor, examples of pupils' work and samples of marking undertaken, written essays and research assignments, as well as some form of personal profile indicating progress against the range of Teachers' Standards (Gifford, in Kerry and Mayes, 1995). The professional portfolio has thus developed as a dossier of evidence tracking the overall progress and development of the student teacher. Practice has varied from one higher education institution to another, but usually the tutor has required the submission of the portfolio, or sections of it, as a part of the overall assessment process. In some partnerships the school mentors have been encouraged to review sections of the file and this has provided opportunity for formative assessment and feedback. The development of the student file or portfolio has also meant that the higher education tutor has been able to get a more rounded perspective of the student teacher's progress than the completed checklist of Teacher' Standards might afford. In the past the Office for Standards in Education, Children's Services and Skills (Ofsted) has routinely asked to have access to student files or portfolios in their inspection of ITE provision. This indicates something of the value placed on these dossiers in terms of the evidence base that they afford on student teacher development. These portfolios provided the tutors and mentors with access to some of the thinking and critical reflection behind the practice and performance of the student teacher in the classroom.

The electronic portfolio is an online programme which serves a similar function to the traditional student file or dossier. However 'unlike the paper-based portfolio, the electronic portfolio is a multimedia approach that allows the teacher to present teaching, learning and reflective artefacts in a variety of formats – audio, video, graphics, and text' (Constantino and De Lorenzo, 2002: 48). The electronic portfolio is already widely used in the USA in initial teacher education (Adamy and Milman, 2009: viii) and it is now a part of staff development and assessment in many educational institutions in the UK. Electronic portfolios have taken different forms in different contexts. Some electronic portfolios are closely aligned to the process of accountability or certification and so are geared to a summative assessment designed to judge attainment against a set of teacher competences. This has been true of some of the 'assessment only' routes into teaching. Other examples of electronic portfolios have been built around a more developmental approach to the assessment of the teacher. Research indicates that generally these are more successful in terms of encouraging the reflective practice that enhances teacher development (Beck and Bear, 2009), in Adamy P. and Milman, N. B. (2009).

Some research on electronic portfolios has been focused on an approach that takes its structure from a process of reflection or evidential reasoning and decision-making (ERDM) rather than from the list of teacher competences or standards (Recesso et al., 2009). As we have seen, there is much more that we are looking for in the assessment of the student teacher than can be captured in a list of Teachers' Standards. A part of this is the ability to give a meaningful account of personal learning and growth during school experience, to see connections, to learn from mistakes and failures as well as from the successes on the journey into teaching. It is this readiness to engage in critical reflection, self-assessment and the ability to see the bigger picture that helps empower the student teacher to become a successful practitioner. In assessing the progress of the student teacher, we need to build in opportunities or tasks to help initiate this process of critical reflection and deeper learning. Some would argue that the electronic portfolio offers tools and structures that we can harness to help us with this process of gathering evidence to support the assessment of the student teacher.

Research suggests that while the electronic portfolio has much potential as an assessment tool for those learning to teach, there are some important considerations to take on board. We need to ensure the learning and the reflection is the main focus and not the technology (Bartlett, 2009: 59). It is therefore important to ensure that the student teacher is equipped early in the programme with the necessary skills for engaging with the electronic portfolio so that it becomes a tool or vehicle rather than an end in itself. The technology must not get in the way. It is also essential to be very clear about the purpose of the portfolio (ibid.: 57). We must be transparent about what we expect in terms of its use in supporting critical reflection and structuring the range of evidence needed for the assessment process. We also have to be realistic about the time that must be invested in this process of critical reflection and completion of the portfolio. As one user said:

> Meaningful reflection is the key to the whole process. Without reflection, a portfolio is pretty meaningless; it's just a collection of data points. It needs to be more than just showing a collection of work to your supervisor; it should support your personal growth … seeing reflection in the context of a data point related to a goal or standard is critical. (Havelock and Sherry, cited in Adamy and Milman, 2009: 73)

The research in this area draws attention to the need for 'customisation' (Havelock, in Adamy and Milman, 2009: 85). In other words it is important to build an electronic portfolio that is designed for the specific context of the potential users; 'the match between an e-portfolio structure and the culture in which it is meant to be used is a critical aspect of implementation' (ibid.). Research also suggests that electronic portfolios employed in the assessment of those learning to teach were most successful when they enabled them to reflect on their experience and 'if novice teachers were able to narrate coherent stories of their learning experiences, most could achieve personal growth and transformation in the process of becoming teachers' (Beck and Bear, 2009).

PRACTICAL IMPLICATIONS FOR SCHOOLS

While there remains a requirement that the Teachers' Standards are the measure by which we judge whether the student teacher has attained QTS, this can only be one component in the overall assessment. The debate surrounding the use of teacher competences makes us aware that we should map out the bigger picture of what we are looking for in the accomplished teacher and then try to see these Teachers' Standards as one part of the assessment process. We do not want to be in the game of ticking boxes. The research and debate requires us to ask questions about the structure of the assessment process and whether we structure it around the Teachers' Standards or do we look at the big picture first and then draw up a structure of assessment that takes a more holistic approach to teacher development and incorporate the Teachers' Standards within this wider framework.

The research and debate on the use of teacher competences requires us to ask how we ensure that we take account of context in the assessment of the student teacher. For example, do we secure assessment opportunities across the age and ability range? We might want to ask what systems we want to put in place to ensure that we take account of the different contexts within our own school and look for the student teacher's ability to adapt the skills and strategies to each new context. We will want to engage the student teacher in conversation about how they are adapting their strategy or approach in response to the change in context. We might consider how we work with other schools within a teaching alliance to give the student teacher appropriate opportunity to teach within a contrasting context. This raises questions about the need for a consistent approach to assessment across the teaching alliance schools.

Research also raises questions about interpretation of the Teachers' Standards and the need to develop a shared understanding among those involved in the assessment process. We will want to consider how to ensure consistency and fairness and look for opportunities for discussion between mentors and other staff on the interpretation of the Teachers' Standards so that there is an equal chance to succeed for our student teachers. The science teacher should sit alongside the history teacher in looking at the profile of a student or the Key Stage 1 (KS1) teacher can compare the performance of their student with that of the Key Stage 2 (KS2) teacher who also has a student teacher. All staff involved need to work as a team when they observe and assess their student teachers.

It is clear from research findings that we need to take account of the stages of development in becoming a teacher. Do we begin the assessment process by identifying existing skills and previous relevant experience so that we ensure that we value prior learning? How can we take account of the different stages in the development of the teacher as we design the assessment process and the paperwork that goes with it? Are our strategies for assessment enabling the student teacher to progress from one stage to the next or are we making the mistake of judging the beginner against the expectations for the experienced teacher? We also need to ensure that our assessment process models best practice and that it is both formative and summative assessment.

One of the most difficult areas of assessment we can see from the research is that of the professional values, qualities and attributes. We need to ask ourselves whether we are completely 'up front' about this dimension from the beginning of the student teacher's time in school. We will want to look at whether we have opportunities for student teachers to engage in dialogue on professional values and moral responsibilities of the teacher. It will be important to share with our student teachers the values and moral objectives of the school so that we encourage them to feel part of a moral community. What do we want them to tell us in terms of their reasons for coming into teaching and their own values and moral starting point? What activities will we give the student teacher that will provide them with the opportunity to show that they are engaging with this important values dimension of teacher development?

We will want to ask whether there is good opportunity for formative assessment in the process of lesson observation and feedback. It will be important to ask whether all the student teachers in school have the same entitlement to regular lesson observations and formative feedback; if so, then to what extent is there an agreed process for this method of assessment? Is there a shared understanding in school of the purpose of observation and the nature of the follow-up? Is it important that every student teacher is observed by someone other than their own mentor? This raises the question of whether we want to build in that element of 'triangulation' that was once afforded by the presence of the higher education tutor. We will also want to develop an approach where the feedback and dialogue that follows observation provides opportunity for the student teacher to learn the 'language' of their own reflection on their teaching – so that they become self-critical (DfE, 2011) and develop the skills of the reflective practitioner. Will we provide opportunity for the student teacher to talk to other colleagues or to read different points of view from books and journals and bring these to their discussion?

The academic assignment required by the HEI can help the student teacher to engage in this process of critical reflection and professional dialogue. The role of the school can be to ensure that the academic assignment is meaningful, relevant and an integrated part of the overall assessment process. It will be essential that the school works closely with the higher education institution to secure the right kind of assignments and modes of assessment for student teachers working at master's level. Those members of teaching staff who are engaged in studying for an MA themselves may help to engender a sense of a learning community within the school. Perhaps the assignments for the higher education institution can become an opportunity for wider staff development, and schools might want to think about a conference day for sharing findings from action research.

We will need to ask to what extent do we want to use technology to support our assessment of student teachers in school and whether we use the electronic portfolio to structure and streamline the process? If we do decide to develop the use of an electronic portfolio then we will need to invest time in the setting up of the portfolio to get the student teachers in the habit of updating their professional portfolio from their first day in school. All those involved in the assessment process will need to think ahead about the range of activities and tasks that will serve as evidence in the student teacher portfolio. This includes thinking about how we want them to collect and present the evidence of progress against the Teachers' Standards. The electronic portfolio, if it is to be successful, must be designed for the context and the specific needs of the users.

CASE STUDIES OF STUDENT TEACHER ASSESSMENT IN SCHOOLS

CASE STUDY 7.1

This case study is from a school that has adapted the process of assessment that was used in the previous partnership model of collaboration with the local institute of higher education. It is based on a personal mentoring approach and a student profile that is mainly structured around the Teachers' Standards. There are weekly lesson observations and written feedback with judgements against the standards. Each week a particular focus is agreed with the student teacher, such as classroom management strategies or starters and plenaries. There are weekly review meetings between the student teacher and their personal mentor. On these occasions targets are set which are based on the feedback provided by the mentor with reference to the Teachers' Standards. At the end of term the student teacher completes a self-assessment form which is structured closely on the list of Teachers' Standards. The pro forma for this process is designed to take account of the phase or level of development of the student teacher. Term One is called the Foundation Phase, Term Two is regarded as the Developmental Phase and Term Three is conceived in terms of achieving 'Mastery' of the range of skills and standards. At the end of each phase the mentor completes a detailed report based on the Teachers' Standards. At the end of the foundation phase, for example, the progress of the student teacher is judged as Satisfactory or Adequate. Sometimes it is recorded that the particular Teachers' Standard has not been achieved. Each section of the pro forma is set out in detail and Table 7.1 shows the section for number 8 of the Standards for the Foundation phase. The mentor highlights the appropriate column on the basis of their own observations and discussion with the student teacher. Targets are set for the next phase on the basis of these judgements.

Table 7.1   Extract from a mentor report

Foundation Phase Teachers' Standard 8: Fulfil wider professional responsibilities	Foundation Phase Satisfactory	Foundation Phase Adequate	Foundation Phase Not yet achieved	Comment Action planning
8:4 Take responsibility for improving teaching through appropriate professional development, responding to advice and feedback from colleagues	Now taking some responsibility for own professional development and beginning to seek out advice from colleagues. Able to put advice into action through identifying practical steps on how to improve. Beginning to set own targets for development	Beginning to switch from relying on external prompts to taking responsibility for improving own teaching. Beginning to translate advice and feedback into practical steps for improvement	Fails to take responsibility for issues with planning and teaching and tends to blame others for problems. Resists advice or practical suggestions for improvement. Unable to translate feedback into practical steps for action	

The overall assessment of the student teacher includes three written assignments, one on classroom management/behaviour, another on assessment for learning and the third is a critical reflection on a curriculum development project that they carry out in school. The school is not involved in the marking of this work and the tutor from the institute of higher education comes into the school twice a term to support the student teachers with the essays and research projects. The student teacher must pass all three assignments to be successful in securing the HEI award, and two of these assignments are assessed at master's level.

What are the strengths and issues with this approach?

- To what extent is there going to be an equal chance of success for all student teachers in the school?

- Is this process of assessment all about making judgements on whether the standards have been met or is it about teacher development?

- To what extent does this take account of the 'whole' teacher and what it means to become a teacher?

- Where are the opportunities for assessing the development of professional attributes and values?

- What are the opportunities for building on early potential or for celebrating success?

- To what extent is the process encouraging the student to become a reflective practitioner?

- To what extent is the academic and master's-level assessment integrated with the school-based judgements?

CASE STUDY 7.2

The second case study is one where the student teacher begins from day one to complete an electronic portfolio and the first activity is a critical reflection on prior learning and previous relevant experience. This first section of the portfolio is submitted online and it can be accessed by those who will be involved in mentoring the student teacher. The electronic portfolio is structured primarily around 'whole-teacher' development. It requires the student teacher to develop their own 'philosophy' and think about the values that underpin their professional role as teacher. As a part of the electronic portfolio the student teacher has to keep a learning journal in which they reflect on their own professional development. In this process they analyse and reflect on critical incidents as well as a range of experiences in school. As they log their initial observations and first steps in teaching they are encouraged to draw on educational theory and relevant research to enhance the level of their critical reflection. Sections of the electronic portfolio are structured around the Teachers' Standards, giving the student teacher opportunity to reflect on progress made and to bring together a range of supporting evidence to show how they are working towards the successful attainment of these standards. Lesson plans or units of work are uploaded in time for the mentor to read and provide feedback before the lessons are taught. After teaching a lesson or part of a lesson, the student teacher is required to submit a critical evaluation to demonstrate the thinking behind their strategies for teaching and learning and to highlight aspects of their development. They identify their targets and plans for action, taking account of any feedback provided by their mentor. All academic assignments are submitted online and integrated within this larger e-portfolio. As the ability to analyse learning and to reflect critically on teaching is regarded as working at master's level, a section of the learning journal itself is submitted electronically as a part of the formal assessment. One of the assignments for the university is built around a small-scale professional inquiry on an aspect of differentiation or meeting children's needs. Tutorials are arranged with the university tutor and the mentor attends these in order to ensure that the school can facilitate the professional inquiry. At the end of each phase of their development the student teacher is expected to submit evidence to demonstrate that they are making progress at the expected level. The mentor is able to engage with this before the assessment meeting at which strengths and targets are agreed. This presents an opportunity for formative feedback which informs the student teachers' next entry in the reflective journal.

CONCLUSION

We can raise the same questions that we asked about the first case study as we consider the example of the electronic-portfolio case above. And there are other questions to ask, for example, how much of it should be made accessible to those involved in assessing the student teacher and how do we make sure that the reflective journal does not become just an added burden? It is likely that many schools involved in ITE through a more school-based approach will begin by introducing the electronic portfolio for tracking key aspects of the progress of the student teacher, including those related to the Teachers' Standards. In the longer term the electronic portfolio may have a much larger part to play in the overall process of assessment, and schools may build it into their continuing professional development programme. Many ITE programmes are in the process of trying to develop the use of the electronic portfolio in a way that really meets the needs of the student teacher, and getting this right is going to take time. It will be important for those involved in school-based approaches to carry out further research on the use of the electronic portfolio in the context of ITE. Whether the schools involved in the school-based approaches decide to use the electronic portfolio or not, the same key issues arise in relation to the assessment of the student teacher. We need to ensure assessment is about development of the whole teacher and not just focused on a set of Teachers' Standards. We need to consider how we build in the opportunities for addressing the 'values' dimension to teaching. We must ensure that our processes model good practice in assessment generally. It is essential that the approach to assessment builds the student teacher's confidence in terms of critical reflection and professional dialogue, as these are essential to ongoing teacher development and school improvement.

FURTHER READING

Adamy, P. and Milman, N.B. (2009) *Evaluating Electronic Portfolios in Teacher Education: A Volume in Research Methods in Educational Technology*. Charlotte, SC: Information Age Publishing.

Blatchford, R. (2013) *The 2012 Teachers' Standards in the Classroom*. London: Sage.

Bubb, S. (2005) *Helping Teachers Develop*. London: Sage.

Bryan, H., Carpenter, C. and Hoult, S. (2010) *Learning and Teaching at M-Level*. London: Sage.

REFERENCES

Adamy, P. and Milman, N.B. (2009) *Evaluating Electronic Portfolios in Teacher Education: A Volume in Research Methods in Educational Technology*. Charlotte, SC: Information Age Publishing.

Arthur, J., Davison, J. and Moss, J. (1997) S*ubject Mentoring in the Secondary School*. London: Routledge.

Bailey, M. and Sorenson, P. (2013) 'Reclaiming the ground of master's level education for teachers: lessons to be learned from a case study of the East Midlands Master in Teaching and Learning', *Journal of Education for Teaching*, 39(1): 39–59.

Beck, R. J. and Bear, S. L. (2009) 'Teachers' self-assessment of reflection skills as on outcome of e-portfolios', in P. Adamy and N. B. Milman (eds) *Evaluating Electronic Portfolios in Teacher Education: A Volume in Research Methods in Educational Technology*. Charlotte, SC: Information Age Publishing.

Berliner, D. (1994) 'Teacher expertise', in B. Moon and A. Shelton Mayes (eds), *Teaching and Learning in the Secondary School*. London: Routledge.

Blatchford, R. (2013) *The 2012 Teachers' Standards in the Classroom*. London: Sage.

Briggs L.D., Richardson, W.D. and Sefzik, W.P. (1985) 'Comparing supervising teacher ratings and student teacher self-ratings of elementary student teaching', *Education*, 106(2): 150–59.

Brooks, V. and Sikes, P. (1997) *The Good Mentor Guide: Initial Teacher Education in Secondary Schools*. Buckingham: Open University.

Bryan, H., Carpenter, C. and Hoult, S. (2010) *Learning and Teaching at M-Level*. London: Sage.

Bubb, S. (2005) *Helping Teachers Develop*. London: Sage.

Burke, C. and Grosvenor, I. (2003) *The School I'd Like*. London: Routledge Falmer.

Calderhead, J. (1989) 'Reflective teaching and teacher education', *Teaching and Teacher Education*, 5(1): 75–83.

Cain, T., Holmes, M., Larrett, A. and Mattock, J. (2007) 'Literature-informed, one-turn action research: three cases and a commentary', *British Educational Research Journal*, 33(1): 91–106.

Constantino, P.M. and De Lorenzo, M.N. (2002) *Developing a Professional Teaching Portfolio*, Boston, MA: Allyn & Bacon.

Department for Education (DfE) (1992) *Initial Teacher Training*. Circular Number 9/92. London: DfE.

Department for Education (DfE) (2011) *Teacher's Standards: Guidance for School Leaders, School Staff and Governing Bodies*. London: DfE.

Department for Education and Employment (DfEE) (1997) *Teaching: High Status High Standards*. Circular 10/97. London: DfEE.

Elliott, J. (1991) *Action Research for Educational Change*. Milton Keynes: Open University.

Furlong, J. and Maynard, T. (1995) *Mentoring Student Teachers*. London: Routledge.

Furlong, J., Barton, L., Miles, S., Whiting, C. and Whitty, G. (2000) *Teacher Education in Transition*. Buckingham: Open University Press.

Johnston, P., Almerico, G. M., Henriott, D., Shapiro, M. (2011) *Education*, 132(2): 391–401.

Jones, L. and Moore, R. (1993) 'Education, competence and the control of expertise', *British Journal of Sociology of Education*, 14(4): 385–98.

Kerry, T. and Mayes, A.S. (eds) (1995) *Issues in Mentoring*. London: Open University and Routledge.

Lockney, K. and Proudfoot, K. (2012) 'Modelling classroom-based action research for PGCE students', roundtable for Teacher Education Action Network: Shaping the Learning of Teachers, 27 November, available at www.cumbria.ac.uk/Courses/SubjectAreas/Education/Research/TEAN/TeacherEducatorsStorehouse/Partnership/ShapingTheLearningOfTeachers.aspx (accessed 7 February 2014).

Montgomery, D. (1999) *Positive Teacher Appraisal Through Classroom Observation*. London: David Fulton.

Norman, A.D. (2010) 'Assessing accomplished teaching: good studies, great challenges', *Theory into Practice*, 49(3): 203–12.

Norris, N. (1991) 'The trouble with competence', *Cambridge Journal of Education*, 21(3): 331–41.

Recesso, A., Hannafin, M., Wang, F., Deaton, B., Rich, P. and Shepherd, C. (2009) 'Direct evidence and the continuous evolution of teacher practice', in P. Adamy and N.B. Milman (eds), *Evaluating Electronic Portfolios in Teacher Education: A Volume in Research Methods in Educational Technology*. Charlotte, SC: Information Age Publishing.

Shiveley, J. and Misco, T. (2010) 'But how do I know about their attitudes and beliefs? A four-step process for integrating and assessing dispositions in teacher education', *The Clearing House*, 83(1): 9–14.

Song, K.H. (2006) 'A conceptual model of assessing teacher performance and intellectual development of teacher candidates: a pilot study in the US', *Teaching in Higher Education*, 11(2): 175–90.

Sotto, E. (2007) *When Teaching Becomes Learning: A Theory and Practice of Teaching*. London: Continuum.

Stern, J. (1995) *Learning to Teach: A Guide for School-Based Initial and In-Service Training*, London: David Fulton.

Teacher Training Agency (TTA) (2002) *Qualifying to Teach: Professional Standards for Qualified Teacher Status and Requirements for Initial Teacher Training*. London: TTA.

Tickle, L. (1992) 'Professional skills assessment in classroom teaching', *Cambridge Journal of Education*, 22(1): 91–103.

Tomlinson, P. (1995a) 'Can competence profiling work for effective teacher preparation? Part 1 General issues', *Oxford Review of Education*, 21(2): 179–94.

Tomlinson, P. (1995b) *Understanding Mentoring: Reflective Strategies for School-Based Teacher Preparation*. Buckingham: Open University Press.

Training and Development Agency for Schools (TDA) (2007) *Professional Standards for Teachers*. London: TDA.

Voss, T., Kunter, M. and Baumert, J. (2011) 'Assessing teacher candidates' general pedagogical/psychological knowledge: test construction & validation', *Journal of Educational Psychology*, 103(4): 952–69.

Whitty, G. and Willmott, E. (1991) 'Competence-based approaches to teacher education: approaches and issues', *Cambridge Journal of Education*, 21(3): 309–18.

CHAPTER 8

HOW DO YOU CREATE SYNERGY BETWEEN DIFFERENT SCHOOL PRIORITIES?

Simon Asquith

This chapter explores:

- the value of initial teacher education (ITE) among the conflicting priorities placed on schools
- how ITE can contribute to school improvement
- how involvement in ITE can help foster a research community within a school.

RESEARCH AND THEORY; ITE AND THE CONFLICTING PRIORITIES OF SCHOOLS

The overarching priority

There can only be one overarching priority for any school, the very best education for each of its pupils. The route to realizing this priority is, however, a complicated one, interwoven with constituent sub-priorities.

Initial teacher education is an important contributor to schools' core work and role, and a systematic or structured approach to ITE within the work of schools can provide a critical contribution to overall success. Further to this it is impossible to ignore the place of individual schools within an overall system and the notion of a 'self-improving system' (Hargreaves, 2010, 2011, 2012a, 2012b) and the increasingly important positions of Teaching School Alliances, Academy Chains and Groups, School Direct groupings and other systematic responses. The increasing shift to more autonomous schools is undoubtedly of key importance in this (Higham and Earley, 2013), as is the increasing emphasis on school leaders working beyond their own schools (Chapman and Gunter, 2009; Gunter, 2012; Higham et al., 2009).

ITE as a driver for improvement

In a detailed study focused on primary schools in the north west of England, a significant exploration of ITE and its relationships with continuing professional development and school improvement found positive links to be often-reported but challenging to quantify (Hurd et al., 2007). An often posited assumption is that student teachers can themselves be agents of change within schools but while Hurd et al. and others rightly point to clear examples of how this can be the case, we have to be very careful about what research tells us on this in broader terms (Zeichner et al., 1987). Particularly 'that it is generally counter-productive to expect the least expert and least established members of organisations such as schools to be the key agents of change' (Hagger and McIntyre, 2006: 7).

Models of ITE and the varied role of the school in ITE

There is a significant history and literature on models of teacher education prior to the recent, largely unprecedented, government-driven increased emphasis on school-led ITE. Notable studies include those of the Oxford Internship Scheme (Benton, 1990; McIntyre, 1997) and the Modes of Teacher Education (MOTE) studies (Furlong et al., 2000). This chapter, while examining competing demands on schools, will inevitably remain mindful of the varied views of what makes the most effective teacher education itself while looking at ITE in the broader context of 'what schools do'.

   Retaining a view on this is important. For example, Hagger and McIntyre (2006) acknowledged that while they were able to espouse structured school-based ITE curricula, emphasizing 'professional craft knowledge' of experienced practitioners and 'practical theorizing', such curricula could ignore subject knowledge and its transformation via effective pedagogies. One of the key findings of the MOTE studies has, similarly, remained important as a question – ensuring that school/ university partnerships do not suffer from an over-managerial response to the need to quality-assure diverse partnerships over and above sustained critical dialogue between school and university partners, and the professional expertise of school-based colleagues themselves (Furlong et al., 2000).

School priorities and communities of learning

The simplest view is that a school is a community. First and foremost it is a community of learning, dedicated to the realization of the best possible learning outcomes for each of its members. This is clearly attractive as a notion to school leaders (Day, 2004, 2008). What, perhaps, sets the most effective schools apart is that they are communities where every member is a learner – the students of course, but also each member of staff. The overarching priority – the best education for each pupil – is most likely to be realized when every member of the school community works to advance their own learning. Work in the USA developed the idea of 'Professional Learning Communities' (Hord, 1997) and Hargreaves and Fullan (2012: 128) expand this to emphasize how the *professional* learning community is a community of learning but is also one where improvement is evidence based, guided by experienced collective judgement and advanced by challenging conversations about effective and ineffective practice. In this environment each advances together, teacher, teaching assistant and headteacher, challenging themselves and, through this, recognizing the challenges faced by their students as each works to advance their own learning.

The idea of the learning community is most obviously traced to the work of Jean Lave and Etienne Wenger on 'communities of practice' (Lave and Wenger, 1991; Wenger, 1999) and to subsequent work on teacher learning within such communities (Habhab, 2008; Hord, 1997). Others have increasingly focused on the system of the school and the human, social and decisional capital that contribute to the professional capital (Hargreaves and Fullan, 2012) that drives and supports successful schools. Hargreaves and Fullan (2012) suggest 'five Cs of professional capital' for an effective teaching workforce: capability (or expertise), commitment, career, culture and contexts or conditions of teaching. These 'five Cs' and how a school invests in these aspects of professional growth are highly pertinent to its perspective on, for example, initial teacher education.

The 'bigger view' is that schools themselves are part of a wider community. They are a 'player', 'member' or 'stakeholder' of their local area, their 'catchment' – along with a range of social, political, housing, social care, health, recreational, employment and other factors – but, they are also in a community that includes other educational players: feeding and receiving schools, colleges and other settings (as relevant), local collaborator schools and those further afield where partnership or alliance might serve mutual and greater good. A 'self-improving system' (Hargreaves, 2010, 2011, 2012a, 2012b) relies on schools impacting on each other in ways greater than was often the case in the past. Hargreaves, building on some of the principles laid out in earlier policy by, for example, David Miliband (2002), has moved forward the expectations of school-to-school working and impact, from the challenges identified by authors such as Fullan, who, in 2003, was reflecting that '(a) it is difficult for schools to learn from each other, (b) the culture and propensity to do so is missing, and (c) the resources and related capacity are limited' (Fullan 2003). The current expectations of National Leaders in Education, National Support Schools and Teaching School alliances, as further championed in the 2010 White Paper (DfE, 2010), have now substantially built on the notion of 'moral imperative' as discussed by Fullan (2003).

School priorities within governmental policy context

Within all of this there continue to be significant changes to the ways that ITE is combined into the mix. Schools have always seen the initial preparation of teachers as something they need and want to be involved in and government, as it has increasingly taken a role in the overview of teacher supply, training routes and quality of training, has supported a trend towards greater involvement of schools in training their own teachers. As this chapter is written an almost unprecedented governmental policy environment is seeing rapid growth of school-led ITE (DfE, 2010, 2011b; NCTL, 2013).

The real context for this discussion, though, is the policy assumption that school improvement and all that it involves – leadership and management development, staff talent management, continuing professional development, initial teacher education – is most effective within a 'self-improving system' enabled by 'system change' and, importantly, 'system leadership' (Higham et al., 2009; Hopkins, 2009; Hopkins and Higham, 2007). Government, through 'New Labour's' administration up until 2010 and since under the Conservative and Liberal Democrat coalition, increasingly finds itself in the sometimes contradictory position of wanting school improvement to be handed to 'the market' via a principle of 'smaller government' while at the same time having to force operational policy roll-out to make this happen. The challenge of balancing conflicting priorities in schools is contextualized by smaller government and the acceptance of free schools and academies, which even critics (Hyman, 2011) seem to be able to support if accountability, funding and admissions safeguards are in place (Gunter, 2012).

Governing for reduced government (Glatter, 2012), when combined with a political mistrust by some in government of the role and effectiveness of some higher education ITE partners in their working with schools, has led to a present climate of significant change with school-to-school alliances and school-led and situated solutions being the order of the day. Both neo-liberal and neo-conservative perspectives challenge university-based training models (Furlong et al., 2000). It is within this context that a careful look at the conflicting priorities and competing demands existent in schools needs to be situated. Initial teacher education is clearly a 'priority' but also a 'demand', as are all elements of workforce development, and the 'holy grail' for any school leader has got to be the operational realization of positive linkage of time and money spent on staff development to pupil achievement and attainment.

As schools balance the competing demands placed upon them, they are faced by the often contradictory positions of a government that is keen to emphasize market forces and leader autonomy but that also places massive pressure on the sector to engage in its own solution schemes (for example, Teach First, School Direct). In this context Hargreaves and Fullan warn of the dangers of government investing in such shorter-term 'business capital' solutions rather than in the 'social capital' resulting from teachers being developed carefully within a professional community of learners so that they might ultimately become part of the 'decisional capital' of experienced and sagacious professional leaders (Hargreaves and Fullan, 2012).

Competing demands: school performance

This brings us to one of the most contested and difficult debates within contemporary education in the UK – that associated with a culture of performativity and accountability through attainment data in schools. Although critiqued, for example by Gorard, 'school effectiveness' measures (Gorard, 2009) continue to be increasingly important across the sector. It is clearly the case that schools have had no choice other than to apply real focus to their attainment data as measured through performance tables and by the Office for Standards in Education, Children's Services and Skills (Ofsted). Any school leader has to regard the maintenance or improvement of their school's data on levels of student attainment and student progress as of critical priority. It is, arguably, an interesting facet of teacher training courses nationally that they model the culture of performativity from day one with their students (Perryman, 2011).

Ofsted was explicit when, in 2003, it reported that secondary schools were 'sometimes reluctant to become involved in ITT [initial teacher training] because of concerns about the effects on pupils' achievement and examination results' (Ofsted, 2003: 20).

Research conducted in secondary schools has certainly borne this out, with schools sharing a concern about perceived possible links between the 'surrender' of pupil groups to the planning, teaching and assessment of learning teachers and concern about pupil achievement and attainment. In a focused look at the views of secondary schools on involvement in ITE, one study in 2008 concluded that schools' placement of student teachers appeared to have 'no significant effect on performance in national examinations at GCSE and A-level or in the value added between ages 14 and 16' (Hurd, 2008: 34). However, it was noted that some schools 'choose to stay out of ITT partnership arrangements altogether and many that do participate take steps to restrict the exposure of examination classes to trainee teachers' (Hurd, 2008: 20).

Prioritizing ITE engagement within a self-improving system

So, within a self-improving school system, energized by system change and contextualized by reduced government and the increasing power of 'the market', what are the various approaches to prioritizing ITE engagement? What are the processes and patterns determining the emerging new reality of the ITE landscape? How are the processes informed and influenced by the conflicting roles that schools now see for themselves and what, therefore, are the emerging patterns of school response?

One set of processes is associated with schools grouping, building pacts, semi- or more formal alliances and occupying 'market share'. The growth of academy chains and groups, including multi-academy trusts and umbrella trusts (DfE, 2013), and the growth of teaching school alliances are the most obvious examples of this. The processes by which these happen inevitably involve strong and ambitious leadership by system-changers (Higham et al., 2009; Hopkins, 2009). The growth of the executive head or the 'super-head' and of the commonly reported phenomenon of the 'school rescue' are examples of these processes in action, and patterns are increasingly evident such that groupings of schools are becoming the norm and executive leadership more common. 'In our experience, reform of school structures and the identification of outstanding schools that can lead the school improvement, initial teacher training and professional development agendas are already resulting in positive changes and a better deal for the children and young people in our schools' (Ofsted, 2012b: 8). The Chief Inspector for Schools' statement that schools in rural, coastal and 'leafy lane' locations are more likely to have pupils that underperform (Ofsted, 2013b, 2013c) could be argued to reflect the fact that these schools have been more difficult to reach by the national wave of schools working closely together in increasingly formal alliances.

Quoting examples for the USA, however, Fullan points to an inevitable challenge, that of the rapid turnover of leaders (Fullan, 2003), especially in more challenging schools and areas. He talks, as have political leaders and commentators in the UK (DfE, 2011a), of the 'moral imperative' of the school leader, and indeed the teacher. In the UK, system change clearly relies on moral purpose being shared by leaders within and across schools and delivering systematic improvement that recognizes that some headteachers will make their mark and then move on. In Australia, Barnett and McCormick (2012) have emphasized the resultant importance of the need for shared and distributed leadership models and team processes, and in the UK Lumby (2013) reminds us of the challenges in getting distributed leadership right.

Models of training and teacher professionalism

Having focused on the positioning or approach of schools to ITE and some of the system relationships that contextualize the links between ITE, continuing profession development (CPD), leadership and management development, and the key school priorities associated with pupil attainment, it is useful to return to the key areas of professionalism and professional learning themselves. How do schools manage competing priorities so that the skills, knowledge and values of teachers that contribute to teacher professionalism, are securely framed and developed?

The much reported MOTE studies of the early and mid-1990s which evaluated the variation emerging in teacher education models up to and through this period (Barton et al., 1994; Furlong et al., 1995, 2000; Whitty et al., 1992) heralded an increasing view that the 'simplistic association of higher education with "theory" and schools with "practice" had started to break down' (Furlong et al., 2000: 130).

Concerns about the relationships between theory and practice in ITE are as central to contemporary analysis of developments as they were through and after the MOTE studies. Drawing on the work of Lave and Wenger (1991), one teacher educator's view is that 'Always and everywhere, it would seem, learning is sociocultural, involves observation and talk, involves narrative; it is through such means that the neophyte gradually moves from legitimate peripheral participation to full participation in a community of practice' (Yandell, 2011: 26). Defining the 'community of practice' (Lave and Wenger, 1991) in teacher education itself always brings us back to the interrelationship of theory and practice and of the players that contribute to the relational growth of the learning teacher. Heilbronn (2011) is clear that teachers must be research literate so that they can effectively evaluate theories, policies and strategies in relation to the aims of their own teaching. Further to this Heilbronn emphasizes the particular power in at least some teachers engaging in action research, and she amplifies the earlier suggestion that 'the unique feature of the questions that prompt teacher research is that they emanate from neither theory nor practice alone but from critical reflection on the intersection of the two' (Cochran-Smith and Lytle, 1993: 15).

ITE within schools as researching communities

So, within schools and within groupings of schools it is particularly important to examine how such learning communities maintain a focus on and a desire to enable continued research into both the community's direct educational activity and the broader frame that determines that activity. How does the changing landscape of schooling allow for and encourage a critical and learning culture within schools themselves and, within this, what is the place of ITE and those involved in it?

Once again we see an interesting positioning by government itself and, therefore, a response from actors including schools, groupings of schools, higher education institutes (HEIs) and individuals. Gunter (2012) argues that the 2010 election by which the Conservative and Liberal Democrat coalition government replaced the New Labour project was truly a 'watershed' because 'the *disposition* to accept how neoliberal ideas frame a problem and provide answers is very strong within knowledge production in education' (Gunter, 2012: 145).

In this context, and specifically following the White Paper of 2010 (DfE, 2010), the present government's Teaching School initiative has adopted as one of its 'Big Six' key responsibility areas for schools that of 'research and development' (DfE, 2011b). In so doing it has encouraged research activity in schools and alliances focusing initially on both pedagogies and gap closure. What is interesting is that the neoliberal framing referred to by Gunter seems alive and well in Department for Education (DfE) and National College for Teaching and Leadership (NCTL) discourse on this element of Teaching Schools' work. Emphasis is on Teaching Schools engaging in evidence-based research and bringing existing data to play on leadership and management decision-making based on this in-school evidence-based research. Teaching Schools are encouraged to engage in randomized control trials providing robust quantitative evidence to sit alongside that made available from within the DfE. The DfE and NCTL cite an analytical review undertaken for them by Ben Goldacre who comments on the difficulties of bringing research findings to teachers. He states that

> it's clear that we need better systems for disseminating the findings of research to teachers on the ground. While individual studies are written up

in very technical documents, in obscure academic journals, these are rarely read by teachers. And rightly so: most doctors rarely bother to read technical academic journals either.

(Goldacre, 2013: 13)

Interestingly, throughout the documents produced as a part of the analytical review, including the DfE's response to them, searches for the word 'university' result in no returns.

It could be argued that this is a shame. Teaching School Alliances have to cite a university partner and many work with a number of universities, but the DfE's framing of 'research and development' as one of the 'Big Six' actually seems to refer to schools playing their part in identifying and better using data – undoubtedly a critically important area of challenge – but does not connect this to broader communities of research expertise and broader research questions. This is in the context that the 2011 *National Teaching Schools: Handbook* (NCSL, 2011) puts some emphasis on the roles higher education institutions (HEIs) can play in delivery against the 'research and development' element of the Teaching School brief.

Importantly, then, within the range of conflicting demands on schools that of developing improved responses to the school's own data is an increasingly high priority and the definition of 'research and development', specifically within the Teaching Schools' range of responsibilities, seems to have been subsumed into this. Initial teacher education must compete as a priority in this culture of a school needing to commit middle and senior leadership to in-school evidence-based research aimed at gap-closing and better use of data.

'System improvement' – beyond individual schools

It is now useful to return to the much discussed idea of the school as a system but importantly, also of schools as a part of a bigger system. Following the conclusion of the then Teacher Training Agency's 'National Partnership Project', Edwards and Mutton (2007) concluded, in 2007, that the future should see an increased emphasis on networks with distributed expertise that benefit the professional learning of all involved and that isolated closed systems should be avoided.

Hargreaves puts significant emphasis on what he calls 'joint practice development' (Hargreaves, 2012b). In describing his 'maturity model' for realization of a truly self-improving system, he starts by rehearsing the value of a professional development approach that includes knowledge transfer as jointly owned between learner and mentor or coach, that is, based in practice or 'doing' and not just described, and that is genuinely developmental and thus leading to school improvement. At the individual professional to individual professional level, then, good practice is increasingly exemplified by a coaching and/or mentoring approach, by learning in and on the job and by development of the practice and not only simple knowledge transfer. Initial teacher education docs inhabit this space in many cases with supporting colleagues in schools and universities playing roles with learning teachers where the models are creatively designed.

In considering how this scales up to how schools themselves can act together in a self-improving system, Hargreaves ultimately takes us to the idea that there is a 'collaborative capital dimension' (Hargreaves, 2012b). Here it is not the individuals only that are engaging in joint practice development but institutions within an inter-school or wider partnership. At the heart of such partnerships Hargreaves sees 'alliance architecture' as critical, with an emphasis on mature partnerships having achieved a deepening of what they are about and how they work with such basic principles as 'joint practice development' as building blocks. He suggests that schools leading such groups must be clear about their narrative:

> This new narrative must inevitably focus primarily on collective moral purpose, the shared commitment to the achievement and success of all the students in the partnership, with a supportive narrative about how high social capital, joint practice development and evaluation and challenge – though expressed more simply – play their roles in realising the vision of collective moral purpose.
>
> (Hargreaves, 2012b: 33)

The conflicting demands on schools that include ITE are, then, increasingly contextualized and handled from within partnerships, alliances, network and groupings, and the bigger question about the integration of ITE becomes one about how effective a particular inter-school partnership has become – in Hargreaves's terms, how mature.

PRACTICAL ACTIONS; SCHOOL PERFORMANCE AND ITE AS A PRIORITY

School data and Ofsted standing

In England the Department for Education's performance tables (DfE, 2012) provide information on student achievement and attainment in primary, secondary and 16–18 schools and colleges, and make comparisons with other schools in the same local authority and with England as a whole. Importantly, the tables provide a very publicly available view of how a school is performing in the following key areas:

- end of Key Stage 4 GCSE attainment
- percentage of pupils meeting English Baccalaureate requirements
- percentages of pupils meeting at least expected progress in English and in mathematics at the end of Key Stage 4
- percentage of pupils achieving A*–C grades in GCSE English and mathematics
- 'value added' progress between the end of Key Stage 2 and the end of Key Stage 4

- attainment of five or more A*–C grades including English and mathematics

- overall and persistent absence rates for Key Stage 4 pupils

- income and expenditure performance

- data on the school's workforce including average teacher salary

- the most recent Ofsted judgements.

Clearly it is of great importance that a school is placed in a healthy position locally within the league tables. A school that is not positioned favourably will be concerned to change the situation and a school in a strong position will see as paramount the need to retain that position. The senior leadership in most schools has to be clear about its development and improvement planning and the part that continuing professional development, leadership and management development and the school's involvement in the initial training of teachers plays in this. When we add the pressure of retaining or improving a school's Ofsted grading then the 'focusing of school leaders' minds' becomes even greater.

The inspection of schools in England is determined by the Education Act (amended) 2005 and is detailed in Ofsted's framework (Ofsted, 2013a). Inspection aims to provide parents with a view of the school's performance, provide the Secretary of State with a view of whether the education it provides is at least acceptable and what any required improvements might be, and aims to promote individual school and sector-wide improvement (Ofsted, 2013a).

Ofsted cites a number of ways that inspection can 'drive and support improvement' as follows, saying that it:

- raises expectations by setting the standards of performance and effectiveness expected of schools

- provides a sharp challenge and the impetus to act where improvement is needed

- clearly identifies strengths and weaknesses

- recommends specific priorities for improvement for the school and, when appropriate, checks on and promotes subsequent progress

- promotes rigour in the way that schools evaluate their own performance, thereby enhancing their capacity to improve

- monitors the progress and performance of schools that are not yet 'good', and challenges and supports senior leaders, staff and those responsible for governance.

(Ofsted, 2013a: 4–5)

So, with the combined necessities of retaining or improving the school's position in the league tables and, similarly, maintaining or improving the school's grading with Ofsted – the need to focus strategically and developmentally on pupil attainment and progress and on matters such as pupil absence rates have to be the senior leadership team's first concerns. Clearly, retention of a clear view on the link between recruiting and developing the best teachers and success in terms of both performance data and inspection outcomes should always be a key focus of senior leadership in all schools.

Teacher recruitment and 'buy-in' to teacher preparation

Given the obvious linkage between all of this and staff development, including the initial training of the teacher workforce, the importance of medium- and long-term planning by schools becomes obvious. Where there is a culture and an effective approach to improvement and enhancement planning in schools, clear consideration will be given to each and every member of staff's ongoing development needs, the balance of staffing expertise and the need to introduce new members to a team (Fullan, 2003).

The recruitment and selection of new staff inevitably brings a number of key questions for a management team: what will be the changes to internal dynamics by bringing in someone new; given this, is an experienced person needed or might a recently or even newly qualified teacher be better suited? What sort of skill set and, perhaps, subject or age-group expertise is the school looking for? If a newly qualified teacher is sought then there are a range of options available to the school in sourcing the right person, including, most obviously, selecting applicants who have trained via:

- an undergraduate university partnership-based course

- a postgraduate university partnership-based course

- a School-Centred ITT (SCITT) course either with or without a university award to accompany the QTS

- the Teach First employment-based programme which includes PGCE and is leadership development based

- a School Direct place, based in a school, possibly including a university postgraduate award such as a PGCE

- a School Direct (Salaried) employment-based place which may include a university postgraduate award such as a PGCE.

Clearly, these separate into two basic types of training – that which is school or employment based, and that which is via a university partnership-led route.

In planning for staff recruitment a school can engage in two different strategies – or a blend of both, and this is of real relevance to how the school plans for its improvement and enhancement through its recruitment practice. The first approach is the more 'traditional' – that of advertising regionally, nationally (or even internationally) and waiting to see who applies. The second is to ensure a direct role in the preparation and training of the person they recruit – perhaps by the school being a member of a SCITT or more directly by training a School Direct teacher either within the school itself or within a group of schools coordinated by a School Direct 'lead school', or by providing school-based training within an HEI-led partnership.

A specific school's response to these key contemporary options for recruiting newly qualified teachers provides a thought-provoking view of how it sees ITE within the blend of its conflicting responsibilities and priorities. The obvious 'spectrum' of involvement might be described as follows:

a. No direct involvement – recruit from the sector as a whole.

b. Provide placements/training context for a university partnership-based provider – recruit from the sector as a whole including, possibly, those placed in own school.

c. Provide placements/training context for a range of providers – recruit from the sector as a whole with an increased likelihood that this will include those placed in own school.

d. Provide training as part of a SCITT partnership – recruit from the sector as a whole but a likelihood of recruiting from within the SCITT.

e. Provide training as part of a group of School Direct schools – recruit against an expectation by the DfE that the group of schools will employ their trainees.

f. Provide training as an individual School Direct school – recruit against an expectation by the DfE that the school will employ the trainee.

g. Provide training as an employment-based provider – recruit, for exsmple, through the mechanism of School Direct (Salaried) or by taking a Teach First trainee.

However, this 'spectrum' might be reconfigured if we consider that it is not just the way that a school engages with ITE but the quality and the quantity of that engagement. A school that might be characterized as type 'b' above, for example, might provide a much higher calibre of mentoring, it might provide trainees with deeply impactful training opportunities and it might place significant numbers of trainees in a year. Of course, a school can prioritize making the right appointment via any of the above approaches or, indeed, a combination of them. In involving itself in at least one of the approaches 'b'–'g', above, an individual school might take a position on whether it sees a resulting individual newly qualified teacher as having been well prepared for working specifically at that school or as having been well prepared for the wider profession and potential employment in any school.

The relevance of all of this to how ITE fits within the contrasting priorities faced by schools is perhaps best explored by considering how clear a school is on how its strategies for engagement in ITE form part of its overall strategy for: pupil achievement, attainment and progression; school improvement overall; leadership and management development; continuing professional development, and other priorities depending on the school's own improvement planning.

The simplest approach to this is to put a clear improvement plan in place as a school, identify within this how engagement in ITE contributes, and act accordingly. The converse is to engage in ITE in a range of ways and to monitor and evaluate which seems most impactful against the aims and objectives of the school improvement plan, and then to manipulate future engagement based on this.

Teacher recruitment and linkage to retention and a continuing career

Government has increasingly taken a view that it is the whole career of the teacher that should be the principal focus and there are increasing examples of school leaders and teacher educators responding to this agenda. Examples include an increasing emphasis on clear linkage of recruitment and selection for ITE to employability into a first post, retention and career development. School-led ITE routes have a heavy emphasis on linkage to employability with, for example, School Direct schools or groups of schools working to a 'lead school' being expected to employ the trainee. The National College for Teaching and Leadership states clearly that, under School Direct, schools must 'recruit trainees with an expectation that they will be employed in your school partnership once they are qualified' (NCTL, 2013: 7).

Inspection methodologies and reporting, since September 2012 particularly, have put increased focus on the desirability of clear linkage of recruitment to teacher education, the teacher education received, successful employment into a job and, increasingly, the linkage of the quality of newly and recently qualified teachers' own teaching, when inspected, to the initial teacher education they received. Since September 2012, for example, ITE Ofsted inspections have commonly included a focus on newly and recently qualified teachers who trained in the partnership being inspected. Ofsted's handbook for ITE inspection is clear about practice during inspection, saying that inspection activities 'are likely to include observations of trainees' and former trainees' teaching, discussions with trainees, former trainees, mentors and induction tutors, and time to read trainees' files' (Ofsted, 2012a: 14).

CASE STUDIES

CASE STUDY 8.1 SCHOOL LEADER VIEWS ON ITE AND CONFLICTING DEMANDS ON THEIR SCHOOLS

Examples of the positions adopted by a selection of senior colleagues, who have key responsibilities for ITE in schools, shed light on their view of ITE's place within the complex demands on their own institutions.

Five such colleagues contributed viewpoints to the author on ITE's place among conflicting priorities. To help contextualize each of their responses it is helpful to know their positions:

- Colleague 'Sec A' is a deputy headteacher in a secondary Teaching School in the Midlands and has responsibility for teacher education
- Colleague 'Pri B' is the headteacher of a primary school in the Midlands which has recently become involved in School Direct through another 'Lead School'
- Colleague 'Sec C' is an assistant head in a secondary school in the Midlands which is seeking Teaching School status and which has a long history of ITE partnership working
- Colleague 'Sec D' is the headteacher of a secondary Teaching School in the Midlands which has a broad range of involvements in ITE and CPD
- Colleague 'Pri E' is the headteacher of an established primary Teaching School in London which has a broad range of involvements in ITE and CPD

Having worked closely for over a year with each of the school leaders referenced here, the author elicited brief written responses to specific questions regarding involvement in ITE, including how this involvement relates to other possibly conflicting priorities. Direct quotes from these colleagues are used here by way of five parallel case studies on the issue of whether ITE has a 'formal' place in the publicly declared purpose of their school as an institution.

'Pri B' said not, but all four of the colleagues from Teaching Schools and the school aspiring to this status were clear that it did. 'Sec A' comments,

> It is stated within our action plan that part of our success as a Teaching School depends on us working collaboratively with partners to increase School Direct numbers.

'Pri E' states,

> Prior to receiving this status . . . the school was very actively involved in ITE with two providers and as such the school sees ITE has a formal place in the purpose of the school.

'Sec C' has ITE

> in the Leadership section of our school development plan

and 'Pri E' refers to ITE as

> referenced in the mission statement which introduces our school development plan.

Interestingly, two colleagues go beyond this and refer to ITE's 'formal place' in their schools' work as contributing to a bigger purpose, with 'Sec A' stating that they:

ensure that a planned programme of high quality school-based training is in place which will enhance the quality of teaching and learning across the alliance and our region

and 'Pri E' saying

The school's mission is to ensure we train all teachers from placements for potential recruits through to headship.

When asked how, as school leaders, they see any relationship between ITE within the school and the success of the school overall, a number of themes emerge:

Referring to the professional development of those who support ITE students, 'Sec A' states

I think there is huge potential for ITE to contribute significantly to school improvement . . . in terms of affording excellent CPD opportunities to mentors who in their role are inevitably compelled to reflect on their own practice and model outstanding practice.

'Pri B' goes further, saying

To provide a vehicle for the development of conscious competence by experienced staff around best class based practice through the necessary discussion, evaluation and review of the practice of another . . . This is almost 'self-driven' CPD by the teacher or mentor hosting a placement or training programme.

Going further still, 'Pri B' and others talk about the link to recruitment and to a quality workforce in the school, and some specifically refer to advantages in training their own teachers through school and employment-based models

by engaging directly with ITE we have the opportunity to invest time and skills in the long term game of ensuring 'success of the school overall' through supporting the availability of new high quality professionals.

'Sec D' says

The recruitment of high quality teachers is crucial to the success of the school and therefore so is their training and I do like the notion that you 'train your own' . . . I am also a big fan of talent management and succession planning and regard excellent ITE recruitment as a foundation to this

and, as a primary Teaching School headteacher, 'Pri E' agrees:

All the school staff are involved in the process of both training our own as well as training for the wider profession. Staff value the opportunities this presents in terms of mentoring, coaching, leading training and working with external providers.

Only 'Pri B' disagrees with this, expressing a view held by many in smaller primary schools that

> our engagement with 'training our own' is pragmatic at this time. As a Head with a long . . . experience of supporting ITE, my view is that schools overall do not have the capacity to ensure consistent high quality training by training our own teachers.

When asked if they can point to any examples of ITE activity within the school putting adverse pressure on key priority areas for the school, there is some reference by all the schools to pressures put on identified training and mentoring staff.

'Sec D' goes further, however:

> ITE can be more difficult if you commit to taking student teachers in a particular area and then there are major staffing changes or a fall in results. You are then forced to rethink priorities, capacity and commitment.

'Pri B' is the only school that has actually restricted involvement in ITE as a result of actual examples of conflicting priorities,

> We . . . needed to shift our CPD capacity to ensuring NQTs [newly qualified teachers] have the best possible induction programme to ensure all teaching rapidly progresses to 'good' or better in support of ensuring positive internal and external school evaluation. The current expectation of the new teacher standards . . . pulls on school capacity to support and address any 'dip' in performance . . . and this in turn pulls on capacity to support new professionals.

However, 'Pri E' is able to talk about how the school has brought involvement in ITE to bear directly on attainment and achievement outcomes for pupils in the school, saying

> We run an immersion model for trainees whereby they will work closely with a group of pupils to plan and deliver . . . ensur(ing) pupils make good progress. This has had an impact on our data as well as (having) provided the trainees with clear insights into strategies that both hinder and improve progress.

'Sec C' agrees, saying trainee teachers

> are a brilliant support for intervention groups and more than anything keep the focus tight on pedagogy

and 'Sec A' says it 'takes advantage' of its trainees

> in terms of increasing capacity to provide intervention either on a small group basis or one to one.

When asked if broader collaborative or partnership approaches with other schools has been able to harness ITE to the benefit of the school or a wider group of schools, all but 'Pri B' are able to do this, 'Pri E' stating, for example,

> With the development of the School Direct programme we now lead on much of the training for the trainees in collaboration with a group of schools in our alliance. Trainees therefore don't go to one place for their training but to different schools and are trained by current practising teachers.

'Sec A' adds

> There is such strength in collaboration. Working together on ITE has strengthened those partnership relationships. We work collaboratively with CPD opportunities, sharing good practice.

These parallel case studies of school leaders' positions seem to generally reflect at least some adoption of system change (Higham et al., 2009; Hopkins, 2009) and in four of the cases, at least, some move towards what Hargreaves has termed a maturing model (Hargreaves, 2012b). The headteachers of four of these schools are National Leaders in Education (NLEs) and espouse at least some of the rhetoric of 'moral imperative' or 'moral purpose' (DfE, 2011a; Fullan, 2003).

The one primary headteacher who is not an NLE is involved in the ITE route School Direct but has not gone as far as seeking Teaching School status. This school leader is less convinced about the school's ability to ameliorate conflicting priorities to ITE and perhaps represents a common position among many headteachers in primary schools. Initial teacher education allocations across university and school- or employment-based providers in the early years of School Direct certainly demonstrate substantially less of an increase in more demanding approaches to ITE taking hold in primary schools (Howson and Waterman, 2013).

In contrast to this, the primary NLE Teaching School headteacher is prepared to go as far as asserting that a link can be identified within the school between involvement in ITE and pupil progress. This is the link searched for in some research studies but seldom clearly identified (Hurd, 2008; Hurd et al., 2007). There is likely to be real impetus for further proof of such a link as the increasing shift towards school-led ITE, started under Labour and continued by the coalition government that followed, develops further.

CONCLUSION

In this chapter I have identified a number of ways in which schools can engage with ITE and I have contextualized these within an exploration of broader school priorities. All of this has been set within a developmental milieu of governmentally encouraged system change founded on the notion of a self-improving school system which, arguably, is beginning to exhibit the characteristics of 'maturity' (Hargreaves, 2012b).

The responses of a small group of school leaders, all committed to their schools' roles in ITE, signal the commitment they have to 'training the next generation' and a range of views – from the pragmatic to the passionate – on how ITE involvement can co-exist with other priorities or overtly support them. In 2007 Hurd et al. found it challenging to substantiate any clear link between involvement in ITE and pupils' achievement and attainment, but one school leader questioned here feels confident that such a link can now be made.

It is certainly the case that these school leaders include some with real reservations about their ability to consistently sustain ITE within their schools, particularly given the way that priorities can suddenly shift – for example, when attainment data exhibit a shift or an aspect of the school's improvement planning suddenly creates a call on middle and senior leadership time and energy. Interestingly, though, there is clearly evidence that some of the potential benefits of a self-improving system are beginning to impact through the creation of new approaches to ITE and its relationship to wider school priorities when supported by sound partnerships and school-to-school working. The overarching priority – the best education for all of a school's pupils – is increasingly being seen as positively supported by involvement in the initial education of teachers.

 ## FURTHER READING

For useful perspectives on the pressures on increasingly autonomous school leaders in England, see:

Glatter, R. (2012) 'Persistent preoccupations: the rise and rise of school autonomy and accountability in England', *Educational Management Administration and Leadership*, 40(5): 559–75.
Higham, R. and Earley, P. (2013) 'School autonomy and government control: school leaders' views on a changing policy landscape in England', *Educational Management Administration and Leadership*, 41(6): 701–17.

For a comprehensive view of system leadership and system change processes, see:

Higham, R., Hopkins, D. and Matthews, P. (2009) *System Leadership in Practice*. Maidenhead: Open University Press.

For an influential view on a self-improving schools system very relevant to recent policy roll-out, see:

Hargreaves, D. (2010) *Creating a Self-Improving School System*. Nottingham: NCSL.
Hargreaves, D. (2011) *Leading a Self-Improving School System*. Nottingham: NCSL.
Hargreaves, D. (2012a) *A Self-Improving School System in International Context*. Nottingham: NCSL.
Hargreaves, D. (2012b) *A Self-Improving School System: Towards Maturity*. Nottingham: NCSL.

For a clear commentary on and explanation of the challenges that school leaders face in recent policy change contexts, see:

Gunter, H. (2012) *Leadership and the Reform of Education*. Bristol: Policy Press.

For an exploration of the place of school-based ITE as a key activity for schools:

Hagger, H. and McIntyre, D. (2006) *Learning Teaching from Teachers: Realizing the Potential of School-Based Teacher Education*. Maidenhead: Open University Press.

Key governmental overview documents impacting on Teacher Education include:

DfE (2010) *The Importance of Teaching: The Schools White Paper 2010*. Norwich: TSO.
DfE (2011b) *Training Our Next Generation of Outstanding Teachers: Implementation Plan*. London: DfE.

REFERENCES

Barnett, K. and McCormick, J. (2012) 'Leadership and team dynamics in senior executive leadership teams', *Educational Management, Administration and Leadership*, 40(6): 653–71.
Barton, L., Whitty, G., Miles, S., Barrett, E. and Furlong, J. (1994) 'Teacher education and teacher professionalism: some emerging issues', *British Journal of Sociology of Education*, 15(4): 529–43.
Benton, P. (ed.) (1990) *The Oxford Internship Scheme*. London: Calouste Gulbenkian Foundation.
Chapman, C. and Gunter, H. (2009) *Radical Reforms: Perspectives on an Era of Educational Change*. Abingdon: Routledge.
Cochran-Smith, M. and Lytle, S. (1993) *Inside/Outside Teacher Research and Knowledge*. New York: Teachers College Press.
Day, C. (2004) 'The passion of successful leadership', *School Leadership and Management*, 24(4): 425–37.
Day, C. (2008) 'Successful leadership: an intelligent passion', in B. Davies and T. Brighouse (eds), *Passionate Leadership in Education*, London: Sage. pp. 75–90.
DfE (2010) *The Importance of Teaching: The Schools White Paper 2010*. Norwich. TSO.
DfE (2011a) Speech: Michael Gove on the moral purpose of school reform, available at www.gov.uk/government/speeches/michael-gove-on-the-moral-purpose-of-school-reform (accessed 14 September 2013).
DfE (2011b) *Training Our Next Generation of Outstanding Teachers: Implementation Plan*. London: DfE.
DfE (2012) *School and College Performance Tables: Statement of Intent – 2012*. London: DfE.
DfE (2013) *e-Bulletin Issue 20: Academy Factsheets*, available at: www.education.gov.uk/aboutdfe/executiveagencies/efa/efaebulletins/h00219864/issue-20/article-07 (accessed 26 November 2013).
Edwards, A. and Mutton, T. (2007) 'Looking forward: rethinking professional learning through partnership arrangements in initial teacher education', *Oxford Review of Education*, 33(4): 503–19.

Fullan, M. (2003) *The Moral Imperative of School Leadership*. London: Corwin Press.

Furlong, J., Barton, L., Miles, S., Whiting, C. and Whitty, G. (2000) *Teacher Education in Transition: Re-Forming Professionalism?* Buckingham: Open University Press.

Furlong, J., Whitty, G., Barrett, E., Barton, L. and Miles, S. (1995) 'Integration and partnership in initial teacher education – dilemmas and possibilities', *Research Papers in Education*, 9(3): 281-301.

Glatter, R. (2012) 'Persistent preoccupations: the rise and rise of school autonomy and accountability in England', *Educational Management Administration and Leadership*, 40(5): 559–75.

Goldacre, B. (2013) *Building Evidence into Education*. London: DfE.

Gorard, S. (2009) 'Serious doubts about school effectiveness', *British Educational Research Journal*, 36(5): 745–66.

Gunter, H. (2012) *Leadership and the Reform of Education*. Bristol: Policy Press.

Habhab. S. (2008) 'Workplace learning in a community of practice: how do schoolteachers learn?', in: C. Kimble, P. Hildreth and I. Bourdon (eds), *Communities of Practice: Creating Learning Environments for Educators*. Vol. 1. Charlotte, SC: Information Age Publishing. pp. 213–32.

Hagger, H. and McIntyre, D. (2006) *Learning Teaching from Teachers: Realizing the Potential of School-Based Teacher Education*. Maidenhead: Open University Press.

Hargreaves, A. and Fullan, M. (2012) *Professional Capital: Transforming Teaching in Every School*. Abingdon: Routledge.

Hargreaves, D. (2010) *Creating a Self-Improving School System*. Nottingham: NCSL.

Hargreaves, D. (2011) *Leading a Self-Improving School System.*, Nottingham: NCSL.

Hargreaves, D. (2012a) *A Self-Improving School System in International Context*. Nottingham: NCSL.

Hargreaves, D. (2012b) *A Self-Improving School System: Towards Maturity*. Nottingham: NCSL.

Heilbronn, R. (2011) 'The nature of practice-based knowledge and understanding', in R. Heilbronn and J. Yandell (eds), *Critical Practice in Teacher Education: A Study of Professional Learning*. London: Institute of Education, University of London. pp. 2–14.

Higham, R. and Earley, P. (2013) 'School autonomy and government control: school leaders' views on a changing policy landscape in England', *Educational Management Administration and Leadership*, 41(6): 701–17.

Higham, R., Hopkins, D. and Matthews, P. (2009) *System Leadership in Practice*. Maidenhead: Open University Press.

Hopkins, D. (2009) *The Emergence of System Leadership*. Nottingham: NCSL.

Hopkins, D. and Higham, R. (2007) 'System leadership: mapping the landscape', *School Leadership and Management*, 27(2): 147–66.

Hord, S. (1997) *Professional Learning Communities: Communities of Continuous Inquiry and Improvement*. Austin, TX: Southwest Education Development Laboratory.

Howson, J. and Waterman, C. (2013) *The Future of Teacher Education in England: Developing a Strategy*. Amersham: Iris Press.

Hurd, S. (2008) 'Does school-based initial teacher training affect secondary school performance?', *British Educational Research Journal*, 34(1): 19–36.

Hurd, S., Jones, M., McMamara, O. and Craig, B. (2007) 'Initial teacher education as a driver for professional learning and school improvement in the primary phase', *The Curriculum Journal*, 18(3): 307–26.

Hyman, P. (2011) 'The Tories want to send schools back by 50 years', *New Statesman*, 24 January: 25–7.

Lave, J. and Wenger, E. (1991) *Situated Learning: Legitimate Peripheral Participation*. New York: Cambridge University Press.

Lumby, J. (2013) 'Distributed leadership: the uses and abuses of power', *Educational Management, Administration and Leadership*, 41(5): 581–97.

McIntyre, D. (ed.) (1997) *Teacher Education Research in a New Context: The Oxford Internship Scheme*. London: Paul Chapman.

Miliband, D. (2002) *Speech: Annual Meeting of the Association for Foundation and Voluntary Aided Schools*. London: DES.

NCSL (2011) *National Teaching Schools: Handbook*. Nottingham: NCSL.

NCTL (2013) *School Direct: Quick Start Guide for Schools, 2014/15*. Manchester: NCTL.

Ofsted (2003) *Quality and Standards in Initial Teacher Training: Inspected 1999/2002*. London: Ofsted.

Ofsted (2012a) *Initial Teacher Education (ITE) Inspection Handbook: For Use from January 2013*. Manchester: Ofsted.

Ofsted (2012b) *The Report of Her Majesty's Chief Inspector of Education, Children's Services and Skills 2011–12: Schools*. Manchester: Ofsted.

Ofsted (2013a) *The Framework for School Inspection*. Manchester: Ofsted.

Ofsted (2013b) *Unseen Children: Access and Achievement 20 Years On. Evidence Report*. Manchester: Ofsted.

Ofsted (2013c) *Unseen Children. Sir Michael Wilshaw, Her Majesty's Chief Inspector. 20 June 2013, Church House, Westminster*. Manchester: Ofsted.

Perryman, J. (2011) 'Performativity versus engagement in a social science PGCE', in R. Heilbronn and J. Yandell (eds), *Critical Practice in Teacher Education: A Study of Professional Learning*. London: Institute of Education, University of London. pp. 138–53.

Wenger, E. (1999). *Communities of Practice: Learning, Meaning and Identity*. Cambridge: Cambridge University Press.

Whitty, G., Barrett, E., Barton, L., Furlong, J., Galvin, C. and Miles, S. (1992) 'Initial teacher training in England and Wales: a survey of current practices and concerns', *Cambridge Journal of Education*, 22(3): 293–306.

Yandell, J. (2011) 'Sites of learning', in R. Heilbronn and J. Yandell (eds), *Critical Practice in Teacher Education: A Study of Professional Learning*. London: Institute of Education, University of London. pp. 15–28.

Zeichner, K., Tabachnick, B. and Densmore, K. (1987) 'Individual, institutional and cultural influences on the development of teachers' craft knowledge', in J. Calderhead (ed.), *Exploring Teachers' Thinking*. London: Cassell. pp. 21–59.

CHAPTER 9

INITIAL TEACHER EDUCATION AND PROFESSIONAL DEVELOPMENT

Alison Chapman

By the end of the chapter you should be able to:

- understand how working with initial teacher education (ITE) can positively impact on the professional practice of a teacher
- reflect on your personal perspectives and context and identify some ways to integrate working with ITE and professional development
- identify some key issues to support you in leading a team of school-based teacher educators.

Until fairly recently there has been little research that directly links involvement in ITE with the professional development of teachers and measuring the impact on pupil outcomes and school improvement (Hurd et al., 2007). This chapter identifies how becoming involved in teacher training can impact positively on the professional development of the school teacher and in particular those who take on the new role as school-based teacher educator and how this can be of benefit to the individual and the wider group of professionals. The final part of the chapter will give some practical ideas for how to ensure you develop a team of school-based teacher educators within the school or across an alliance of schools that will contribute to a community of people working together to provide the very best teacher training experience and sustained capacity for high quality delivery.

THE PROFESSIONAL BENEFITS OF WORKING WITH ITE

Since the early 1990s there has been a shift towards increasing the role schools play in contributing to the training of teachers and from 1994 onwards (Brooks et al., 1997; DfE, 1992), at least two-thirds of the time for secondary teacher training has to be spent in school. The primary phase has the same requirements from September 2013. With the increase in school-based teacher education courses there is a renewed view that practising teachers are well placed to train new teachers for the profession (Bryan and Carpenter, 2008; NCSL, 2012). The National College for Teaching and Leadership (NCTL, previously the National College for School Leadership, NCSL) recognizes the potential benefits of being involved in ITE and wants to increase the involvement of schools in training teachers:

> Encouraging greater involvement in ITT across their strategic partners and supporting their partners in improving the quality of their ITT provision ... Teaching schools will need to plan and manage a coherent, school-led approach to teacher and leadership training and development, linking this to the priorities of their alliance and their own school improvement planning. (NCSL, 2011: 9)

Even though research measuring the impact of ITE on professional development is fairly new, there is a range of research linked to why schools become involved in ITE. Hurd et al.'s (2007) study of more than 3,000 primary schools identified that those schools which were involved in teacher training tended to perform better with regard to Office for Standards in Education, Children's Services and Skills (Ofsted) and pupil achievement outcomes. Of course there are many facets to that claim, none more prevalent than questioning whether this is coincidence or do teacher training institutions select the 'better' schools to work with in teacher training. However, Child and Merrill (2003) found that teachers who were not involved in training new teachers were disadvantaged with regard to their own professional development. It is widely recognized that being a mentor is very demanding on time but the majority of research advocates that the benefits far outweigh the effort involved (Beutel and Spooner-Lane, 2009; Brooks et al., 2007; Hurd et al., 2007, Skinner, 2010). Hurd et al. (2007) go further and advocate that if teachers experience professional learning from working with ITE, then the knock-on effect should be that school outcomes improve over time.

Harland and Kinder's (1997) model identifies three tiers of benefits that teachers and schools perceive to be the benefits of being actively involved in the training of new entrants to the teaching profession:

1. New teaching ideas and resources are brought into schools.

2. Teachers become excited about their work with ITE and this invigorates them in their role and improves their mentoring skills.

3. The process of reflection on mentoring and their own professional practice leads to subsequent improvements.

From my discussions with teachers involved with ITE, they agree with this model but feel there are two additional reasons for being involved:

a. Improving mentoring and coaching skills and having a greater understanding of teaching and learning can lead to whole-school improvement through the sharing of good practice and working with established staff in schools to further their practice.

b. A moral sense of purpose to support the training of the next generation of outstanding teachers for the pupils in the education system.

Being involved in initial teacher education can take many forms, from being a class or subject mentor who supports a traditional placement in a 'university-led' teacher training programme to being the programme lead for a school-based teacher training course. Each of the roles has distinct characteristics and responsibilities and they in themselves provide a framework for professional development.

Class mentor or subject mentor

In a traditional university-led course these often focus on supporting the trainee teacher on a day-to-day basis; observing lessons and giving formative feedback; setting targets to ensure the trainee teacher progresses; monitoring the trainees' documentation and evidence for meeting the Qualified Teacher Standards (QTS), working closely with university-based tutors and the school professional mentor, or lead for ITE, and modelling good practice to support the development of teaching, learning and classroom management. In a school-based programme, the mentor may take on a larger role supporting the development of subject knowledge and teaching pedagogy in addition to taking on the role of pastoral support.

Professional mentor/school lead

This person usually oversees and supports the mentors in school and is responsible for overseeing the quality assurance of the provision at the school. They usually arrange a timetable of sessions within school for the trainee teachers to learn about professional and whole-school issues such as assessment or behaviour management. They are usually more strategic and have oversight of the whole-school policy for ITE within the school and will carry out joint observations with subject or class mentors. This person is usually the link with the higher education institution (HEI) and attends regional meetings on behalf of the school. For school-based programmes, this person will also be responsible for the academic and professional progress of the trainee teachers based in the school. With the increase in drive for more school-based approaches to teacher training and especially with the introduction of School Direct, where schools are encouraged to take a larger role in training teachers, the involvement from school staff is likely to increase, with staff taking on more responsibility.

The majority of teacher training is still via a postgraduate (PGCE) route (DfE, 2013) and this brings academic as well as professional requirements. If school staff are to support and deliver aspects of teacher training beyond the 'placement' experience, then they need to have a strong understanding of the requirements of ITE. For example, the academic components and assessment that make up the award of PGCE and how that is integrated into the training for QTS; the ebbs and flows of a training year and logical sequencing for integrating learning and practice. For someone taking on the role of a leader in ITE in school there are many other elements to understand, such as recruitment and retention, academic regulations, the importance of employment and the Ofsted inspection framework for initial teacher training. For those new to teacher education, it is possible to feel like a new entrant to the profession again, this is what Murray and Male (2005) called a 'second order practitioner', meaning that you are moving from being an 'expert' in your original field of teaching (children, first order practitioner) to learning a new field. However, with these challenges come many opportunities for professional development that will enhance the individual, school and wider community. It is within this context, where ITE in school is increasing and the role of the university diminishing, that the quality of mentoring is more important to meet the increased demands placed on mentors (Bryan and Carpenter, 2008). With this comes a greater need for continuing professional development (CPD) and an induction into higher education and teacher training.

According to Brighouse (2008: 321), teachers blossom and prosper if four needs are met:

1. They thrive on responsibility and are recognized as the trusted expert.

2. They enjoy an environment that encourages professional dialogue and excites them about the contribution they can make to education.

3. They feel their hard work is appreciated and recognized.

4. They have the opportunities to consult with others in similar roles and can access a network and study beyond the immediate school environment.

Being involved in ITE can provide an environment where these four needs can be met, which can then invigorate teachers' work within the school. There is an increase in popularity of school-based teacher education courses as experienced mentors are excited about having opportunities to build on their mentoring experiences and to take on a fuller role with teacher training. Being part of a team across an alliance of schools can stimulate professional discussions about the vision and philosophy of teacher training and how to train outstanding teachers for their schools. There are also networks where school-based teacher educators can discuss together and compare their courses and experiences which ensure they are not isolated within a school context. Finally the school and student teachers are enthused and appreciative for the hard work, seeing the trainee teachers flourish and develop into excellent new entrants into the profession is personally rewarding.

Referring back to Harland and Kinder's (1997) model for the professional development benefits of working with teacher training, the most common development cited was that student teachers bring new ideas into the classroom and the teacher benefits from receiving these resources and new approaches to teaching, especially the integration of technology into teaching, which trainee teachers are often more adept at than more established teachers (Hurd et al., 2007). These types of development can be described as at a surface level with little long-lasting effect or change on the personal practice of the teacher, but they should not be undervalued. For an experienced teacher, having new resources or approaches to teaching a topic can certainly help the teacher ensure their practice does not stagnate, and the trainee teacher may give ideas the teacher has not thought about before. Moving down Hurd et al.'s model towards stage three (reflection on practice and mentoring), the potential impact on a teacher and the wider school increases.

From my discussions with many school teachers who work with trainee teachers, they cite working with ITE as their main source of professional development as they learn from the trainee teachers. It also encourages them to reflect on their own practice (Beutel and Spooner-Lane, 2009), especially through discussions when they articulate the underpinning principles of why something was or was not successful or how to approach a specific topic or adopting a teaching style with a class. Working with ITE can offer opportunities to debate with trainees and other professionals and, for the open minded, to extend their pedagogies through learning from others. Many school mentors feel that their teaching has improved because they have to be role models for trainee teachers and ensure they thoroughly plan their own lessons so that they engage the children in their classes and demonstrate to the trainee teachers how learning takes place in many different forms.

WORKING WITH ITE TO DEVELOP PERSONAL SKILLS: REFLECTIONS FROM SCHOOL-BASED TEACHER EDUCATORS

The importance of developing observation, mentoring and coaching skills cannot be underestimated. It is widely accepted that those with leadership potential require a range of interpersonal skills and being able to observe, coach and mentor are important skills for a middle leader or subject leader in school. Phelps (2008) advocated teachers taking on wider roles outside their classroom as a way of developing leadership potential. The role of an ITE mentor is usually the first step for a relatively new teacher to start to develop these skills. Knowing how to observe, what to look for, how to break down teaching into components and how to give feedback are not learnt overnight and it is a fine skill to be able to distinguish between when mentoring is more appropriate than coaching to help the trainee teacher to develop their craft of teaching (Alred and Garvey, 2000, cited in Beutel and Spooner-Lane, 2009; Feiman-Nemser, 2003). A head of humanities at a secondary school reinforced this view:

> Working with a student teacher helps me to be a more effective head of faculty as I am regularly observing and giving feedback to the student, this improves the quality of feedback I give and sharpens my observation skills which helps me as I observe the staff in my department.
>
> (Teacher 1)

Hurd et al.'s study (2007: 315) quoted school mentors attributing their ITE coordination role as contributing to gaining promotion; for example one subject mentor suggested the mentor role was used as part of an assessment for the National Professional Qualification for Headship (NPQH) and another felt the whole-school role helped to secure a deputy headteacher position.

With a greater emphasis on the school-led system where schools support their own and other schools' improvements in teaching and learning, the use of coaching and lesson observations has become more important. For some staff, observing a trainee teacher can be a way of gaining confidence, developing those skills before observing and giving feedback to an experienced colleague in the school. This type of approach can improve the teaching and learning in the classroom. If a classroom teacher is familiar with observing and giving feedback on lessons, they are developing a strong understanding of what makes good learning and teaching. This knowledge can then be applied to their own classroom teaching. A number of experienced teachers have mentioned to me how observing others gets them to think carefully about their own practice, question whether their teaching maximizes learning opportunities and demonstrates the same good practice that they have observed in others. The process also often reminds them about key aspects of teaching that they take for granted, such as questioning techniques, differentiation by task and noticing what the children are doing in lessons.

Teacher 2 said:

> My involvement with teaching PGCE students about behaviour management has forced me to retain a focus on the most effective strategies and to use them consistently, and so my behaviour management has improved.

Examples such as this are important in ensuring teachers stay fresh and do not become complacent about their teaching, and in time should contribute to maintaining and improving the standards of teaching and learning in the school.

Teacher 3 said,

> I have seen a marked improvement in the ability and confidence of the school staff to observe lessons and give feedback to their peers after they had supported and mentored a trainee teacher. The most significant longer term impact had been the development of a community of staff who openly discuss teaching and learning strategies and we have implemented a coaching model in the school.

This is in line with Engestrom's (2001) work, who advocated developing a culture of sharing ideas in the workplace, the principles of which can be applied to the school setting. He also advocated that where there was a culture of staff collaborating and learning from each other, student teachers were part of the wider community and no one worked in isolation.

New school-based teacher educators (SBTE) need to support their existing classroom experience with clear pedagogies in order for the trainee teachers to understand why certain approaches and behaviours are successful (White and Jarvis, 2013). It is important that SBTEs are part of a team and not isolated individuals in a school, as this will allow them to have affirmation and gain in confidence and to be a part of a wider community to share ideas (White and Jarvis, 2013).

Papastamatis et al. (2009) felt there is no real difference between the type of professional development a teacher and a teacher educator requires. The most important aspect is to ensure the culture and climate for learning is conducive to professional growth. Referring back to Engestrom's (2001) findings that working with ITE impacts the most positively on schools who have a culture of the whole school sharing ideas and collaboration between staff, this links to Hargreaves's (2011) model of schools as learning communities at all levels, with education, training and staff development as a lifelong process which will sustain long-term growth. (Papastamatis et al., 2009)

The role of the teacher educator is often more challenging than the experienced teacher thinks, for this reason being part of a wider team is important. As the leader for teacher education within a consortium of schools you may find many teachers say that they have been mentors for years and are confident in their ability to support the trainee teachers. Many fall into the trap and assume that they can just transfer their knowledge about the classroom, teaching children and subject knowledge to the adult learner through 'telling the trainee' (Casey and Fletcher, 2012; Murray and Male, 2005). They soon find that they have to learn new pedagogical approaches for adults and engage with academic study that is different to the classroom setting and to that of delivering short CPD courses.

One of the main challenges for SBTEs taking on the role of leading academic, theoretical and professional aspects of teacher training is to be able to articulate pedagogic content knowledge, putting the art of teaching the subject into words. Good teachers do not always know why they do something, because it has become second nature to them and they find it difficult to unpick their tacit knowledge about teaching practice and put it into words (Clandinin, 1986; Skinner, 2010).

Embedding action research into schools

You will have read a chapter earlier in this book about the importance of the academic aspects of teacher training and will have learnt about integrating this into a programme. Although the past six years have seen an increase in the number of teachers studying towards a higher degree, the delivery of the 'theoretical' master's-level work is the aspect where SBTEs report they are the least confident, especially if it has been some years since they carried out any academic research.

Working closely with a higher education partner is essential for those schools which embark on leading the majority of the training. The school must consider how SBTEs can deliver the academic aspect and support trainee teachers in their assessments and research skills. Embedding action research into the culture of a school is the long-term way to develop the climate for research that will seamlessly integrate research and professional practice, but this takes many years to accomplish across a whole school or alliance. There are many stages on the way to this goal which can help staff to develop their research skills:

- Have a small group of staff who all embark on studying towards a higher degree and organize half-termly meetings where they meet and discuss their work, issues, and have tutorials for carrying out research.

- Encourage twilight sessions where teachers can briefly present or talk about any small-scale research projects they have carried out with their classes.

- Create a small template for a basic impact study which teachers can complete and have an area of the school Virtual Learning Environment (VLE) for sharing work

- Organize a session 'an introduction to action research' for staff to learn about how to go about conducting a small-scale piece of research in their classroom with subsequent sessions on how to access research journals, how to write up your study, how to present at a school in-service training poster presentation.

- Organize a mini-conference within your school or network where staff can briefly share what they have found out with others.

These could be organized within a school or for staff from a number of schools including the trainee teachers so there is a community of teachers all learning together, sharing their ideas, issues, problems and lessons learnt; having a culture where it is safe to say, 'I tried this, but it didn't quite work; I read about this and tried it with a group and the results were … ; I had this problem and I found a study which had a similar issue; I learnt from …'. The higher education institution could help support this research community and by being involved in action research as a teacher, this develops the reflective practitioner who has more confidence and experience in supporting the trainee teacher with their action research projects. My own personal experience with working in a large teacher education university is that those new to the role were concerned that they did not have the 'academic' experience to support master's-level work and the level of confidence increased after gaining the qualification. I would recommend anyone having a significant role in training teachers to study for a higher degree. The benefits of doing so are confidence-building; re-engaging with recent educational literature, which increases the ability to support trainee teachers and to contribute with formative feedback on assessments; and you will take back the skills of a reflective practitioner into your school community, which will benefit your teaching and contribute to a self-improving school community.

The final real challenge for the teacher educator and the strongest justification of all for developing a team is that the trainee teachers should learn a broad range of techniques and experiences. You might argue that traditional courses provide two different school experiences, and often the experience from a university tutor, and this is not a range of techniques. However, that tutor draws on their own personal experiences as a teacher and has over the years developed a wealth of knowledge through training many teachers and spending time in many different schools while working with ITE. This wealth of experience can only be replicated by a school-based teacher educator if two main conditions are met:

- Breadth and range develop over time after supporting many trainee teachers and visiting different contexts.

- There is a team of people working together to provide the training so the trainee teachers learn from more than one mentor, or teacher educator, and experience contrasting styles of teaching and delivery. Skinner (2010) and Hodkinson and Hodkinson (2005) advocate that school-based programmes should only be run in expansive learning environments that value and support learning and provide an openness to diverse learning opportunities.

Teacher 4 said,

Being involved in ITE has given me the opportunity to work with a wide range of colleagues from my school, other schools and also with university staff. This 'melting pot' is very stimulating and it is always a pleasure to work with a team of dedicated professionals all willing to share ideas and talk education. All with a common goal.

Practical ideas to develop a team of school-based teacher educators

The lead teacher educator for any school-based programme will need to have a strong understanding of the training requirements for ITE, a strong personal philosophy and pedagogy, and appropriate personal attributes to support the trainee teachers and to lead the experienced teachers who form the school-based teacher education team. This may involve changing mindsets and established practice because the schools are now taking on a more significant role in the training of teachers and the school and staff simply cannot do the same as they always have done. If schools are delivering more of the training, then the staff involved need to have knowledge of the academic components of the training. As student teachers are based in school from the start, this gives more opportunities for them to see the application of the principles of teaching in practice from an early stage. Teachers who play a role in this need to be able to articulate the link between theory and practice for those students. It is important that all staff can consistently apply the principles and pedagogy, knowing what the focus for the week is and the structure and content of the course. It is widely recommended that the School Direct leads do not do so in isolation but engage with others in similar roles through networks (White and Jarvis, 2013) or even the NCTL online community.

A few easy steps to help with this are:

1. Establish the key people working with the school-based training to include:

   programme lead, professional mentors (school lead), subject mentors (secondary), classroom mentors, and staff delivering key parts of the course.

2. Plan (jointly with the HEI if appropriate) some training events where the key people meet together (either all or in specific groups, dependent on the size of the project). Here are some ideas for the focus of these events:

   recruitment and the interview process, an introduction to the course (philosophy, structure and assessments), how to have a professional learning conversation, how to observe lessons (to ensure all mentors are applying the same processes and consistency of judgements), and quality assurance processes.

3. Carry out an audit of the expertise within the schools working on the project to find out about the special characteristics of each school, school improvement priorities and the areas of expertise within the school. This will help to identify a range of professionals who can contribute to the taught elements of the course or which schools will offer excellent opportunities for immersion experiences and visits.

4. Create a small core working group who plan the overall structure of the programme. This will ensure that ideas from a number of professionals input into the design and the programme is not just one person's opinion. It will be part of a capacity-building process and succession planning in case a key person leaves the group and is a step process for teachers who have aspirations of taking on a leading role in teacher training.

5. In developing pedagogical subject knowledge, pairing staff to develop the subject-specific input will ensure no one is isolated and those staff can work as a team, sharing ideas and developing a pedagogical underpinning together. This also ensures that the trainee teachers benefit from at least two different teaching styles and personalities, and the staff can interact together to critically analyse the work they are doing. For some smaller primary subject inputs, it might not be feasible for pairs as the level of input is minimal. I would recommend you do not have large numbers of staff working together as this makes planning more challenging to get larger numbers of people together, which may also lead to additional costs. These small subject clusters could cross reference with other subjects to ensure a parity of experience and coverage. At a time where education is changing, these planning meetings will no doubt be useful in informing professional practice through discussions about changes to the national curriculum and examination projects.

In an ideal situation, each school involved in a school-based teacher education project will recognize the professional learning benefits from being involved in teacher education. Hurd et al. (2007) recommend a whole-school approach to ensure it forms part of the planned professional development provision for a school. Initially this could involve some mentor training for all teaching staff, which would enable any of the teachers to act as a mentor, to observe and have a professional learning conversation with trainee teachers and to raise awareness of how teacher training was integrated within the school.

One of the perceived strengths of a school-based teacher training programme is the reduction of the theory–practice divide. This divide is only reduced if the learning environment has carefully designed the learning opportunities to facilitate this. Hutchinson's (2011) research shows that, in general, students talk about school-based experience but do not reference teaching theories in their discussions. Van Velzen and Volman (2009) state that the link to education theory has traditionally been carried out by university lecturers. Just basing a course in a school setting does not reduce the divide; the knowledge and understanding must be constructed. Hegender (2010: 151) refers to Cochran-Smith and Lytle's (1999) description of teacher knowledge being a combination of knowledge *for* practice (research-based) or knowledge *in* practice (experience-based); having a grounding in both aspects will enable SBTEs to successfully integrate the theoretical and practical components of teaching. An example could be the articulation and explanation of the underpinning knowledge of approaches to behaviour management and the practical application and role-modelling with pupils in a learning environment.

Integrating ITE into schools

Schools embarking on leading a School Direct course must ensure that it becomes an important focus for the school. In traditional courses, ITE is not the main activity of a school, as educating the school pupils is the priority and is subject to scrutiny from Ofsted. If a school becomes a lead for a school-based teacher education programme, then it has a moral duty to provide an excellent training provision jointly with the accredited provider for the future of the teaching profession and for the students studying on the course. If a school becomes an accredited provider such as School-Centred Initial Teacher Training (SCITT), then the Ofsted scrutiny will be with the school as the ITE provider. Sufficient provision of resources must be made, including dedicated staff time to work with the student teachers, school mentors and staff involved in the delivery of the course from across a network of schools.

Working with many new school-based projects, the biggest challenge the SBTEs face is the recognition that this work should be viewed in the same way as teaching a class of pupils. As teaching children is the main priority of a school, involvement in teacher training is often seen as additional to the role and often very little dedicated time is given to those involved. For those who will be taking a leading role in supporting the personal, academic and professional development of new teachers, the workload needs to be allocated accordingly and this should be timetabled and seen as a part of that person's workload.

Hurd et al. (2007) suggest that many schools undervalue the professional learning benefits from being involved in school-based teacher education and recommend a whole-school approach to ensure it forms part of the planned professional development provision for a school.

> Having lots of trainees in school I feel gives a school a more modern professional feel. School students observing lots of trainees discussing teaching issues with more senior colleagues improves our professional standing and makes them feel that they are in a more dynamic, forward thinking school. The same holds true for teaching staff and parents.
>
> (Teacher 5).

Extending from the previous comments about learning from a range of professionals, trainee teachers report most favourably on courses that allow them to visit and experience more schools than the minimum requirement of two. There are rich learning opportunities from spending time in different schools, seeing how schools approach learning in different ways, especially in contrasting types of schools and catchment areas. These learning opportunities can then feed into a school placement school which allows for a discussion about teacher pedagogy and reinforces the dynamic teacher environment Teacher 4 discusses above.

The real strength of a school-based training course is the opportunity to learn from the best practitioners. No one person is an expert in all parts of education. Some schools, for ease of organization reasons, tend to have the ITE lead for the course and the trainee teachers predominantly based in one school for the non-placement activity with sessions led by one main person. Although this is a very valid experience and no doubt the course is professionally planned and delivered, it is suggested that this does not give the most richness to the training. In planning your course, consider having the ITE lead as the 'glue' who pulls the training together, who supports the personal and academic development of each trainee teacher, but plan for specialists from a range of schools to deliver the sessions. For example, in primary ITE, have an outstanding phonics teacher deliver phonics training, but ensure that the trainees work in different schools to see a range of phonics approaches and give them the opportunity to come back together and share and reflect on what they have seen, critically evaluating the merits of the different approaches.

Another example could be an introduction to special educational needs led by a special educational needs coordinator (SENCO), observe meeting the needs of all pupils in a school setting and then have an immersion experience in a special school, again sharing and reflecting on their experiences, what they have learnt and what they will apply to their teaching.

This type of approach allows for a richness of experience, scaffolding the learning, enabling the trainees to learn from different approaches and to reflect and apply them to their own teaching. There is no one 'best method' for teaching as teachers are individuals and develop their own craft. We must ensure that SBTEs do not give a narrow training experience, it is more important that skills are developed that can then be adapted as the situation changes, rather than rehearsing and learning techniques that have been applied to one type of school or situation. Otherwise we are developing mini-versions of ourselves instead of skilful teachers who can then, in time, be employed to teach in any school.

Schools want to take on a wider role in teacher training because they want to train the teachers for their group of schools, which means they have a vested interest in ensuring the training is of high quality. To maximize the potential, it is recommended that leads plan how the ITE trainees can contribute to school improvement. This contribution can be through intervention projects, such as reading and writing interventions, or through deliberately planning for existing school staff to be involved in ITE as a programme of professional development, from mentoring a trainee, to leading a session for the group of trainees, to a book scrutiny or sample lesson through to being a personal tutor or the school lead. Involvement at any level will have a positive learning effect on the teacher and contribute towards the learning environment of the school.

CASE STUDY 9.1 LESSONS LEARNED: THE EXPERIENCES FROM SOME SCHOOL-BASED TEACHER EDUCATORS

Perspective from a primary teacher who is responsible for leading a school-based teacher education programme:

> This year has been amazing for me as a professional and the best form of continuing professional development (CPD) and new experiences I have ever had. By taking on the lead for teacher training on behalf of a Teaching School alliance of eighteen schools I have developed a totally new skill set that has helped me grow in confidence both in terms of learning about ITE but also for my role as a senior leader in school. The aspects that have had the largest impact on me are communicating, presenting and negotiating with Headteachers and other senior leaders in schools. In launching the ITE project I have presented at national events such as the North West NCTL Teaching School conference, this in itself was very daunting talking to 300 successful school leaders about my experiences of school-based ITE. I have learnt about the requirements for ITE, validation procedures and assessments for the academic award of a PGCE and learnt about how theoretical sessions and courses are devised. I am an experienced ITE school mentor but had no idea about the regulations, marking, quality assurance requirements or Ofsted framework for ITE and I feel empowered in ensuring that our course is the best experience for training outstanding teachers that hopefully will be employed in the alliance schools.
>
> (Teacher 6)

This statement demonstrates how involvement in ITE can support the development of personal skills by providing many new opportunities that would not normally arise in the day-to-day operations of teaching and leading within a school. However, through ITE, this teacher has worked collaboratively with other schools, which has enabled a new skill set to be developed.

I have worked with 15 lead schools to develop School Direct projects and some advice is consistent from all in advising others of the key things they have learnt.

Time is the most challenging aspect of developing school-based teacher education. When there is a lot of change in education, such as a new National Curriculum and examinations, to develop a teacher training programme which can respond to these changes and deliver high-quality training can take time.

> Teachers are very busy people, doing the day job. To be successful requires full buy in from the school management in order to afford appropriate time to do a good job. I would recommend a memorandum of understanding of roles and responsibilities is agreed for all schools participating in the project
>
> (Teacher 5)

This statement aligns with the requirements of a traditional university-led course where a partnership agreement must be signed by the accredited provider and school. If schools are taking on a leading role in a consortium, it seems appropriate to mirror the expectations, which also provides clarity for all partners involved.

The school-based teacher educator programme leads have all enjoyed working with staff from other schools. To share expertise and learn about how teachers approach an issue in other schools has been enlightening but also a form of CPD, as those teachers have taken ideas back to their own schools. All agreed it is reassuring to have a shared vision which has evolved and all are striving for excellence, both in educating the trainee teachers and for the children within their schools. A phrase I often hear is 'quality first teaching'; by ensuring the very best teachers are employed in our schools we will enable pupils to attain to the best of their ability. Most of the schools have audited their schools and staff to ensure that appropriate expertise is utilized in the training. For many this has raised awareness of untapped expertise within schools, and with new opportunities has invigorated and excited staff, with many volunteering to be involved. Teacher 6 advocated an extended team to be involved in developing School Direct to develop capacity and for succession planning. In many cases the most gifted teachers and leaders in school are involved in teacher education; for sustainability a team should be developed that ensures that, if the lead should be promoted, the programme can still be successful. Another advocated a rotation of responsibility in order that the professional development a person gains from leading ITE can then be experienced by other staff; the personal gains are great and are then fed back into the school to continue to improve the teaching and educational standards within the school.

When I entered the teaching profession it was because I wanted to help people and make a difference. Teaching has done this for me but working with ITE is the icing on the cake. I unreservedly recommend it to any teacher if the opportunity arises.

(Teacher 3)

CONCLUSION

To conclude, with the increased role schools are taking on in training teachers, it seems sensible to strategically plan to ensure that high-quality teacher training is coupled with opportunities for the professional development of the existing school staff, whether through taking on the role of mentor, leading some taught aspects of ITE, reflecting on personal professional practice or being part of a team who are developing and leading action research projects which complement the academic projects that the trainee teachers participate in. Involvement in initial teacher education gives many opportunities for the personal and professional enhancement of teachers and leaders at all levels in school.

 ## FURTHER READING

National College for Teaching and Leadership online network: www.nationalcollege. org.uk/signin

There is a wealth of useful documents about professional development, coaching, the self-improving school system and joint practice development published by the NCTL and available online, you also have the opportunity to engage with online discussion forums, a good example is the School Direct discussion forum where you can share ideas and experiences with other school-based teacher educators nationally.

Engestrom, Y. (2001) 'Expansive learning at work: toward activity theoretical reconceptualisa-tion', *Journal of Education and Work*, 14(1): 133–56.
White, E. and Jarvis, J. (2013) *School-based Teacher Training, a Handbook for Tutors and Mentors*. London: Sage.

REFERENCES

Beutel, D. and Spooner-Lane, R. (2009) 'Building mentoring capacities in experienced teachers', *International Journal of Learning*, 16(4): 351–60.
Brighouse, T. (2008) 'Putting professional development centre stage', *Oxford Review of Education*, 34(3): 313–23.
Brooks, V., Barker, S. and Swatton, P. (1997) 'Quid pro quo? Initial teacher education in second-ary schools', *British Educational Research Journal*, 23(2): 163–78.

Bryan, H. and Carpenter, C. (2008) 'Mentoring: a practice developed in community', *Journal of in-Service Education*, 34(1): 47–59.

Casey, A. and Fletcher, T. (2012) 'Trading places: from physical education teachers to teacher educators', *Journal of Teaching in Physical Education*, 31(4): 362–80.

Child, A.J. and Merrill, S. (2003) 'Professional mentors' perceptions of the contribution of school/ HEI partnerships to professional development and school improvement', *Journal of in-Service Education*, 29(2): 315–24.

Clandinin, D.J. (1986) *Classroom Practice: Teacher images in action*. Lewes: Falmer Press.

Cochran-Smith, M. and Lytle, S.L. (1999) 'Relationships of knowledge and practice: teacher learning in communities, *Review and Research in Education*, 24: 249–305.

Department for Education (DfE) (1992) *The New Requirements for Initial Teacher Training*. Circular 9/92. London: HMSO.

Department for Education (DfE) (2013) *Initial Teacher Training Allocations in England for Academic Year 2013/14 – Final Update*, www.gov.uk/government/uploads/system/uploads/attachment_data/file/229468/SFR_ITT_allocations_August_2013.pdf (accessed 7 February 2014).

Engestrom, Y. (2001) 'Expansive learning at work: toward activity theoretical reconceptualisation', *Journal of Education and Work*, 14(1): 133–56.

Feiman-Nemser, S. (2003) 'What new teachers need to learn', *Educational Leadership*, 60(8): 25–9.

Hargreaves, D. (2011) *Leading a Self-Improving School System*. Nottingham: National College for School Leadership.

Harland, J. and Kinder, K. (1997) 'Teachers' continuing professional development: framing a model of outcomes', *British Journal of in-Service Education*, 23(1): 71–84.

Hegender, H. (2010) 'The assessment of student teachers' academic and professional knowledge in school-based teacher education', *Scandinavian Journal of Educational Research*, 54(2): 151–71.

Hodkinson, H. and Hodkinson, P. (2005) 'Improving Schoolteachers' workplace learning', *Research Papers in Education*, 20(2): 109–31.

Hurd, S., Jones, M., McNamara, O. and Craig, B. (2007) 'Initial teacher education as a driver for professional learning and school improvement in the primary phase', *The Curriculum Journal*, 18(3): 307–26.

Hutchinson, S.A. (2011) 'Boundaries and bricolage: examining the roles of universities and schools in student teacher learning', *European Journal of Teacher Education*, 34(2): 177–91.

Murray, J. and Male, T. (2005) 'Becoming a teacher educator: evidence from the field', *Teaching and Teacher Education*, 21(2): 125–42.

National College for School Leadership (NCSL) (2011) *National Teaching Schools: Prospectus*. Nottingham: NCSL.

National College for School Leadership (NCSL) (2012) *System Leadership Prospectus*. Nottingham: NCSL.

Papastamatis, A., Panitsidou, E., Giaurimis, P. and Papanis, E. (2009) 'Facilitating teachers' and educators' effective professional development', *Review of European Studies*, 1(2): 83–90.

Phelps, P. (2008) 'Helping teachers become leaders', *The Clearing House*, 81(3): 119–22.

Skinner, N. (2010) 'Developing a curriculum for initial teacher education using a situated learning perspective', *Teacher Development*, 14(3): 279–93.

Van Velzen, C. and Volman, M. (2009) 'The activities of a school-based teacher educator: a theoretical and empirical exploration', *European Journal of Teacher Education*, 32(4): 345–67.

White, E. and Jarvis, J. (2013) *School-based Teacher Training, a Handbook for Tutors and Mentors*. London: Sage.

CHAPTER 10

HOW CAN ACTION RESEARCH BE USED TO ENHANCE SCHOOL-BASED ITE?

Carey Philpott

This chapter has three purposes:

- to identify some of the main differences and debates between approaches to action research
- to explore, in principle, what adopting action research as a key part of your initial teacher education (ITE) provision will mean for the organization of ITE in your school
- to give some case study examples of ways that action research has been used in school-based ITE to enhance the experience for all participants.

As well as these three key purposes, this chapter will draw together some of the ideas explored in other chapters in order to show how action research can be a useful vehicle for achieving these. This includes using ITE for staff development, creating synergy between ITE and other school agendas, and creating the best conditions for professional learning for ITE students.

Action research, sometimes called practitioner research, has become increasingly popular in recent decades. This growing popularity is evidenced by library shelves full of 'how to' books on action research and the establishment of several academic journals devoted exclusively to action research. The rising popularity of action research in education has also given it increasing perceived legitimacy as a way of researching education and improving educational practice, evident in its increasing use as a method of teaching, learning and assessment in university-based ITE and master's courses. It has also been given official approval through government schemes such as the Master's in Teaching and Learning, Best Practice Research Scholarships and networked learning communities (Bartlett and Burton, 2006; Cain, 2011; Noffke, 1997).

However, despite its growing currency as a term and its popular and, to some extent, official adoption, action research is a diverse and sometimes complex practice, and it is arguable that many of its advocates and users only have a partial understanding of this diversity and complexity (Bartlett and Burton, 2006; Cain, 2011; Noffke, 1997). In order to use action research in the most effective ways, it is important that teachers have at least an overview of the key differences and debates in action research theory and practice so that they can make informed choices about what they do and how they do it.

The purpose of this chapter is not to provide a 'how to' guide to doing action research. As previously mentioned, there are shelves full of these already and many of them are very good.

AN OVERVIEW OF ACTION RESEARCH

Before addressing some of the complexity and diversity of action research theory and practice, it is worth briefly recapping the basic nature of action research.

In its simplest form, action research is often represented in the form of a cycle, as in Figure 10.1. You will find variations on this type of diagram, including some that are simpler and some that are more complex.

What this cycle seems to show is a step-by-step process for learning how to improve practice in the classroom. Action research is often succinctly characterized as research to produce change rather than just research to produce knowledge. This process starts at stage 1 in Figure 10.1 by identifying something that we want to improve. Let us say, for example, that you think pupils in your class would benefit from being better at self-assessment. The data collection stage involves thinking about the evidence we already have, or can generate, about the initial situation. So, in the example given, this could involve thinking about the evidence that made us believe that pupils could be better at self-assessment in the first place. It could also involve looking at existing written records of self-assessment. You might also decide to gather additional observational data by watching and listening carefully while pupils are engaged in self-assessment and noting down your observations. You might decide to talk to pupils about self-assessment to get their views. This stage can also involve looking for information and evidence in what other people have written about self-assessment. So this could mean searching academic journals and other sources to find out if there is anything that would give you a better understanding of the initial situation.

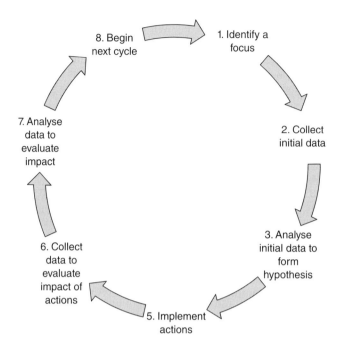

Figure 10.1   Typical action research cycle

Stage 3 involves you in reflecting on what you have got from your data col-
lecting and what this might tell you about the situation you want to improve. It
is about arriving at a more analytical and informed understanding of your initial
situation. The idea is to use this more informed understanding to generate a
hypothesis or plan about what could be done to improve the situation. This plan
is then implemented and the effects of it are monitored by continuing to gather
and generate data about the situation. This allows you to evaluate the success of
your plan and, by implication, the 'accuracy' of your hypothesis about the situation. It is usually envisaged that you might need to go through this cycle more
than once in the process of improving practice.

It might strike you that this cycle is similar to the reflective practice that teachers are encouraged to engage in, and indeed often do engage in as part of their
normal work. There clearly are similarities between the two and some education-
alists have sought to explore the similarities and differences between reflective
practice and action research (Dana and Yendol-Hoppey, 2009; Leitch and Day,
2000; McIntosh, 2010). Among the differences that have been suggested is that
action research is thought to be more intentional, focused and systematic in its
approach through its emphasis on gathering and generating data that might not
be immediately apparent and using other perspectives and sources of information such as reading. This greater emphasis on a deliberate and systematic
approach can, arguably, overcome limitations to reflective practice such as being
bounded by our own world view, beliefs and assumptions. This deliberate and
planned approach might also overcome obstacles to more spontaneous reflection
on practice such as those identified by Cole (1997) in which we might not tend

to ask searching questions about our practice because of the discomfort or other types of challenges this brings. Further distinctions can be the often collaborative nature of action research, whereas reflection might be a more individual activity, and the greater visibility of action research as something that can be shared.

I wrote that the cycle in Figure 10.1 'seems to' show a step-by-step process. I used the phrase 'seems to' because in practice the process of action research is rarely as straightforward and 'step-by-step' as Figure 10.1 and my explanation of it suggest. To begin with, 'identifying a focus' might not be straightforward. In the complex and sometimes messy situation of the classroom it might be difficult to know what the focus is or to narrow it down sufficiently to make it manageable. For example, if I am concerned about pupils' ability to maintain their attention on my whole-class teaching, what type of problem is this? Is it a problem of their behaviour? Is it a problem of my teaching? Is it a problem of the content of the lesson? Is it a problem of the environment of the classroom? Sometimes the business of deciding on the focus can require quite some work in itself. In addition, each stage of the cycle in Figure 10.1 might cause us to go back and review earlier stages. For example, I might start by thinking that pupils' inability to maintain attention on my whole-class teaching is a problem of their behaviour, so I probably need to look for behaviour modification solutions. However, as I gather data, either from my classroom or from reading, I might decide that this was a mistaken view and I need to reformulate my understanding of the situation at that stage to thinking about it as a problem of the content of the lesson. Once I have planned my set of actions based on my view that the content of the lesson is the issue and implemented them, the data I generate and gather as part of my monitoring of the situation might lead me to believe that content is not the issue but perhaps my teaching strategies are. This might mean that I have to go back to searching for additional reading to help illuminate this situation.

So, in practice, the action research cycle might involve moving backwards and forwards recursively between stages rather than just moving through them in a straightforward sequence. This is one of the ways in which action research might be more complex in practice than frequent references to it acknowledge. However, I do not propose to write much more about these issues here as many of the available 'how to' guides for action research address these issues in useful practical ways.

The diversity and complexity within action research that we explore in this chapter, relates to how different approaches to action research are related to different beliefs about the nature of the social world of teaching and learning, and different beliefs about what it is possible to know about that world and how we can come to know it. The action research cycle as I have so far presented it, even in its more uncertain, recursive form, is presented as a value-free, neutral technique for improving teaching and learning practice. It does not seem to commit us to any view about what improving teaching and learning might actually mean. So it could apparently be just as suitable for developing effective behaviour modification techniques or effective routines for rote learning as it could be for creating a greater role for pupil voice in the classroom or for responding effectively to diversity in the classroom.

Similarly, the process of action research as it has so far been presented has nothing explicit to say about how we view the nature of reality and how we can come to know what it is. Does the data we gather or generate show us something that is objectively true about the situation or does it just allow us to construct a version of the situation that is no more or less true than many other possible versions of the situation that we could construct? Can my analysis of the data reveal 'the truth' of the situation or is my analysis inescapably subjective and would someone else analyse it differently? And would their analysis be just as 'correct' as mine? Although the account of action research I have given so far has had nothing to say on these questions, they are of central importance to many of the leading advocates of action research and are central to these advocates' views of what is important about action research and how it is carried out. So in order to have an informed understanding of action research and, therefore, to carry it out in informed ways, we need to explore them.

NAVIGATING THE DIVERSITY OF ACTION RESEARCH THEORY AND PRACTICE

People who spend large parts of their professional lives thinking about what is real and what is not, and how we can come to know, often refer to questions about what actually exists as questions of ontology. They refer to questions about how we can come to know about the world as questions of epistemology. There are differing views on ontology and epistemology.

For the sake of simplicity we can think about different ontological beliefs as lying along a scale. At one end of the scale would be the view that there is ultimately a single thing called the real world that actually exists (Cassell and Johnson, 2006, call this realist ontology). At the other end of the scale would be the view that ultimately there is no such thing as the real world, there are only various subjective models of it in the minds of different people and communities (ontological subjectivism – Cassell and Johnson, 2006). This second view might seem difficult to accept if we are thinking primarily about the physical world. It seems like an extreme and unsustainable position to say that ultimately nothing is real beyond our own beliefs about it. Does this mean that this book is not real, nor is the chair you might be sitting on? However, it might seem like a more plausible view if we think primarily about the social world; the world of human identities, relations, thoughts, intentions and actions. For example, in a classroom a pupil might believe they have been treated unfairly by a teacher. The teacher might believe they have treated the pupil fairly. Assuming that neither is intentionally misrepresenting what happened in the classroom or their thoughts about it, which one of these accounts is the real world? Did the teacher treat the pupil unfairly or not? We cannot reduce these different versions of reality to a single version that we would call what really happened.

We can also think of different epistemological views as being along a scale. At one end would be the view that if we use the right methods in the right ways we can discover what the objective reality or truth of a situation is (objectivist epistemology – Cassell and Johnson, 2006). At the other end of the scale is the view that we can only ever have a subjective understanding of the world. Even if there is a single thing called reality, we cannot know what it is (subjectivist epistemology – Cassell and Johnson, 2006).

These different positions in relation to ontology and epistemology can be combined in different ways. It is possible to believe that there is one thing called reality and that by using the right methods it is possible to find out what it is. This combination of positions is sometimes known as positivism. This is the combination of views that many of us would ascribe to science, although not all scientists would agree. A second combination is to believe that ultimately there is a single state of affairs called the real world but also to believe that it is not actually possible to know what that is no matter what we do. This is because our attempts to understand the world are inescapably filtered through our own subjective positions and ways of making sense. In some forms, this combination is called critical realism (Bhaskar, 1998). A third combination arises if you believe that there is no single reality outside of individual or community interpretations or models of the world. Then, of course, it is not possible to find out about the nature of reality because there is no single reality. You can only find out about the different ways in which different people make sense of the world. This combination of beliefs is sometimes called an interpretivist approach.

These distinctions are important for understanding what many leading advocates and practitioners of action research think is important about action research as a way of finding out about the world and the way in which we try to change the world.

Theories about action research and approaches to it are very diverse (Cassell and Johnson, 2006; Chandler and Torbert, 2003; Noffke, 1997; Reason and Bradbury, 2001). Mills (2011) claims that there is a fundamental distinction in action research approaches between what he calls practical approaches and emancipatory approaches. By practical approaches Mills means the application of action research as a process or technique that does not necessarily commit itself to any particular view of ontology, epistemology or any particular agenda of social and educational reform. Mills defines action research generally as:

> any systematic inquiry conducted by teacher researchers … in the learning/ teaching environment to gather information about how their particular schools operate, how they teach, and how well their students learn. The information is gathered with the goals of gaining insight, developing reflective practice, effecting positive changes … and improving student outcomes and the lives of those involved. (Mills, 2011: 5)

This definition of a neutral technical process finds echoes in many 'how to' guides to action research. However, other prominent proponents of action research place more emphasis on what Mills calls the emancipatory approach:

the political commitments that they believe action research entails and the challenge to positivist thinking about reality that it presents. These two ideas are linked because, according to these action researchers, positivist views about reality are linked to claims by some people to superior, authoritative knowledge, which are in turn linked to the exercise of social and political authority. Reason and Bradbury claim that action researchers 'undercut the foundations of the empirical-positivist worldview that has been the foundation of western inquiry since the Enlightenment' (Reason and Bradbury, 2001: 4). They link this rejection of a single authoritative view of reality through 'the connections between power and knowledge' (Reason and Bradbury, 2001: 9) to:

> A political form of participation [that] affirms peoples' right and ability to have a say in decisions which affect them and which claim to generate knowledge about them [that] asserts the importance of liberating the muted voices of those held down by class structures and neo-colonialism, by poverty, sexism, racism and homophobia. (Reason and Bradbury 2001: 9)

Within this view of action research, the fact that understanding of situations is generated locally by people closely involved in them is a way to emancipate them from beliefs, identities and practices imposed on them by those in authority who use their control of supposedly authoritative knowledge about the world to achieve this imposition. An important part of this emancipation is achieved by the participation of everyone concerned in the situation in the action research. So often action research is not done *to* the groups being researched but is done *with* them so that their voices are heard equally.

A similar view of action research can be found near the beginning of the first paper in the first edition of the academic journal *Action Research* in which Brydon-Miller et al. (2003: 13) assert that 'Action research rejects the notion of an objective, value-free approach to knowledge generation in favour of an explicitly political, socially engaged and democratic practice'. The salience of this assertion in the first issue of the journal suggests that this is a non-negotiable position to many involved in action research. However, this has not always been recognized by proponents of action research, particularly those in positions of authority, such as government agencies (Bartlett and Burton, 2006; Cain, 2011). Official endorsement of action research has often been based on a view that it is just a neutral technique for improving the technical aspects of practice rather than a fundamental challenge to existing hierarchy, power and status.

As an alternative to the binary opposition represented by Mills's definition of action research as a neutral technique for developing practice and Reason and Bradbury's commitment to emancipation through the rejection of positivist views of knowledge and reality, Cassell and Johnson (2006) use different beliefs about epistemology and ontology as a way of trying to organize the diversity of existing action research practice into five broad approaches. Other aspects of the research practice, such as the role given to participants, also play a part in their categorization. Table 10.1 summarizes the main features of each of these approaches.

Table 10.1   Types of action research practice (after Cassell and Johnson, 2006)

Experimental action research	Realist ontology, objectivist epistemology. Little participation from community researched apart from as sources of data
Inductive action research	Recognizes that for different participants reality might be different, so some recognition of subjectivist epistemology. Yet this acknowledgement of subjectivist epistemology is not also applied to the views of the researchers who are still seen as having a privileged neutral perspective on the situation researched. So an objectivist epistemology is retained for the researchers
Participatory action research	Involves some of the community researched in defining the problem to be researched and in diagnosis. However this tends to be the 'elite' within the community. This approach, therefore, privileges the knowledge, understanding and perspectives of the elite in defining and understanding the situation and in generating solutions to problems
Participatory research	Subjectivist epistemology, realist ontology. The subjectivist epistemology is extended to the researcher too, who cannot claim authority from having a privileged perspective on what is true. Gives equal voice to all participants in the research at all stages. All members of the community are equal in defining the problem, generating and interpreting data and proposing solutions. The approach is intended to empower currently marginalized groups within the community. The realist ontology is clearest in the certainty that marginalization and oppression are objectively existing facts and not just a subjective creation
Deconstructive action research	Subjectivist epistemology, ontological subjectivism. No form of change to practice in the community can be justified on the basis of being objectively better or fairer. The value of research is for the multiplicity of voices to challenge any single dominant voice

This is only one way of trying to organize the diversity of action research approaches. Chandler and Torbert use three 'dimensions' of action research (voice, practice and time) to create a typology of '27 flavors of action research' (Chandler and Torbert, 2003: 133). Tekin and Kotaman (2013) use three epistemological perspectives (positivism, post-positivism and interpretivism) to explore the diversity of action research belief and practice. Post-positivism is similar to what I have called critical realism. They also call interpretivism anti-positivism. Noffke (1997) identifies three areas, the professional, the personal and the political, that are present in varying degrees and relationships in different approaches to action research. In some cases, she argues, these variations 'are reflective of fundamentally different assumptions about the processes and purposes of action research' (Noffke, 1997: 307). All of these ways of trying to navigate the territory of action research have value. However, for the remainder of this chapter, I use Cassell and Johnson's categories of action research to explore the practical implications of action research for ITE in schools. This is for the sake of simplicity rather than because I am suggesting that these categorizations have more value than others.

WHAT CAN ACTION RESEARCH BE USED FOR IN SCHOOL-BASED ITE AND WHY DOES VARIETY MATTER?

Action research can have a number of uses in school-based ITE. This discussion focuses on three such uses, as:

- a vehicle for student teachers' learning (and assessment of their learning)
- a way of combining school improvement with student teachers' learning
- a way of improving school-based ITE and providing staff development.

A vehicle for students' learning

Action research can be a powerful vehicle for students' learning in school-based ITE. This is because it manages to bridge the so called theory–practice divide (Bartlett and Burton, 2006; Cain, 2011) and because it addresses some of the possible challenges of learning through work-place experience that are explored in more detail in Chapter 3 of this volume.

The theory–practice divide refers to the perceived gap that can exist between the generalized and relatively abstracted form of educational theory and the specific detail of daily practice in any given context. One form that the theory–practice gap can take is the challenge of knowing how to apply educational theory to the specific circumstances of practice. The amount of work that can be needed to close this gap has been identified by City et al. (2009) and Eraut (1994). City et al. (2009: 9) claim that 'the problem is not that schools don't have access to knowledge. The problem is that they don't have a process for translating the knowledge systematically into practice'. This gap has led some people to claim that educational research and theory generally has no direct impact on practice. It can certainly be the case that students in ITE can find the theories they learn, traditionally in the university, of questionable relevance to the actual situations of practice they encounter and this can lead them to neglect these theories in favour of more localized ways of making sense of experience and planning actions (Philpott, 2006). Action research can bridge this gap by starting from the specific experiences that students have and considering how existing research and theory can be used to understand these.

Approaching theory from this 'direction' has the advantages of demand-side learning that Brown and Duguid (2000) identify and of disembedding transferrable learning from specific experiences in a way that Billett (1996, 1998) argues is an effective model for professional learning. Because action research makes explicit use of other forms of educational research during its cycle of trying to improve practice, it is also likely to avoid the risk of restrictive learning (Evans et al., 2006) or single-loop learning (Argyris, 1999) that can result from experiential learning that does not explore different ways of understanding experience (Chapter 3 in this volume has a more detailed discussion of each of these ideas). In addition, Brookfield (1995), when considering teachers' critical reflection on practice, identifies academic literature and pupils' views as two key 'lenses' with which to 'hunt assumptions' about practice that might ultimately be preventing teachers from developing their practice in the most effective ways. Action research makes use of both of these 'lenses' during its cycle.

The greater visibility and share-ability of action research also means that students can learn from one another's experiences as they share what they have done or collaborate in carrying out action research.

Taken collectively these advantages of using action research as a vehicle for students' learning in school mean that it is more effective than either 'supply side'-led (Brown and Duguid, 2000) teaching of educational theory and practice in advance of experience or expecting students to learn from experience without explicit consideration of how different research and theories can illuminate our experiences.

A final advantage of using action research as a vehicle for students' learning is that its reflective evidence-based cycle, supported by what we can learn from others through collaboration and educational literature, models the process of autonomous professional learning that students will need to continue with once they have qualified. So the process of learning during ITE will also equip them with the skills and dispositions necessary to continue career-long learning.

As well as providing a powerful vehicle for learning, action research can also provide an opportunity for valid assessments of the academic component of ITE, as it combines practice and literature-based knowledge. The possibility of students sharing action research can be combined with assessment through the practice of peer presentations.

A way of combining school improvement with students' learning

The collaborative and shareable nature of action research provides an opportunity to create synergy between student teachers' learning and school improvement. As the nature of continuing professional development (CPD) has changed in recent years, less emphasis has been put on teachers attending externally provided courses to improve practice, and more emphasis has been put on teachers working together to develop and share their practice. One idea that has gained currency is that of professional learning communities. Bolam et al. (2005: iii) state that 'An effective professional learning community has the capacity to promote and sustain the learning of all professionals in the school community with the collective purpose of enhancing pupil learning'. They report that their evaluation shows that an effective professional learning community 'exhibits eight key characteristics: shared values and vision; collective responsibility for pupils' learning; collaboration focused on learning; individual and collective professional learning; reflective professional inquiry; openness, networks and partnerships; inclusive membership; mutual trust, respect and support' (Bolam et al., 2005: i). In national guidance on professional learning communities, the Welsh Government (2011) sets out the defining features of a professional learning community shown in Table 10.2.

Table 10.2 Features of a professional learning community (PLC) (adapted from Welsh Government, 2011)

A PLC	Not a PLC
Group of professionals working as a team to address specific learner needs arising from the analysis of data/ evidence	Formally established or existing group with a continued focus on a theme, subject or topic
Chooses the focus of inquiry and the membership of the group	Prescribed focus and membership (e.g. a working party is given its task or brief)
Imperative to generate new ideas and new practice	Expectation of sharing of existing knowledge, information or practice
Operates within a clear cycle of action inquiry.	Inquiry is not an expectation.
Leadership is widely distributed and the group chooses its own facilitator	There is a designated or pre-existing leader of the group
Each member is accountable for the outcomes of the PLC – there is reciprocal accountability	One person is responsible for producing minutes, sharing the outcomes, reporting, etc.
Disbands and reforms with a new focus on inquiry and changed membership	Continued membership and work of established group is ongoing
Assesses its impact directly on learner outcomes and has a responsibility to share these outcomes with others	Engages in reporting and written dissemination
Independent and interdependent learning. Reflection upon individual and collective learning based on evidence	Dependent learning
Active community of learners	Passive participants

Many of the features identified as central to effective professional learning communities by Bolam et al. (2005) and the guidance from the Welsh Government (2011) overlap with the collaborative practice of action research. Using action research as a vehicle for student teachers' professional learning, it is possible to include them in the wider professional learning community to the benefit of both the student teachers and the school.

A way of improving school-based ITE and providing staff development

Inevitably, if a school is committed to school-based ITE it will also be committed to making that ITE as effective as possible and to improving ITE provision year on year. Action research can provide the process for evaluating the effectiveness of current provision and for improving that provision. The staff who engage in this evaluation will be gaining valuable professional development themselves as they develop their understanding of the most effective ways of supporting other colleagues' professional development. This capacity in the school can enable it to become ever more effective at developing its own staff, not just ITE students.

Why does the variety of approaches matter?

The variety of views about action research is connected to the particular ways that it is carried out in practice and the kinds of benefits that are likely to result from it. What Cassell and Johnson (2006) call experimental action research can be used for narrowly conceived improvements to the technical aspects of practice without fundamentally challenging our wider understanding of the situation we are engaged in or the relationships that are part of it (consider the teacher and her test scores in Chapter 3 in this volume). Engaging in what they call collaborative research will cause us to give equal value to the experiences, opinions and world views of all participants in our practice, for example, pupils, teachers, learning support assistants, student teachers, managers, parents, and so on.

This latter situation of openness, sharing and community has obvious benefits for the effective development of practice. Findings on effective professional learning communities, reported earlier in this chapter, indicate that these are important values. In addition, more active pupil involvement in understanding their learning has been promoted through a number of initiatives because it is believed that this will result in better school communities and better outcomes for pupils. A recent Joseph Rowntree Foundation report on closing the achievement gap for learners from disadvantaged backgrounds has found that one effective strategy is for schools to have a better understanding of the views of the pupils and parents they serve in order to adapt the school's practices accordingly (Hirsch, 2007). The advantages of collaborative research will be for teachers as well as pupils. Approaches like collaborative research also value and empower teachers' local understandings of practice over centrally provided prescriptions.

For these reasons it is important to be wary of experimental action research style approaches as they can be restrictive (Evans et al., 2006) and to understand the values and approaches of other forms of action research. Bartlett and Burton (2006) identify that government-backed approaches to action research often treat it as a straightforward technical process without sufficient acknowledgements of its social and cultural implications. Understandings of action research that do not allow for its full benefits have also been identified among teachers. Adelman (1993) suggests that the collaborative nature of action research is overlooked by many teachers who tend to pursue it as a form of individual reflection. Cain (2011) claims that teachers often do not see the need for 'politics' and that they overlook the value of collaboration and self-reflexivity in their uses of action research. By self-reflexivity we can mean questioning our own beliefs, values and assumptions. We can also mean recognizing that other people's understandings of a situation can have equal weight with ours.

While collaborative research approaches have obvious benefits, they also bring challenges. Brydon et al. (2003: 21) write: 'You have to be willing to be wrong, to trust that other people know their own lives and their own interests better than you do. This comes hard to those of us who have been trained to believe that we are smarter than everyone else.' Collaborative research approaches require willingness from everybody to let go of some of their authority and flatten the hierarchy. This means that school managers need to cede authority to teachers, teachers to student teachers, and everyone to pupils and parents. This can be risky and scary but it is what is needed if we are to achieve 'openness, networks and partnerships; inclusive membership; mutual trust, respect and support' (Bolam et al., 2005: i).

CASE STUDIES

Note: the names of schools in these case studies have been changed.

 ## CASE STUDY 10.1

St Jean-Baptiste de la Salle Technology College joined up their whole-school improvement plan with master's-level accredited staff professional development and the learning and assessment of the ITE students in the school. They used action research as the main method for achieving this. In partnership with a local university, some members of staff enrolled on a master's level practitioner research module. These teachers used the support offered by the module to plan and implement action research on key areas of the school improvement plan. Student teachers at the school were required by their course to carry out a curriculum development project using an action research approach. The teachers and the student teachers worked together to coordinate the focus of their action research so that it all fed into the school improvement plan. Student teachers and teachers presented their action research to wider groups of colleagues so that what had been learned could be shared as widely as possible in the school.

This case study shows a way of integrating school improvement, professional development, school-based ITE and action research. School improvement, professional development and ITE benefited from this mutual support. Student teachers were given a legitimate role in the school community which made a resource of their particular identity as *students* of education rather than just less-experienced teachers (see Chapter 3 in this volume). This use of the student teachers also emphasized what they could give to colleagues in the school rather than just what colleagues needed to give to them. The professional development of the teachers benefited not only the school improvement plan but also created extra capacity for future action research and for supporting ITE students' action research in future. The greater possibility for sharing action research compared to other forms of reflective practice or ITE assessment meant that the benefits of the activity could be maximized in the whole school community.

 ## CASE STUDY 10.2

Egdon Heath Community School hosted ITE student teachers who were required, as one of their assessments, to carry out a small research project modelled on practitioner research approaches. One student teacher, Lakshmi, had planned a project to raise achievement with her low-achieving Year 7 class. As part of the data-gathering for this she observed her class in other subjects being taught by other teachers. Many pupils in the class struggled with reading and writing. During her data-gathering she noticed that the teachers whose lessons she was in were aware of the pupils' difficulties with reading and writing and attempted to compensate for this with teaching strategies that minimized reading and writing demands. This is an understandable strategy and made sense in terms of allowing pupils access to the content of the subject and allowing them to express their understanding without the barrier of the writing they found difficult. However, taken collectively it meant that pupils were not regularly experiencing the demands or support that would develop their reading and writing ability. Although this was not the initial focus of the student teacher's research she did feed back on this during her presentation to school colleagues on what she had been doing.

One thing that is significant about this case study is that the particular role of the student teacher gave Lakshmi the possibility of an overview of this class's experience that no one else had. This shows the benefits of giving proper space and legitimacy to the role of the student teacher as a student and how this can feed into school improvement and wider staff development. At the same time, her activities were not seen as marginal or contained within an enclave of student teachers that had little to do with colleagues in the rest of the school. It is also important that hierarchy was not an issue and the views and insights of the student teacher were seen as worth listening to. This was facilitated by the approach to assessing students that made use of action research and presentations to a wider staff group.

CASE STUDY 10.3

The Nethertarn Federation is a group of schools that work together. They have used the existing infrastructure of the federation as an infrastructure for school-based ITE. Initial teacher education students within the federation are expected to carry out a project based on practitioner inquiry as one of their assignments. The federation has agreed that the main form of assessment of these projects will be through presentations of action research to peers. Peer assessment contributes to the assessment of the projects. To this end the federation gathers all ITE students together for a conference day. This is an opportunity for assignments that could be 'invisible' to everyone apart from the student who produced them and the marker to be shared more publicly. This maximizes the benefit of the work and provides a rich opportunity for student teachers to discuss ideas and develop their understanding.

CONCLUSION

Action research approaches can be a useful 'engine' for driving a number of different agenda in relation to school-based ITE. One of action research's potential advantages is that it brings together the theory and practice that can, if we are not careful, end up in separate places in ITE. These can be the separate places of the university and the school or the training room and the classroom. They can also be separate 'places in the head' of student teachers.

Action research approaches also potentially create a useful synergy between what might otherwise seem like competing demands on schools so that, for example, ITE and school improvement can join up. The shareable nature of action research when compared with other forms of reflective practice also means that it can be used as a resource for a rich professional learning environment that can take in and join up improving teaching, learning and assessment and improving support for professional development.

 ## FURTHER READING

Altrichter, H., Feldman, A., Posch, P. and Somekh, B. (2007) *Teachers Investigate their Work: An Introduction to Action Research Across the Professions*. London: Routledge.
Mills, G.E. (2011) *Action Research; A Guide for the Teacher Researcher*. London: Pearson.

REFERENCES

Adelman, C. (1993) 'Kurt Lewin and the origins of action research', *Educational Action Research*, 1(1): 7–24.
Altrichter, H., Feldman, A., Posch, P. and Somekh, B. (2007) *Teachers Investigate their Work: An Introduction to Action Research Across the Professions*. London: Routledge.
Argyris, C. (1999) *Organisational Learning*. London: Wiley Blackwell.
Bartlett, S. and Burton, D. (2006) 'Practitioner research or descriptions of classroom practice? A discussion of teachers investigating their classrooms', *Educational Action Research*, 14(3): 395–405.
Bhaskar, R. (1998) *The Possibility of Naturalism: A Philosophical Critique of the Contemporary Human Sciences*. London: Routledge.
Billett, S. (1996) 'Towards a model of workplace learning: the learning curriculum', *Studies in Continuing Education*, 18(1): 43–58.
Billett, S. (1998) 'Constructing vocational knowledge: situations and other social sources', *Journal of Education and Work*, 11(3): 255–73.
Bolam, R., McMahon, A., Stoll, L., Thomas, S., Wallace, M., Greenwood, A., Hawkey, K., Ingram, M., Atkinson, A. and Smith. M. (2005) *Creating and Sustaining Effective Professional Learning Communities*. Bristol: University of Bristol.
Brookfield, S.D. (1995) *Becoming a Critically Reflective Teacher*. San Francisco, CA: Jossey-Bass.
Brown, J.S. and Duguid, P. (2000) *The Social Life of Information*. Cambridge: Harvard Business School Press.
Brydon-Miller, M., Greenwood, D. and Maguire, P. (2003) 'Why Action Research?', *Action Research*, 1(1): 9-28.
Cain, T. (2011) 'Teachers' classroom-based action research', *International Journal of Research and Method in Education*, 34(1): 3–26.
Cassell, C. and Johnson, P. (2006) 'Action research: explaining the diversity', *Human Relations*, 59(6): 783–814.
Chandler, D. and Torbert, B. (2003) 'Transforming inquiry and action: interweaving 27 flavors of action research', *Action Research*, 1(2): 133–52.
City, E.A., Elmore, R.F., Fiarman, S.E. and Teitel, L. (2009) *Instructional Rounds in Education: A Network Approach to Improving Teaching and Learning*. Cambridge, MA: Harvard Education Press.

Cole, A.L. (1997) 'Impediments to reflective practice: toward a new agenda for research on teaching', *Teachers and Teaching: Theory and Practice*, 3(1): 7–27.

Dana, N.F. and Yendol-Hoppey, D. (2009) *The Reflective Educator's Guide to Classroom Research; Learning to Teach and Teaching to Learn through Practitioner Inquiry*. Thousand Oaks, CA: Corwin Press.

Eraut, M. (1994) *Developing Professional Knowledge and Competence*. London: Routledge.

Evans, K., Hodkinson, P., Rainbird, H. and Unwin L. (2006) *Improving Workplace Learning*. London: Routledge.

Hirsch, D. (2007) *Experiences of Poverty and Educational Disadvantage*. York: Joseph Rowntree Foundation.

Leitch, R, and Day, C. (2000) 'Action research and reflective practice: towards a holistic view', *Educational Action Research*, 8(1): 179–93.

McIntosh, P. (2010) *Action Research and Reflective Practice; Creative and Visual Methods to Facilitate Reflection and Learning*. London: Routledge.

Mills, G.E. (2011) *Action Research: A Guide for the Teacher Researcher*. London: Pearson.

Noffke, S.E. (1997) 'Professional, personal and political dimensions of action research', *Review of Research in Education*, 22: 305–43.

Philpott, C. (2006) 'Transfer of learning between higher education institution and school based components of PGCE courses', *Journal of Vocational Education and Training*, 58(3): 283–302.

Reason, P. and Bradbury, H. (2001) *Handbook of Action Research; Participative Inquiry and Practice*. London: Sage.

Tekin, A.K. and Kotaman, H. (2013) 'The epistemological perspectives on action research', *Journal of Educational and Social Research*, 33(1): 81–91.

Welsh Government (2011) *Professional Learning Communities*, available at wales.gov.uk/topics/educationandskills/schoolshome/schoolfundingandplanning/plc/?lang=en (accessed 8 February 2014).

CHAPTER 11

PASTORAL CARE FOR STUDENT TEACHERS

Robert Heath and Carey Philpott

By the end of this chapter you should:

- have an overview of recent relevant literature on pastoral care
- understand some key issues and principles in the pastoral care of student teachers
- have considered some examples to explore possible ways to resolve pastoral issues.

One day you get a phone call from your best friend to say he is getting married, you find out a colleague has to go into hospital for a serious operation, and your sister is having problems with a teenage son who stays out late and is not doing any work at school. The response you have to these situations will be different in each case and may range from going out for a drink to celebrate to sitting with your sister while she cries and pours out her heart to you. Assuming that you show care towards the people in these situations, you are exhibiting the quality of pastoral care – you have become a pastoral carer.

Before the techniques of pastoral care are looked at in detail, along with the academic background to pastoral care and case studies, let us consider the origin of the term 'pastoral care'. The word 'pastor' comes from the Latin and means 'shepherd' and is found in use today in many Christian churches for both an ordained minister and a leader of a church. The word 'care' comes from a Gothic word *kara* which means 'to journey with' or 'to be with'. So the idea of a caring shepherd (Carroll, 2010), someone with whom you can take a journey, is a useful one when thinking about the role of pastoral care in any situation.

In the context of students undergoing training for teaching, the aspect of pastoral care is essential but is often overlooked, sometimes because it is done so well and also because it is not done at all. Most universities have an established tutorial system whereby students are assigned an academic member of staff as a personal tutor who will look after their pastoral needs. This is particularly important in the case of a student training to be a teacher as, when faced with the reality of school life and all the interpersonal skills that have to go with that situation, many students find it hard to make sense of the situations they find themselves in. In many initial teacher education (ITE) establishments the personal tutor is often the placement tutor and will see the student in schools and can deal with any situations that may arise. The move to school-based training means that this role might increasingly have to be undertaken by the training school, and this chapter provides some typical situations that students find themselves in and some guidance on how to set up an effective pastoral care scheme for your school. Also included are some real case studies that will allow the reader to reflect on real situations and how they may have reacted in those situations.

CURRENT LITERATURE ON PASTORAL CARE FOR STUDENT TEACHERS

An explicit focus on the idea of pastoral care in (largely secular) education does not have a very long history (Carroll, 2010). Arguably it made its appearance as a topic of consideration for educators when ideas about the purposes of education were broadened, around the turn of the twentieth century, from a relatively narrow focus on knowledge and skills to a focus on developing the whole person (Carroll, 2010). Carroll draws on Armstrong (2008) to suggest the term itself did not 'enter the lexicon of education' (Carroll, 2010: 147) until the 1950s. It is perhaps worth noting particularly this connection between pastoral care and the particular view we have of the objectives of education as this creates a link between some of the ideas explored here and the ideas you will find in Chapters 3 and 4 of this book.

Definitions of pastoral care are numerous and contested (Carroll, 2010) and come from a diverse range of literature including a substantial literature from religious sources. Carroll (2010: 146) states that many writers on pastoral care 'choose to ignore the matter of definition altogether'. However, for the purposes of this chapter, a useful starting point could be Carroll's definition of pastoral care as going 'beyond uniform legislative industrial requirements and general professional support, to be concerned with personal, individual recognition, needs and welfare' (2010: 147) or Grove's (2004: 34) definition of it as 'all measures to assist an individual person or community reach their full potential, success and happiness in coming to a deeper understanding of their own humanness'.

There is little if any academic literature on the pastoral care of student teachers. There is literature on the pastoral care of students in higher education (HE) but perhaps it is more relevant for the purposes of this chapter to focus on the literature that exists on the pastoral care of teachers. This is because the experiences and organizational context of students in school-based ITE are more likely to correspond to the experiences of teachers than they are to the experiences of HE students who are mostly located in the university. However, it is worth remembering that, although there will be significant overlap between teachers and students, their experiences and needs will not be exactly the same.

There is an existing body of literature on the pastoral care of teachers but it is very small. Arguably this is because teachers are usually thought of as the providers of pastoral care rather than its recipients (Askelton, 1991; Brockie, 1992; Lawley, 1985). For this reason the literature on teachers as providers of pastoral care is vastly larger than the literature on their needs. This is probably also the reason why school training programmes for student teachers focus more often on the role of students as providers of pastoral care to pupils than they do on addressing the pastoral needs of those students rather than their professional development needs. Brockie (1992) suggests that the sense that teachers have of themselves as the providers of pastoral care may have been an obstacle to them thinking more about their own pastoral needs. He goes on to comment that 'taking time to look after our own needs and those of other colleagues is not considered to be "on-task behaviour"' (Brockie, 1992: 3). However, as Dunham (1987) points out, we will be unable to help others with their pastoral issues if we are not coping adequately with our own. Where there is consideration of the pastoral needs of teachers in academic and professional literature this is most often in terms of career and professional development needs rather than needs such as emotions or well-being.

In fact, recognizing the distinction between professional needs and personal needs or the 'needs of the teacher in role of the teacher' and the 'needs of the teacher *qua* person' (Lodge et al., 1992: 8) is suggested as the key to understanding and developing a pastoral system for teachers.

Lodge et al. argue that a pastoral system for teachers needs to recognize and provide for the teachers' 'role needs' and also for their 'person needs' as 'The person is not just an institutional atom but, rather, a complex and independent entity ... [that] transcends any institutional identity such roles may attempt to give it' (1992: 9). They argue that not understanding this distinction 'makes it difficult to determine whether or not a school has a clear policy and proper mechanism for providing both kinds of support ... [and this] leads to a mixing up of personal and teacher support, which contributes to ambiguity in senior and middle management roles' (1992: 9). Furthermore they argue that some pastoral needs arise from a mismatch between the person needs and the teacher needs. Having a clear view of this distinction enables us to identify this as a source of difficulty and to understand how to begin to address it.

An important feature of pastoral systems for teachers and student teachers is that they need to be more than just reactive to 'casualties' (Carroll, 2010; Chappell et al., 1992; Lawley, 1985; Lodge et al., 1992). They need to be proactive in providing the support that prevents the 'casualties'. As a result of this, they also need to avoid being viewed as something only needed by these 'casualties' but should be viewed as something that is central to all our needs and something that is a regular part of our working life, not just a source of occasional 'first aid' (Lodge et al., 1992) when things go wrong (although they have that function too). To put this in very direct terms, we need to recognize that having emotional, personal and interpersonal needs is not a sign of struggling, weakness or failure.

This need to be proactive leads to a need to structure pastoral support in ways that attempt to predict where pastoral needs are and when they occur. Lawley (1985) suggests key points in the career cycle of teachers when they might need enhanced pastoral support. These include being new to a school, or particular role within the school, and retirement. Although these are linked to the career cycle it is important to note that they are not just professional development needs. While it is the case that teachers new to a school or a role will need professional development support with necessary professional knowledge and skills, they may also need emotional and other kinds of support to deal with feelings such as anxiety or loneliness and issues such as personal relationships. It is easy to imagine similar points in the 'career cycle' of student teachers, such as being new to a school or particular class, applying for jobs and preparing to move to a new school. These are areas where emotional and interpersonal support may be needed as much as support with knowledge and skills.

However, the distinction central to understanding pastoral care between professional and personal needs means that we need to balance this proactive and structured approach based on the prediction of generic needs with a sensitivity and openness to how individual teachers' or student teachers' needs and circumstances are personal, specific and varied. One aspect of this is the sheer diversity of the types of needs that might be located under the pastoral umbrella (Carroll, 2010; Chappell et al., 1992). At heart a pastoral system needs to address personal needs rather than generic ones because of the distinction between the role and the person. We can try to predict generic needs in relation to particular roles; it is less easy to do so on the basis of individual personalities and circumstances. The challenge for the design of any pastoral system is to balance these two requirements. A related issue to this balance between the structure and responsiveness of a pastoral system is the extent to which the system can pick up any trends or patterns in pastoral needs for the whole community it serves through the needs of individual members of the community. While the details of individual cases are of course confidential, it can be useful to use anonymized recording systems to identify whether there are any general needs that have not been previously identified. For example, particular issues, experiences or points in the 'cycle' might show up regularly in the experiences of many individuals.

This then provides information that can be used to adjust the structured and proactive part of the pastoral system (Lawley, 1985).

So, it is important for pastoral systems to be proactive and structured and not just reactive. It is also important for them to be a part of everyone's experience, not just 'first aid' for 'casualties'. However, it is also important that they should not be perceived as top down and hierarchical or mandated as part of a management system (Lawley, 1985). Pastoral systems need a sense of equality and shared participation to be most effective (Grove, 2004). Lodge at al. (1992) make a link between this and the distinction between the teacher needs and person needs when they suggest that it is worth looking for opportunities to use personal groupings (or primary groups, in their term) rather than professional structures as a resource for pastoral care.

A further consideration for pastoral systems is how they relate to the wider culture, structures and practices of the school (Brockie, 1992; Chappell et al., 1992; Grove, 2004; Lawley, 1985; Stibbs, 1987). Obviously an obligation for pastoral care is not just confined to a discrete pastoral care system but must also be exercised and expressed through all features of the school's culture and practices (Grove, 2004). As Askelton (1991) argues, there is not much point in using a pastoral care system to address teachers' needs if they are not being met by the wider culture and practices of the school. There is also a question about the extent to which needs identified through the pastoral system result in adjustment to other aspects of school experience. Obviously one legitimate function of a pastoral care system is to develop teachers' resources and resilience in dealing with challenges and stresses that are not going to go away. However, we also need to consider the extent to which challenges and stresses identified through the pastoral care system should result in changes to practices or culture elsewhere so that the stresses are less likely to arise in future.

A consideration that Dunham (1987) raises is also important. In his paper on providing pastoral care for pastoral carers he identifies that one source of stress for pastoral carers is the belief that they can and should be able to personally solve every problem that comes their way. He argues that disabusing ourselves and others of that notion will be helpful. A good pastoral care system and good pastoral carers will recognize when an issue is beyond their expertise and is best directed towards other sources of support.

PRACTICAL IMPLICATIONS FOR SCHOOL-BASED ITE

Some of the literature on pastoral care for teachers argues that it is not appropriate or possible to prescribe designs for pastoral care systems for individual schools. A better approach is to raise sensitivity to the key considerations and issues in relation to pastoral care systems and then to allow school communities to develop their own. These issues, which have been explored in more detail in the previous section, can be summarized (in no particular order) as in Table 11.1.

Table 11.1   Considerations for a pastoral care system for teachers and trainee teachers

- Be proactive not just reactive
- Make pastoral issues and support mainstream not just for people 'struggling'
- Recognize personal needs as distinct from professional needs (although recognize the relationship between the two)
- Balance a structured approach to identifying likely points of need with openness to individual needs
- Maintain distance between management structures and pastoral structures
- Make the pastoral system non-hierarchical
- Think about the links between the pastoral system and needs and the wider culture and practices of the school
- You cannot solve every pastoral issue for every individual and you will need to refer people on to more specialized sources of support at times

These principles can be useful for guiding the creation of a pastoral care system, reflecting on it and developing it. However, in addition to developing a system, it is important to develop the skills and dispositions to make the system effective.

The basic tools of pastoral care

Although pastoral care and counselling are often linked together, the two are not the same thing and a good pastoral carer must be prepared to refer a client to a counsellor qualified in the specific area of concern if they reach the point at which it is clear the carer can be of little further help. There is an understandable desire of all good pastoral carers to do everything for the person they are caring for and the good pastoral carer is one who knows when they have reached the limits of their expertise.

Some staff in schools will be excellent professional mentors to students and will be able to help them greatly in matters of classroom practice and subject knowledge but may be less suited to a pastoral capacity; other staff will be needed to fulfil this pastoral role. In fact, depending on the structure of the personnel in a school, this pastoral role may be taken on by a variety of people. Indeed, Lawley (1995) makes the point that pastoral care may be in the hands of staff other than the teaching staff and there is no harm in that; equally there is no harm in the pastoral carer changing to suit the needs of the student teacher during the time they spend in the school. The aim of pastoral care is to benefit the student; it is not for the benefit of the carer.

The first skill of pastoral care has to be *listening*; very often pastoral carers will tell stories of seeing students and during the meeting the carer will have said very little, if anything, and the student will leave saying that they have appreciated the help given and they now see their problem much more clearly. Often someone with difficulties may never have laid out their problems or issues to another person and it can be the act of saying out loud what the issues are that will lead to a solution.

Listening carefully will lead to remembering and it is a great tool of pastoral care to remember the details that a person has told you. Just simple things like remembering they were going to visit a friend at the weekend and then asking how the visit went at the next meeting helps to build up this relationship of care and of trust from which will come, or may come, the help needed.

The third skill is one that can be difficult in the current educational setting of a school and that is to *relax and give time* to what is being done. If pastoral care is to be done well it cannot take place in rushed minutes between lessons or before the school day when the pressure of getting ready for a lesson is growing. A pastoral meeting has to be arranged when both parties will not be disturbed and it has to be made clear to anyone who may disturb such a meeting that this must not happen. People may need time to feel comfortable to say what is on their mind and will need to do this in a place and at a time where they can be as relaxed as possible and know that the person listening to them will not be looking at their watch because a meeting or a lesson is about to start.

Next, when listening a good pastoral carer needs to *listen to what is not being said*; how does the person talking look, are they relaxed or anxious, do they look at you or always at the floor or somewhere else, what is not being talked about, is that where the problem lies? An experienced school mentor knew that there was a problem out of school with a student, he did not say anything but what was not being talked about, the home situation and his girlfriend, was picked up on by the mentor who, noticing a very bruised arm one day, said to the student 'All is not well at home is it?' This gave the student the opportunity and the space to reveal that his girlfriend was very violent towards him, especially if he was doing school work in the evening and not paying her any attention. This developed into a situation where the student was referred to a domestic violence counsellor for help. This is an example of the fifth skill, which is listening to yourself and how you may have felt in a particular situation. Always remember, of course, that you are not that person and your reaction may be different, but you will have a reaction to what you are told. Sometimes it is not clear what your own reactions and feelings are and, while there is not space to go into detail about this pastoral care technique here, it is worth mentioning the value of verbatim in pastoral care. Briefly, verbatim involves writing down all the conversations between two people and then playing the other person when reading it back. So, for example, a student may be asked to write up a verbatim of a pastoral meeting and then to play the part of the carer at the next meeting while the pastoral carer takes the part of the student. It can be very revealing to hear your words spoken by someone else and then to discuss what was being said.

The next skill is one that, typically, caring people find difficult and that is *not speaking too soon*! The great temptation when trying to help someone is to want to say 'That's OK I know exactly what your trouble is, what you need to do is …' and it will all be fixed. It will not. What is a good technique is to use your listening skills and help to summarize what may be a very disjointed outpouring of information, in the way you understand it. Something along the lines of 'I think what you are telling me is … have I got that correct?' This can often help a person make some sense of what can often be a disjointed series of facts and feelings that they are struggling to make some sense of. Such a summary could be the starting point for the next meeting – 'Last time you were telling me about … can you say a bit more about that?' or 'How are you feeling about that now?' This highlights the next skill which is to *keep questions to a minimum.*

A pastoral carer is not interviewing or cross-examining a student, he or she is there to help them work through their issues, and so direct questions should only be used when a time has been reached when neither party has anything to say and the interview has come to a halt. Finally, the golden rule, *you are not there to make comment or to pass judgement* on the student. You may be surprised by what someone tells you, you may be deeply saddened by their situation but it is not your place to provide judgement or instant solutions. The best and most permanent outcome of good pastoral care is when the outcome or solution is reached by the person you are working with, your solutions may not be their solution and so 'Leave her and find someone else' may not be a useful suggestion, whereas, 'Do you think there may be some way you can talk this through together?' may be a much better solution.

Finally, a few thoughts on the practicalities of pastoral care. Remember that in a pastoral care situation it is possible that someone may reveal things that are very personal, difficult and/or something they would not normally talk about and so boundaries must be set. An initial agreement that everything said remains confidential and will not go beyond the walls of the room you are in is a crucial starting point but also be clear that, if during a subsequent conversation, it becomes clear that you are going to know something that is so serious you will have to act on it, you should make it immediately clear that you will have to take this further. This needs to be done in a way that will not inhibit the conversation but needs to be made clear to avoid compromise.

The layout of the room is also important; sitting with a low table between you or no barrier at all is far preferable to having the barrier of a desk. Where you sit in relation to the door is also important, a male pastoral carer with a young female student should ensure the student is closest to the door so they may leave without fear of being stopped. Likewise a female carer with a difficult male student may feel safer if she is able to reach the door first and while these may seem extreme situations they are worth thinking through. Also always agree the length of the meeting before you meet, if possible, but allow some time at the end in case you have to continue due to the matters being discussed or because you need some time to process what you have heard. This all sounds as if pastoral care meetings are going to involve revelations about the most serious information and situations and in reality it is rarely like that, it is just good to be prepared.

A good school will already have a good pastoral care system in place. De Jong and Kerr-Roubicek (2007) talk about the ethos of care within a school community and so a student placed in such a school should also receive good pastoral care, and if a school is not providing this care they may well decide to review their pastoral care provision for the whole school, and having to take on the role of pastoral care for a student teacher may well be a good point at which to start such a review.

CASE STUDIES

So far, pastoral care of students has been looked at from a theoretical and idealistic point of view but real life is not idealistic and so in the concluding part of this chapter we will consider a range of real examples of where pastoral care has made a real difference to the performance of students. In each case the initial situation will be outlined. This will then be followed by the actions taken by the tutor and the student, and the final outcome will be indicated. Although these are all real cases, the names used are not the names of the students involved in the examples.

Some of the cases might seem rather extreme and it is true to say that you will not come across many examples of problems as serious as some of these. However, it is worth reflecting that as schools take increasing responsibility for the pastoral care of student teachers, they need to think about aspects of students' lives that would previously have been the concern of the university.

 ## CASE STUDY 11.1 THE POST-CHRISTMAS DROP OUT 'SPIKE'

Over three academic years it had been noticed that there was a 'spike' in student teachers withdrawing from a Postgraduate Certificate of Education (PGCE) course immediately after the Christmas holiday. This particular course had a school placement that ran on either side of Christmas. During November, student teachers were in school four days each week and in the university on the remaining day. At the beginning of December the school placement increased to five days a week in school and after Christmas this five-day-a-week pattern continued for a further five weeks. Colleagues in the partnership reflected on why there was a spike in withdrawal after Christmas. The students who were withdrawing were not necessarily struggling academically or with professional skills (although some were). On reflection colleagues speculated that what was happening was this. Some students were finding the school placement a significant challenge although this was not necessarily evident from what they said or how well they appeared to be doing. They managed to struggle on as long as they could see the Christmas holiday approaching and focused on getting to the end. Once they had been away from the school and perhaps returned home for Christmas they found that they could not face the thought of returning to start another sustained stretch at the school. Some colleagues commented that, even as experienced teachers, they too found returning to school after being on holiday a point of increased stress.

Having identified a possible source of the problem there were two fundamentally different possible responses. The first was to plan to intervene to support students' individual resilience immediately before Christmas. This could take the form of a pastoral session that would explore feelings about the placement just ending and the one to come in an attempt to address concerns and provide resources for dealing with them. The second was to alter the pattern of placement in order to remove this point of increased stress. One way of doing this would be to have a university-based block immediately after Christmas rather than an immediate return to school.

This case study touches on several of the issues raised in the literature section of this chapter. First, it is an example of a number of individual cases adding up to a pattern that might benefit from a structural response. Secondly, it shows two different types of response to these issues. The first is to try to develop the resources and resilience of student teachers to deal with situations that will remain unchanged. The second is to change the situation to try to reduce unnecessary stress points.

CASE STUDY 11.2 PENNY AND A FAMILY ILLNESS

Penny was a secondary PGCE student. Prior to her PGCE she had done an enhancement course in her subject to bring her up to the required level of subject knowledge to start the PGCE course. The enhancement course meant that she was on campus for most of the time and this was good for Penny as she had not been away from home before and she was in a safe and secure environment with her friends always close by for support.

The following year she started the PGCE course and all was going well until in October (her second month of training) she had news from home that her father was ill but the cause was not known. Her performance in school was affected and her tutor was informed by the school that she was having some difficulties. Two weeks later it became clear that Penny needed to go home and see her father and the tutor arranged for this to happen. Penny returned after two days but after a further three weeks she found out that her father had terminal cancer and was not expected to live for more than a few weeks. Her tutor arranged for her to take leave of absence (LOA) and she stayed at home until after Christmas, returning for the start of the Spring term. Sadly, two weeks later her father died and Penny returned for the funeral. Her tutor told her to take whatever time she needed, and six days later Penny returned to school and resumed her training. She was close to her father and did not find the next few weeks easy but regular contact with her tutor, which included a short telephone conversation every day for five weeks and several tutorials, enabled Penny to finish her course with a grade A for teaching and master's credits for her academic work.

In this case the tutor put many hours into the pastoral care of this student due to the student being out on placement. In the situation where the student has a tutor based in the school this would be an easier situation to manage and would be far less time-consuming. The time spent away from the school may seem excessive and certainly not the amount of time a teacher would expect to be away from school in such a situation but for Penny this was an event in her life that she had no experience of. The actions and care shown by the tutor enabled a student to complete her course successfully and Penny now has a full-time teaching position and is very happy.

CASE STUDY 11.3 NARMAD: THE OVERCONFIDENT STUDENT

Narmad was a PGCE secondary student. He had achieved a first class honours degree from a good university and had also completed his master's. While his subject knowledge could not be faulted, his attitude was his main downfall. Narmad was convinced that teaching was so easy that he really needed little by way of professional development and the teaching profession would be all the better for having him as part of it. Consequently, he went into school with an overconfident attitude and towards the end of his first term he was put at risk of failure and a remedial programme was put in place. Narmad was convinced it was 'the school's' fault and it was not until his tutor had been to see him several times and discussed his situation and his attitude that his situation began to improve. His tutor felt that this strong character needed a stronger tutor and so another member of the team, a female tutor, took over the pastoral and professional care of this student. Narmad came from a culture where females were not respected as much as males and found this change of tutor difficult, but their pastoral relationship developed in a positive way, leading to a C grade at the end of the year. Narmad had a shortage subject to offer and so quickly secured a teaching post and made a success of his first year.

The important lesson to be learnt here is that a tutor needs to be able to identify that they are not the best person to give pastoral support to a student and there is a skill in knowing this and being able to find the right tutor who can provide that support. Far from seeing this as failure, a good tutor will see this as a realistic and necessary skill to give effective pastoral care.

CASE STUDY 11.4 JULIE: THE SOLE CARER FOR HER MOTHER AND A

PRIMARY PGCE STUDENT

Julie was a bright and bubbly student in her mid-twenties who had left a job she did not find particularly rewarding to train as a teacher. Julie had a sister but she had left home, leaving Julie to look after her mother, who had mobility problems, an addiction to alcohol and bipolar disease. When she started the course, Julie had few problems juggling her studies and her carer's role. The placement office found her a school close to her home to cut down travelling times and her first placement was successful and her studies continued. Just before Easter, Julie became a concern as lecturers had noticed her 'sparkle' had gone and she was starting to look drawn and tired. Her tutor arranged to see her and it quickly became clear that she was struggling, particularly financially as there was little money coming into the household, and it looked as if Julie was not going to reach her goal of becoming a teacher. However her tutor contacted student support and some money was found through the hardship fund and Julie was also advised of other allowances she could get access to as a carer. Her situation improved and her final placement arrived.

Julie did not find the placement easy; it was a difficult school and the teacher assigned as her mentor spent most of her time out of the classroom, giving Julie very little support and making comments if she was not still in school after 5.00 p.m. In addition, the condition of Julie's mother had deteriorated and her mental condition meant that she was ringing the school asking for Julie to come home several times each day. Julie was managing to go home briefly at lunchtimes but the situation was getting out of hand. Her mentor was not helping the situation, showing Julie no compassion at all and, despite the tutor's intervention, the mentor was not prepared to make any allowances. With two weeks of a nine-week placement to go, Julie walked out of the school and, despite a long tutorial, decided to take a fail for the placement and agreed to reassess her situation after the summer.

At a tutorial the following September Julie was at rock bottom and wanted to leave the course. Her tutor could see a potentially great teacher leaving the profession before she had begun and suggested a series of tutorials over the next four weeks. At each tutorial the majority of time was spent on positive aspects of Julie's life and a short amount of time at the end discussing any problems and talking through solutions. By October Julie was in a different place and agreed to retake her placement after Easter at a local school. Between October and the following Easter Julie was able to arrange some respite care for her mother and started her placement in April. At her pre-attachment tutorial the emphasis was on 'you can do it' rather than looking back at what had happened in the past, and this time her school mentor and her tutor worked together to give Julie positive reinforcement following lesson observations with points for improvement, and this resulted in not only the highest grade being given for the placement, but the school offering Julie a job as an unqualified teacher up to her being awarded Qualified Teacher Status (QTS) and a year's contract for the next academic year. She is still at the school after three years.

This is a good example of pastoral care seeing the student's whole situation and being able to contact the right people to help the student in areas the tutor was unqualified in, such as student finance and care allowances. Undoubtedly it was the faith the tutor had in the student that enabled her to show that she was a quality student and Julie's comment at her final tutorial of 'without your confidence in me I couldn't have done it, you said I could and I did', tells the story on its own.

CASE STUDY 11.5 IT'S MY CLASS AND I DON'T WANT YOU SPOILING IT!

Louise found herself in a Nursery/Reception class (although in this case the setting is not important as this situation could develop anywhere) and it became obvious that the class teacher regarded both the classroom and the children in it as hers and she really did not want anyone spoiling either the room or the education of the children. Louise was very professional about the way she worked with the class teacher and 'did it her way' but she was becoming increasingly frustrated that she was unable to put into place any of the teaching methods that she had been taught about or had read about.

At a weekly meeting with her mentor Louise was clearly frustrated and the mentor sensed that she was holding something back. Using careful questions Louise admitted that there was a problem and all her frustrations came pouring out. The mentor knew that the way forward was not to confront the class teacher as an uncooperative person but met with her and suggested that Louise might be allowed to try out something, as she (the mentor) thought that it may have positive benefits for the children, reluctantly the class teacher agreed.

Louise had found some voice recorders in a cupboard that had never been used. The class teacher had identified that some children were not engaging with the books in the room and Louise had suggested that the recorders could be used with the stories recorded on them, up until this point this suggestion had been rejected. Following a meeting with the mentor the class teacher agreed that Louise could try the recorders out. Louise chose an observed lesson (with the mentor and the class teacher observing) to introduce the recorders, and the way the children interacted with them was noted in the feedback. The class teacher had to admit they were effective and agreed to let Louise introduce other information technology (IT) into the room. This became the start of a relationship between class teacher and student that developed into one of mutual cooperation and respect. What could have developed into a very difficult situation was turned round and a positive made from a negative situation. In this example it was the mentor assessing the situation with care and identifying a problem but then approaching the solution with care, knowing the member of staff well, and 'manufacturing' a situation where the student's contribution to the learning could be identified and shown to be of benefit to the children. In so many cases it is a softer approach that can often lead to the most positive results.

CONCLUSION

As identified in the introduction, pastoral care is all about working alongside another with care for that person. Having said that, not everyone can be a good pastoral carer and it takes someone who can be sensitive to the needs of another to fulfil this role. In the last case study this can be seen very well and it just happened that the student's mentor was the right person to be the pastoral carer and correctly identified a problem that was standing in the way of the student achieving success. In other cases it may be someone who is more detached from the situation that provides the care, and so it is important for a student to be allocated someone identified as skilled in pastoral care as well as a professional mentor. This is not to say the professional mentor cannot fulfil both roles but it is good practice to give the student access to both personal resources. Good pastoral care can mean the difference between a successful placement for a student and failure.

FURTHER READING

Jacobs, M. (1993a) *Still Small Voice: An Introduction to Pastoral Counselling.* London: SPCK.
Jacobs, M. (1993b) *Swift to Hear: Facilitating Skills in Listening and Responding.* London: SPCK.

REFERENCES

Armstrong, A.C. (2008) 'Pastoral care', in G. McCulloch and D. Crook (ed.), *Routledge International Encyclopaedia of Education.* London: Routledge.

Askelton, A. (1991) 'Don't I matter, too? Pastoral needs of staff in educational institutions', *Pastoral Care in Education: An International Journal of Personal, Social and Emotional Development,* 9(4): 3–5.

Brockie, D. (1992) 'Learning to look after ourselves: experiencing pastoral care for pastoral carers', *Pastoral Care in Education: An International Journal of Personal, Social and Emotional Development,* 10(2): 3–6.

Carroll, M. (2010) 'The practice of pastoral care of teachers: a summary analysis of published outlines', *Pastoral Care in Education: An International Journal of Personal, Social and Emotional Development,* 28(2): 145–54.

Chappell, E., Hotham, B., Linge, S., Stedaman, J., Sweetingham, P. and Webb, J. (1992) 'Pastoral support for teachers', *Pastoral Care in Education: An International Journal of Personal, Social and Emotional Development,* 10(2): 13–16.

De Jong, T. and Kerr-Roubicek, H. (2007) 'Towards a whole school approach to pastoral care: a proposed framework of principles and practices', *Australian Journal of Guidance and Counselling,* 17(1): 1–12.

Dunham, J. (1987) 'Caring for pastoral carers', *Pastoral Care in Education: An International Journal of Personal, Social and Emotional Development,* 5(1): 15–21.

Grove, M. (2004) 'The three R's of pastoral care: relationships, respect and responsibility', *Pastoral Care in Education: An International Journal of Personal, Social and Emotional Development,* 22(2): 34–8.

Jacobs, M. (1993a) *Still Small Voice: An Introduction to Pastoral Counselling.* London: SPCK.

Jacobs, M. (1993b) *Swift to Hear: Facilitating Skills in Listening and Responding.* London: SPCK.

Lawley, P. (1985) 'The pastoral care of teachers', *Pastoral Care in Education: An International Journal of Personal, Social and Emotional Development,* 3(3): 202–7.

Lodge, C., McLaughlin, C. and Best, R. (1992) 'Organizing pastoral support for teachers: some comments and a model', *Pastoral Care in Education: An International Journal of Personal, Social and Emotional Development,* 10(2): 7–12.

Stibbs, J. (1987) 'Staff care and development', *Pastoral Care in Education: An International Journal of Personal, Social and Emotional Development,* 5(1): 36–9.

CHAPTER 12

CONCLUSION

Carey Philpott, Helen Scott and Carrie Mercier

Editing this book and writing some of its chapters have been a powerful (and partly unexpected) form of triangulation. By triangulation we mean the process by which different sources of information or evidence tend to confirm, support or strengthen one another. When we started writing this book we used our own experience (and some feedback from school-based colleagues) to identify a list of areas in which school-based initial teacher educators (ITE) might find support helpful. We then identified suitable chapter authors and everyone retired to their diverse parts of the world to write the first draft of their chapters.

What was striking when we received the first drafts of these chapters was the extent to which, quite independently, working on different topics and based in different locations and institutions, chapter authors repeatedly identified similar central issues for school-based ITE. The purpose of this conclusion is to identify these central issues and map some of the ways in which they relate to the differing areas of this book.

Two central issues struck us by the frequency with which they recurred in different guises and different contexts. In some ways the two issues are actually different faces of the same issue. The first of these is the importance of not taking too narrow a view of what there is to be learned in teacher education and how it is learned. The second is not viewing teacher education in isolation but making connections to other issues and activities.

We can start thinking about the first of these issues in relation to Kathryn Fox and Patrick Smith's chapter on recruitment and selection, Chapter 2. When recruiting and selecting future teachers we need to think about what it is we most value in teachers and what it is about possible teachers that we think gives them the greatest potential for development. Subject knowledge can be easy to assess during selection. Knowledge of existing curricular arrangements and teaching strategies can also be assessed, and sometimes applicants have these if they have spent time in school prior to application. However, is this what we value most in teachers? Perhaps we place more value on the ability to form positive relationships with young people or 'habits of mind'. Perhaps, thinking of development potential, we are more interested in a disposition to reflexivity, or resilience, or in the ability to learn new ideas quickly rather than in what people already know. So at this early stage we have to think in the broadest terms about what it is that teachers need to learn to do so we can assess the ability of candidates to learn it.

The idea of the importance of personal characteristics links to Gail Fuller's chapter on the centrality of identity and relationships in learning to be a teacher. Fuller emphasizes the importance of recognizing that the work of learning to be a teacher is not just about developing knowledge and skills, but that there is also work in connection with identity, relationships and feelings. So we must not leave this out of our view. She also emphasizes that we must recognize the ways in which these personal characteristics make the learning journey different for all students so it is difficult to have a one-size-fits-all approach to working with students to develop them as teachers. Given that this work is important to successfully learning to be a teacher, it should not just be relegated to the margins or left to chance. It needs to be focused on in the processes of ITE.

There is a link here to Robert Heath and Carey Philpott's chapter on pastoral care for student teachers. It would be very easy to see pastoral care as an issue that is separate from the process of learning and, perhaps, to see it as something that is only relevant to those who are having particular difficulties. However, if we accept that part of the work of learning to be a successful teacher is processing emotions as much as it is about processing ideas, then we can recognize that pastoral care is an integral part of the learning process and not an add-on.

In some very important ways Gail Fuller's chapter provides a link between Heath and Philpott's chapter on pastoral care and Carey Philpott's chapter on professional learning. The ideas that Philpott explores often emphasize that theories of learning need to take account of values, attitudes and identity as much as they take account of knowledge and skills. This is the values, attitudes and identity that we learn as well as those that influence the learning process. Again, if we want learning to be successful we should not leave these things to chance; we need to pay deliberate attention to them and think about how they are developed and how they influence learning.

Philpott raises the issue of 'horizon of visibility' in relation to learning. This is connected to thinking about the full range of skills, knowledge, behaviour, attitudes and values that successful teachers have and how we make them visible to learners. This idea of ensuring the visibility of what might otherwise be hidden is addressed also in Helen Scott's chapter on mentoring and coaching. So, once again, this is another example of taking a broad and inclusive view of what there is to be learned in the process of becoming a teacher and how it is learned.

This is a theme that Nigel Appleton echoes in his consideration of the importance of academic learning in learning to be a teacher, even in cases where there is no academic award as part of the outcome. Appleton argues that we need to go beyond a model of craft skills to understand the nature of teachers' practice and expertise and recognize the diverse range of understanding and knowledge that is necessary to be an effective teacher.

The theme of the heterogeneous nature of what needs to be learned in order to be a successful teacher is addressed again in Carrie Mercier's chapter on assessment. Typically, assessment in the school-based component of ITE might lean heavily on assessing classroom competence through observations. However, as Mercier points out, there is a lot more to being a teacher than this. So our assessment processes, both formatively as part of learning and summatively, have to consider a wide and diverse range of dispositions, values and understandings and how we might assess these.

The second theme, looking for opportunities to join ITE to other issues or activities, is most obviously addressed in Simon Asquith's chapter on synergies and Alison Chapman's on ITE and the professional development of other teachers. Over the many years that we have collectively worked in ITE partnerships with schools, we have come across a number of schools who were very willing, active and good partners but who, nevertheless, seemed to view ITE as an additional demand alongside a number of other existing demands rather than as something that could be a resource to help in meeting those other demands. It is probably unlikely that this will be the view of schools who opt for a role in more school-centred approaches to ITE. Nevertheless, it is worth emphasizing the potential to join ITE to other school activities to the mutual benefit of both. Carey Philpott's chapter on action research suggests one method that can be used to join up some of the agenda written about by Asquith and Chapman. These include staff development and school improvement. However, this is not the only way that this can be done. Some schools currently offer the learning opportunities planned for student teachers to other staff as well, to the mutual enrichment of all involved.

In terms of joining recruitment and selection to other issues, both Fox and Smith and Simon Asquith in Chapter 8 make links between ITE and the wider workforce planning of schools. While Carey Philpott in Chapter 3 warns against the limitations of thinking of ITE only in terms of the perceived needs of your own school, it is perhaps sensible to think about the general qualities you want from teachers in your school in the future when setting ITE selection criteria.

Leaving aside whole-school agenda, Gail Fuller's chapter on identity and relationships in learning implies a suggestive connection between professional learning and the pastoral issues that Robert Heath and Carey Philpott discuss. This could lead to a view that we need regularly to join the pastoral to the academic and professional if we want to assist student teachers in processing what they need to process in order to become teachers.

In summary, a key message of this book is to recognize the richness and complexity of teachers' knowledge and skills and the richness and complexity of the processes by which these are developed. If we pay deliberate attention to all parts of this process, we can best support the teachers of the future. Equally, if we see teacher education as an integral part of everything we do in schools, both schools and ITE will benefit.

INDEX

Added to a page number 'f' denotes a figure and 't' denotes a table.